Noel Gerard Watson

April 1962.

HARPSICHORD MUSIC

The boy Mozart playing the clavecin.
After a picture by Olivier in the Louvre.

HARPSICHORD MUSIC

A survey of the virginals, spinet, harpsichord and their
Continental equivalents; the people who played
upon them; the composers for them; and
the music they wrote

by MAX KENYON

WITH FRONTISPIECE AND EIGHT PAGES
OF ILLUSTRATIONS

CASSELL
AND COMPANY LIMITED
LONDON TORONTO MELBOURNE SYDNEY
AND WELLINGTON

1949

THE PAPER AND BINDING OF
THIS BOOK CONFORM TO THE
AUTHORIZED ECONOMY STANDARDS

First published 1949

Printed in Great Britain by
Wyman & Sons, Limited, London, Fakenham and Reading

F 948

TO

WHARNCLIFFE

CONTENTS

INTRODUCTORY NOTE 11

INSTRUMENTAL PRELUDE 13

CHAPTER

  I. THE VIRGINALS IN ENGLAND 18
- 1. The Instruments in Society
- 2. The Composers
- 3. The Music

 II. THE CLAVECIN IN FRANCE 58
- 1. The Instruments in Society
- 2. The Composers
- 3. The Music

III. THE CEMBALO IN ITALY 93
- 1. The Instruments in Society
- 2. The Composers
- 3. The Music

IV. THE FLUGEL IN GERMANY 132
- 1. The Instruments in Society
- 2. The Composers
- 3. The Music

 V. THE CLAVICHORD IN GERMANY . . . 169
- 1. The Instruments in Society
- 2. The Composers
- 3. The Music

CONTENTS

VI. THE HARPSICHORD IN ENGLAND .   .   . 200

    1. The Instruments in Society
    2. The Composers
    3. The Music

APPENDIX A: Domenico Scarlatti in the Iberian Peninsula . 238

APPENDIX B: The Ruckers Harpsichords of Antwerp .   . 240

INDEX 243

LIST OF ILLUSTRATIONS

The boy Mozart playing the clavecin . . . *Frontispiece*

Facing page

Virginal and Clavichord 16

Spinets 17

Parthenia and *My Ladye Nevells Booke* 32

The Clavecin 33

'La Leçon de clavecin' 192

Clavichord and Flugel 193

The Harpsichord at home and in public. 208

Ruckers Harpsichords 209

INTRODUCTORY NOTE

K IND friends have read the manuscript for me, and this is the place to say that I am grateful. But the specialists among them say, "But you have not mentioned the Aylesford Manuscript" or, "What about Gerstenberg?"

It will be noticed that this volume has little in the way of scholarly apparatus: few footnotes, the bibliographies are short, nothing (one hopes) to baffle the reader in the train, or reading in the evening at home with one ear compulsorily on the wireless.

The advent of the Third Programme was indeed one of the reasons for the publication of this book: hardly a session goes past without the notes of an harpsichord. There are, too, the public harpsichord recitals and, perhaps above all, the numerous amateur pianists who, wishing to explore the territory for themselves, find themselves puzzled by the different appearance of the music on the page and by its so different pianistic sound from the well-loved and thoroughly explored pages of Beethoven and of Chopin.

A reader of a book on music in the days when the harpsichord flourished might be assumed to have leisure and a library. He could pursue references, write marginal notes, cogitate, and enter into cross-country correspondence with other amateurs. But life is now so different that I have tried to write a self-contained book, one which may be read from page to page, and which will lead to a few other books until anyone sufficiently enthusiastic, working from book to book, may make himself master of the whole subject.

The art of disposing available material to this end is largely the art of exclusion. Many minor English composers are not mentioned: the two English chapters are already quite sufficiently long if any balance is to be preserved. Detailed specialist studies of one aspect of one part of the output of a minor composer, such as Gerstenberg's *Die Klavierkompositionem Domenico Scarlatti*, have rarely been of use to me. For instance, I may not altogether agree with the author, but a sort of learned one-sided argument indulged in before weary readers is bad architecture. In the same way I have not halted the narrative to examine a solitary manuscript merely because it is rare or, in the scholastic sense, important. Importance, to me, is founded upon the amount of music of that composer already known to a reader (e.g. Handel is more important than Telemann) and upon the amount of harpsichord music of that composer which has real aesthetic interest (e.g. François Couperin is very important, but Louis Couperin quite unimportant). A composer like Purcell has therefore a double importance, both in general and as a harpsichordist as well. I have not put forward discoveries or protégés of my own; except possibly in the case of Cimarosa, and then only to a claim for limited admiration.

My gratitude goes to M.W. without whose timely help the book would not have been published.

This is the place to thank Miss Gladys Scott Thomson for allowing me to use material from her *Letters of a Grandmother*, published by Messrs. Jonathan Cape in 1944; and to Professor Gerald Abraham of Liverpool University for reading my MS. and for making suggestions, though I have not followed all of these.

Max Kenyon

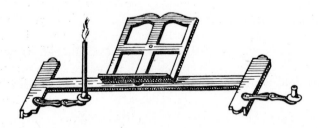

INSTRUMENTAL PRELUDE

T HE various domestic keyboard instruments with which we are
about to deal will be introduced as they are discussed in the
natural course of the narrative. But it will be as well to give a list,
with some details, of the more important of them, so that readers of
this book quite new to the subject will recognize the things I will be
considering.

This book is not, however, about instruments, it is about a special
sort of music. This music differs in quality: and in countries where the
quality of music for one of the instruments is low, that instrument will
be only briefly alluded to, however important and interesting it may
be from a "woodwork" point of view. This word is given in quotation marks because it is in the Woodwork Section of the Victoria and
Albert Museum that the finest specimens of clavichords, virginals and
harpsichords are housed.

And this is why and where our difficulties in nomenclature begin.
In botany it happened that a certain scientist at a certain time renamed
all the herbs, classifying them thus and thus: what he did has been
accepted by all workers in that science. The earlier writers on that
subject are superseded. But in the realms of domestic boxes containing musical instruments, made by man, only some students wish to
agree upon an exact way of naming them. Even these students who
have the same wish will not agree on the same method: the man
who is first of all interested in wood and in decoration will have a
different approach from him to whom the way the music is made
comes first.

My own approach to nomenclature tries to be that of the player
on the instrument when it was in full use. Pepys, in the same sentence,
calls the identical instrument a virginals, a spinet and a harpsicon.
This is not at all surprising, for in the same sentence a modern man will
speak of the cinema, the movies and the pictures.

A man speaking in 1948 means the same thing by these three
nouns, but he meant different things in 1920. The use of the word

"talkies" for a time will give the A.D. 2100 historian the necessary clue. Thus we have to take into account social changes in interpreting old writers: furniture and the domestic arts were plainer in the eighteenth century than in the sixteenth, and one of the real differences between the spinet and the virginals was the absence and presence of case orna- mentation. In the spinet we have a beauty of line, and in the virginals a beauty of encrustation.

As this Instrumental Prelude is written for those with no previous acquaintance with the instruments (though no musical person will be quite ignorant of some of the music), I propose to work from modern days backwards, and take the known family of pianofortes as the basis of comparison. We have the concert grand pianoforte, the baby grand, the upright and the square.

The harpsichord was the equivalent of the concert grand: fully as long, but leaner and cleaner in its lines. This was because it had less range and therefore fewer keys, and because it was made entirely of wood, with no iron or steel. The chief visual difference is that usually the harpsichord has two manuals, even possibly three, so that the key- boards look like those of an organ, sometimes having a few hand- worked stops. The method of making the sound is quite different from that of a piano, in which a felted hammer is thrown upwards against a stretched string. In the harpsichord a plectrum, something which plucks, made of goose quill, or of leather, or with two sets of plectra so as to give a choice of tone quality, comes up beside a stretched string and twangs it. The jack carrying the plectra bounces up against a felted bridge, and is thus knocked downwards with sufficient escaping action as to avoid striking the string twice. These strings were made of various materials: experiment was constant. Bach had a harpsichord with lute strings, so as to give a lute effect to the music. Gut or wire (brass and steel), sometimes silk, was usually used. Sheep's gut was probably the most common sort of gut, but this is a subject upon which authorities are cautious: most of the older instruments have been re- strung more than once in their history, and while we can be sure what the cases and the keys were made of, we can rarely be sure of what the original strings were made.

The harpsichord was the great instrument of Europe: it dominated the opera, the oratorio, what passed for orchestral music, and it was essential for, though it did not dominate, chamber music. It is highly important in every chapter but one of this book, and has been given the most names: thus in England it has generally been known as the harpsichord, in France the clavecin, in Italy the cembalo, and in Germany the flugel.

This is not quite exact: variations in nomenclature are dwelt upon as the instruments come forward for examination. It is a rough working guide. The only other comment which need be made now, is that Germany means anywhere in the Empire where German was spoken, and the word flugel, meaning a wing, alluded to the wing-shaped flap, and therefore meant equally the wing of a grand piano-forte, the early models of which ran concurrently with the later models of the harpsichord for nearly a century.

The spinet is quite unimportant, in exactly the same way as the baby grand, which it vaguely resembles, is unimportant. No music was specially written for the spinet, any more than any music has ever been written especially for the baby grand. In order to take up less room, the harpsichord strings run off from the keyboard at an angle, thus determining the shape of the instrument. The method of tone production is exactly the same as in the harpsichord. But the spinet rarely has more than one manual. There is no need at this stage to trouble ourselves with the names given to this instrument in other countries, partly because of the essential aesthetic unimportance of the spinet, and partly because the subject is a very vexed one: the derivation of the name itself being disputed, the French word for "thorn" and an Italian maker both being put forward as origins. But there certainly was confusion between this instrument and the virginals in various writers. However, of all the old instruments, the general reader is most familiar with the word spinet, because it occurs most often in English eighteenth-century fiction, and in modern advertising is invariably chosen as the epitome of all that is quaint and charming.

One authority claims the name spinet for all single manual instruments of the plucking type, so that the single manual harpsichord, as it has been called in this book, would be a spinet. Another claims the name spinet for what might be termed virginals in rectangular cases, arguing it is the arrangement of wrest plank (where the strings are tied down) and sound board (over which they tremble) which makes the spinet. Clearly, the spinet is something more than a virginals and less than a harpsichord, occurring historically as a contemporary of the latter.

The virginals is like a very small square piano. It is equivalent to an upright piano, the clavicytherium, which was never a popular instrument, and we may pass it by. But the virginals is of great importance, ranking as the supreme instrument of one school of music. In the virginals the strings run left and right, not sideways as in the spinet or away from the player, as in the harpsichord. The shape of the virginals is therefore something like that of the square piano (though the case is sometimes pentagonal), in which the strings are arranged in the same manner.   Like a typewriter, the instrument was carried from room to room and placed on a table.   It was opened up, and the keyboard was disclosed.   The strings were sounded in exactly the same way as in the other members of the harpsichord family, of which the virginals is the smallest and earliest member.   It is not proposed to enter into international nomenclature, because although more virginals were made on the Continent than in England (we imported and did not export virginals, as we were later to do with harpsichords) it was only in England that real music was specially written for them. The English Virginal school is the one branch of instrumental music in which this country is pre-eminent.   Comparison with the square piano and even a portable typewriter needs countering in this sense : the virginals were usually highly embellished, keyed with costly woods, bone or ivory, and the cases painted by the greatest artists.

The clavichord is an instrument so like the virginals as often to be confused with it, the more so as the virginals was sometimes called (though never in the ensuing pages) the "clavicymbolum".   It will be clear that an unmusical person engaged in writing an inventory of furniture would be careless as to the real nature of the instrument, because this had nothing to do with the outer visual shape, but only to do with the inner mechanism.   We have seen that a felted hammer bounces from a pianoforte string, and that a quill, or thorn, plucks an harpsichord string.   In the clavichord, a blade is levered upwards when the finger presses the key in exactly the same way as the prongs of a dinner fork move upwards when, suitably levered, the handle is pressed downwards.   When the blade, usually called a tangent, moves up and touches the string, it causes it to vibrate in two portions, the tangent itself forming a point of rest between the two opposite arcs of vibration.   All that has to be done to secure a pure tone is to damp one of these arcs with a piece of felt.   The string then vibrates only along its unfelted length.   When the finger is on one end of a single piece of wood the tangent, at the other end, touches the string and can remain in contact with it.   This gives much more control over the tone, which may be increased, decreased or prolonged not so well, but in the same manner, as the human voice itself.   Neither

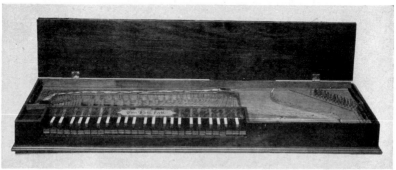

The upper illustration is a virginal made in 1655 by John Loosemore, while the lower is an undated clavichord by Peter Hicks. The juxtaposition of these two photographs shows the visual similarity of the rectangular virginal to the clavichord, though the method of making the music is quite different.

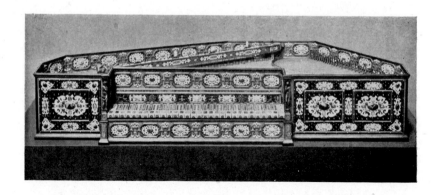

The upper illustration is a spinet by Annibale Dei Rossi of Milan made in 1577. The lower is a spinet by John Player of about 1700. What the sixteenth century Italian called spinets were in England called virginals, and this Milanese instrument belongs to the same family as the virginals of Plate 1.

Both photographs by courtesy of the Victoria and Albert Museum.

the harpsichord nor the pianoforte can achieve this effect. The clavichord is therefore the most singing of the keyboard instruments. But the instrument only exists in the square, portable shape. There is no upright, baby or grand equivalent. This is because the strings cannot be under great tension or else the touch would be too heavy: it would be too much effort to make the strings vibrate. They must be short and comparatively slack. So the instrument is a quiet one, suitable only for the pleasure of the player himself. It was a masculine instrument rather than a feminine one like the virginals, which was named after the young ladies who played upon it. It was a German instrument, and an instrument for poor scholars, organists and schoolmasters. The clavichord, therefore, rarely has an ornamented case like the virginals, but is cased in a plain wooden box. As the tangent falls when the finger is raised from the key, there is no need for a jack-bar of the virginals type: this means the clavichord does not stand quite so high from the table. Therefore, usually the clavichord looks like a small neat black wooden suitcase. Open it, prop up the flap, and you have a perfect means of making quiet music for yourself. Just as the virginals are great because of Byrd's music, so the clavichords are great because of Bach's. But the German word *clavier* means any keyboard instrument, even an organ, and consequently throughout this book when a clavichord is meant, even in Germany, where the instrument is called the clavier, clavichord is the word that has been used. French and Italian words need not bother us.

B

CHAPTER I

THE VIRGINALS IN ENGLAND

1. The Instruments in Society

THE earliest mention of any domestic musical instrument of which the sound is made by vibrating a string, and which is played by the depression of keys, is recorded by the learned Canon Emeritus of Chelmsford, Dr. Galpin. According to this authority, in 1360 Edward III gave an "eschiquier" to John of France, then his prisoner.

King Edward IV had, among many other instruments, a similar one to that given by his predecessor to France, but Edward IV called it "virginals". This is possibly the first mention of the word, a noun designating a tribe of little portable instruments, in which the depressed key causes the string to be plucked, and which, in the fifteenth century, gave out surely so ghostly a sound as barely to be heard by the player herself.

During the fifteenth century the utility of these little boxes of strings seems to have been enlarged, and in 1477 we find that the Master of the Choristers of Lincoln Cathedral, William Horwood, is to teach the boys the use of the "clavychord", an instrument similar in appearance and in strength of sound, but quite different in action and quality of sound, to the virginals. The "clavychord" did not take root in England, and flourished much more in Central Europe, and so will be dealt with in the chapter devoted to the clavichord and the Empire. The word clavichord appears in one of Caxton's *incunabula*, but, in general, the virginals, name and instrument, were much more prominent in the sixteenth century in England.

By 1518 the virginal was sufficiently well known to be used in

poetic simile, on a now destroyed manor house in Yorkshire named
Leckingfield. On a wall of this house was inscribed the following:

A slac strynge in a Virginall soundethe not aright,
It doth abide no wrestlinge it is so loose and light;
The sound-borde crasede, forsith the instrumente,
Throw misgovernance, to make notes which was not his intente.

The year 1529 is important as yielding the name of the first professional keyboard player, apart from organists, for we learn that
John Heywood, the dramatist and poet, was paid fifty shillings a
quarter for playing the virginals at the Court of Henry VIII. He
continued in this pleasant employment for the two successive reigns
of Edward VI and of Mary, retiring to Belgium in his old age, as we
will see other English musicians did. The King's Band of Music
consisted in all of forty-four members, of which John Heywood was
one. Another of the Band was a player upon the regals, a sort of
small organ, hand-pumped by a second person upon bellows on the
same level as the keyboard, projecting, indeed, from behind it.
Rising from what would in a pianoforte be the music stand, were the
pipes, into which the bellows blew the air when the keys were depressed. A two-manual regal might have one keyboard for the pipes
and another to pluck a set of virginal strings. As in the case of the
virginals and the organ, regals were alluded to as "pairs". A pair
of organs, a pair of regals, or a pair of virginals seems to have meant,
however, just the one instrument.

King Henry VIII was one of the most musical of the Tudors.
Of his virginal playing, the Secretary of the Embassy from the Doge
of Venice (himself a skilful amateur of the keyboard) wrote to his
master that Henry "is . . . an excellent musician, plays the virginals
well . . ." and adds, truthfully, that the King also composes "not
badly". One of Cardinal Wolsey's correspondents, reporting on
Royal activities, writes: "The Kynge haith nowe goode passe tyme"
on a new instrument "Mr Rochpotte" had introduced to him.

We have this from the Privy Purse expenses of Henry VIII in
April, 1530, "item the vi daye paied to William Lewes for ii payres
of virginalls in one coffer with iiii stoppes brought to Greenwiche
iii li . . . and for ii payres of virginalls in one coffer brought to the
more other iii li". These "two pairs of virginals" meant, as we
have seen, at the most two instruments, but possibly, considering the
only one coffer and the no less than four stops, there was just the

one instrument, which would be a two-manualled virginal; so that Lewes was paid for two instruments, one landed at Greenwich and the other (it may be conjectured) to the marsh adjoining Whitehall, on the site of which Scotland Yard is built, "divers fair tenements lately built, till ye come to a large plot of ground inclosed with brick, and is called Scotland".

Henry's instruments were by no means all English-made. Some he secured from a Venetian maker named Michael Mercator, who also built them for Cardinal Wolsey.

> And whan it pleased the kyng's majestie for his recreation to repayer unto the Cardynall's howsse, as he dyd dyvers tymes in the yere, at which tyme there wanted no preparations or goodly furnyture. . . . Ther wanted no dames or damselles, meate or apt to daunce with the maskers, or to garnysshe the place for the tyme with other goodly disports. Than was ther all kynd of musyke and armonye set forthe with excellent voyces bothe of men and childerne.[1]

We cannot really tell from this and other passages whether Wolsey was a genuine musician, or merely a sincere flatterer of his master. But no doubt the instruments he imported were in very sumptuous "coffers", perhaps like the Italian instrument now in the Donaldson Museum of the Royal College of Music, garnished with pictures of Cupid tempting an almost naked Venus. In the Victoria and Albert Museum is another instrument of Wolsey's time, built in Rome by Geronimo of Bologna. The case and the actual instrument are separable. These wing-shaped instruments of small compass but considerable length of body, enamelled and adorned with pictorial panels, look most musical and workmanlike in their proportions and almost erotically inviting in their ornament. But what music had they in 1531 to answer these patterns? The charm and allure may, in the absence of a special historical aesthetic sense, it seems to us, have largely resided in the player, or in the overtones of remembered moonlight when a folk-tune or fragment of plain chant was tinkled, repeated, ornamented and adorned with descants. While such lyric poets as Wyatt were mature at this period, poets whose work may compare with the Elizabethans, there was no domestic keyboard composer whose music could at all compare with the work which came a generation later, published in *Parthenia*, or collected in the

---

[1] Cavendish, biographer of Wolsey, in 1557.

manuscript now known as the *Fitzwilliam Virginal Book*. John Heywood was the Court virginal player to Henry VIII, but his virginal music is rarely heard and infrequently reprinted. Perhaps the King himself was as good as any of them. The last of the truly English (as opposed to Scottish or German) royal lines was also the most musical, and reigned during England's greatest musical period. At the time when we began to import our Kings we also began to import our composers: and so we leave the golden years of Henry, playing on his "payre of new long virginalls made harp fashion of Cipres, with keys of Ivory".

The bad years followed: Henry's heavy hand descended upon much English beauty. This man destroyed more than, either directly, or through his patronage, he created. The walker on the grass of Hayles, who looks towards the town of Winchcombe, but fails to see its monastery, may indeed feel bitterness surging within him. This has relevance here, for although Waltham Abbey was not destroyed, its inmates were expelled, and one of them, still a young man, its organist, Thomas Tallis, wandered to London, wrote music for the virginals and became the teacher of Byrd. Much more would be known of Tallis had music printing and publishing been as advanced as the book-publishing trade. Although Caxton printed his first book in 1474, there was, in the time of the youth and exile of Tallis, no printing of music for the virginals whatever, and what he wrote was in manuscript. Holograph manuscripts are rare, transcribed manuscripts were usually made into collections by the scribe or the master for whom he worked, and were the chief means of multiplying the fame of a virginals composer. Yet even such manuscript collections had not started when Tallis came to London, as is supposed, and began to teach William Byrd.

The authority for this relationship between the two great men lies mainly in a Latin quatrain prefixed to one of the first of printed volumes of vocal music which appeared a decade or so later. We may reasonably suppose that Tallis taught Byrd the virginals, as well as the organ, singing and modal counterpoint. As we shall see in the second section of this Chapter, when the tuition was complete, Byrd travelled north to take up the position of organist of Lincoln Cathedral, and there, perhaps, used the nearly hundred-years-old "clavychord", which may, in fact, have been a virginal, used by the Masters of the Choristers.

The instruments, their position in society, and their decoration, were little changed by the deaths of the Tudor sovereigns. Mary was nearly as musical as Henry himself, and perhaps even more so than Elizabeth. Anne of Cleves had a virginal in her house in Lewes, as probably every country house of the gentry class had in the more civilized portions of England, either virginals made in England, or imported from Italy, France or Holland. Queen Mary had three virginal players among the Queen's Music, and had a fourth to tune and repair the instruments. As for Elizabeth, the very name has been supposed to derive from her affection for them; but the Virgin Queen cannot be taken as godmother, seeing the antiquity of the words "a pair of virginals". One of Queen Elizabeth's instruments is still extant: a five-sided model, it might, on the Continent, have been called an espinette, a word (from *spina*, a thorn) not used in England for a hundred years to come. The case bears Elizabeth's royal arms and also those of her mother Anne Boleyn, a dove holding a sceptre.

No instruments have had more names given to them than the virginals. In the chapters dealing with other countries we will meet with these names, and in this chapter with their Englished versions upon importation. The other domestic keyboard instruments with quite a different action from the virginals (the clavichord and the pianoforte) have always had the same names throughout Europe, though there has been confusion, especially between clavichord and virginal, both by contemporary writers of the day, and by modern historical writers and novelists. Readers who do not wish to examine plans of the instruments and understand its very simple mechanism from an engineering point of view, will find their knowledge quite sufficient if they grasp the following points. In the virginals the musical string is plucked by a "thorn": once plucked, its tone cannot be prolonged, nor can the string be plucked softly or loudly. There was no means of making a sudden, or gradual, crescendo or diminuendo. Lastly, the instrument was portable quite easily, a girl could carry it. It would be laid on a table, or a grander model (and the grandeur would be in the case, not the instrument) might have its own legs; but essentially it was a portable musical instrument. Virginals existed in all states: very cheap, like the instrument valued at 10s. in an inventory of a country house near Bury St. Edmunds, to two-manualled affairs in noble casings like the "great payer of dooble virginalls in the parlour" of the same house. In two-manualled virginals with two sets of jacks or with mechanism for altering the plucks, sudden and dramatic changes of tone could be produced by playing on the alternative manual; though "dramatic" is hardly the word, a pleasing change at the repeat of the dance (or folk tune, it would now be called) being all that was usually aimed at. Though some storm music, written by the organist of St. George's, Windsor, and playable on the virginals, might well have delighted those boys of Eton having access to a "payer of dooble virginals", with its possibilities of sudden stop contrasts. Considering, however, the expense of the larger instruments, equal to the annual rent of a large house, while a cottage piano to-day might only be a quarter's rent of a small London flat, and also considering the painted cases and their frequently noble owners, it is unlikely that anyone but a skilled player, or the owner, was allowed to unlock the keyboard cover.

What size and price of virginals it was that the Ambassador of Mary, Queen of Scots, heard the Queen of England play on a much-quoted occasion is not known. In spite of its frequency of quotation, the passage from the *Memoirs of Sir James Melville* must be given: in full and in the original language, not truncated and modernized, for much of the pleasure of reading lies in the details. Here again we are in Royal presence, and we contrast the vanity, diplomacy and flirtation in such an atmosphere with our little instruments, snug in their gorgeous cases, waiting to be touched by the fingers of King, Queen or Cardinal.

Queen Elizabeth had asked Sir James what kind of exercises Mary, Queen of Scots, used.

I said, quhen that I was dispatchit out of Scotland, that the Queen was bot new com bak from the hyland hunting; and when sche had leafer fra the affaires of hir contre, fche red upon gud bukis, the histories of dyvers contrees, and somtymes wald play upon lut and virginelis. Sche sperit gene sche plaid weill. I said, raisonably for a Quen.

That same day efter dener, my L. of Hundsden drew me up till a quyet gallerie that I mycht heir some musik, bot he said he durst not advow it, wher I mycht heir the Quen play upon the virginelis. Bot efter I had harkenit a whyll, I tok by the tapisserie that hang before the dur of the chamber, and seing hir bak was toward the dur, I entrit within the chamber and stod still at the dur chek, and hard hir play excellently will; bot sche left aff sa schone as sche turnit hir about and saw me, and cam forwartis semyng to stryk me with hir left hand, and to think schame; alleging that sche used not to play before men, but when she was solitary hir allaine, till eschew melancholy; and askit how I cam ther.   I said, as I was walken with my L. of Hundsden, as we past by the chamber dur, I hard sic melodie, quhilk ravyst and drew me within the chamber I wist not how; excusing my falt of hamely-ness, as being brocht up in the court of France, and was now willing to suffer what kynd of punissement wald pleise hir lay upon me for my offence.   Then sche sat down laich upon a kusschen, and I upon my knee besyd hir; bot sche gaif me a kusschen with hir awen hand to lay under my knee, quhilk I refused, bot sche compellit me; and callit for my lady Stafford out of the nyxt chamber, for sche was hir allain ther.   Then sche asked whither the Quen or sche played best.   In that I gaif hir the prayse.   Sche said my Frenche was gud; and sperit gif I culd speak Italen, quhilk sche spak raisonable weill.   I said, I taried not abone tua monethes in Italy, and had brocht with me some bukis to reid upon; bot had na leafer to learn the langage perfytly.

A very trying conversation for Sir James, which he seems to have managed "perfytly".

As the sixteenth century drew to a close the virginals came to be a well-established musical instrument for which the greatest composers wrote, but not more established and not with a better repertoire than the lute, we must remember.   The virginals was more for the ladies, while gentlemen played and sang to the lute.   Both instruments, in-deed, were portable, but the keyboard instrument was only suitable for carriage from room to room, while the lute, strung across the body, could be taken out of doors and on horseback.   Perhaps this had something to do with the division of the instruments between the sexes.

These times were great in music as well as in drama.   While in vocal polyphonic writing, Palestrina, Vittoria and the Netherlandish composers must be mentioned along with Byrd, in keyboard writing the English school was supreme, and in songs to the lute, in Dowland and perhaps in Campion we had lyricists of a beauty unparalleled until we come to Schubert.   The several mentions in English literature shows the popularity of the virginals: this quatrain, for instance, from a sonnet of Shakespeare's,

> . . . When thou gently swayest
> The wiry concord thy mine ear confounds,
> Do I envy those jacks that nimbly leap
> To kiss the tender inward of thy hand:

(but Shakespeare should not have said "jacks", "keys" was the right word): and Murray, the lexicographer, quotes from Shakespeare's fellow playwright, Middleton, "her teeth chattered in her head and leaped up and down, like virginal jacks". These quotations show that the sight of a virginal being played was understood to be a common one. In case it be thought that the rebuke to Shakespeare (and to Middleton too) was unjustified, and as a slight contribution to the Shakespeare–Bacon controversy, Bacon can be quoted as getting it quite right, "in a virginal, as soon as ever the jack falleth, and toucheth the string, the sound ceaseth".

With the new century the harpsichord comes into more prominence. It was to play, in the course of time, a new sort of music, and has its place in a later chapter. But it must be considered here in relation to the instrument it was to supplant. Those who look at Jan Vermeer's "A lady at the Virginal" in the National Gallery will notice that the strings, lying within their beautifully painted case, are sideways to the keyboard. This was the usual arrangement, and was rendered suitable by the limited range of the virginals. But when the makers became more ambitious and tried to extend the number of keys, the strings furthest from the keyboard required greater finger leverage and were therefore uncomfortable to play. The obvious way out of this difficulty was to remove the keyboard to the beginning of the strings, when each string could be equidistant from the keys. This was therefore done on the larger instruments, and although authorities differ on the exact meaning of the words "harpsichord", "spinet" and "virginal", a good working definition is, that a harpsichord is a virginal with the keyboard set at the terminus of the strings. And it will be remembered that a virginal and a pair of virginals are one and the same instrument. The difference between a harpsichord and a spinet need not detain us: there seems to have been no essential difference in principle between a virginal and a spinet, the latter word being the Englishing of the current French word, espinette.

Florio's *New World of Words*, 1611, gives these definitions:

> SPINETTA: a kind of little spina . . . also a pair of Virginalles.
> SPINETTEGIARE: to play upon the Virginalles.
> SPINETTO: a thicket of brambles or briars.

In spite of the competition of the largely foreign imported harpsichords, virginals continued to be made in England: Gabriell Townsend made one in 1641 for that daughter of James I who had been the

"Winter Queen": the instrument bore the Palatinate Arms impaling those of Great Britain and an ER, for Elizabeth of Bohemia. The painting inside the lid shows Orpheus enchanting the animals. And musicians were still appointed to the Court under the style of "musician for the Virginall", a title to become meaningless in the civil broils of Charles I.

As the dissolution of the monasteries under Henry VIII turned organists out into the fields, to drift to London to teach (as we have seen in the case of Tallis), so the Cromwellian wars turned out the Cathedral organists. Playford, the great editor and publisher of Stuart times, quotes a long, ominously long, list of teachers of the virginals in London, putting at the head of them the ex-organist of Westminster Abbey. This gentleman, one Portman by name, also wrote a successful book, going into a second edition and being read for a decade or so, aptly named *The Soule's Life, exercising itself in the sweet fields of Meditation, collected for the comfort thereof, in these sad days of distraction.*

But the very business of these ex-organists teaching the virginals shows the kindness the more moderate Puritans had for chamber music. Solomon Eccles was another fashionable teacher: reputed indeed to make £200 in tuition fees. But religion was too much for him, he turned fanatic, and burnt his harmless little instruments publicly on Tower Hill, changed his name to Solomon Eagles, and was lost to music.

However, the influence of Eccles (quite a charming composer) seems to have been but moderate, and at least two virginal makers pursued a lucrative trade, White and Loosemore. A Loosemore of 1655 is still with us: it is on its own stand of black wood, and opens top and front. The front flap drops down to disclose the keyboard, while to the right of the player the strings project. The drop flap is painted with a pastoral scene of pheasants and peacocks, and the inside of the top flap is painted with several scenes merging into one another: Adam and Eve stand under a most luscious and large tree, like a huge mandarin tree, only with fruit more red than mandarins. Huntsmen, in pink and with greyhounds, obtrude on their garden, while large green trees close the prospect. As for the keyboard itself, the naturals are white and the sharps black in the modern manner, but the ends of the keys are gilded.

In the indeterminate period when the virginals were going out and the harpsichord coming in, writers and amateurs, such as Pepys, would sometimes use both words for the one instrument, perhaps even in the same sentence. Those who considered the name to be derived from the player, as does Blount in this quotation from his *Glossographia* (London, 1656) "Virginal (virginalis), maidenly, virginlike, hence the name of that musical instrument called Virginals, because maids and virgins do most commonly play on them", might be justified in calling any boudoir instrument a virginals, even if the keyboard was set end on to the strings. The harpsichord, then, would be the splendid male instrument used in the Opera. However, this theory, like most of the others about instrument nomenclature, is not watertight, for on the Restoration Christopher Gibbons became "musician upon the virginalls in place of Thomas Warwick deceased, with the yearly wages of £86 to be paid quarterly". This was good pay: Pepys, a civil servant (clerk to one of the four Tellers of the Receipt of the Exchequer) got only £50 in 1660.

Nell Gwynn perhaps could play the virginals, for Adam Leversidge made her an instrument, and the lid was painted with a subject as popular as the conventional castle and river scene, or the beasts listening to Orpheus, for it shows the Mall in St. James's Park.

A last sight of these charming little instruments, the bringers forth of so much excellent music, may be had in reading Pepys's report on that fatal evening of the third of September, 1666.

> Met with the King and Duke of York in their barge [for Pepys had gone to the waterside to see the fire] and with them to Queenhithe, and there called Sir Richard Browne to them. Their order was only to pull down houses apace, and so below bridge at the water-side; but little was or could be done, the fire coming upon them so fast. River full of lighters and boats taking in goods, and good goods swimming in the water, and only I observed that hardly one lighter or boat in three that had the goods of a house in, but there was a pair of Virginalls in it.

2. The Composers

Byrd, when in Lincoln, was much cut off from English musical life and was as far away from London as almost to belong to another country. While in Lincoln he married, Fellowes says Juliana Birley, correcting his predecessors, who say Ellen Birley: two children were born, and then the Byrd family moved south, into civilization indeed, for William Byrd was appointed joint organist of the Royal Chapel with Thomas Tallis.

We know little of this period, and the steps by which Tallis secured this appointment under Queen Elizabeth, the daughter perhaps being anxious to make recompense for the wrongs of the father or, more likely, that Tallis was the best organist available. That he should suggest Byrd as collaborator is natural enough.

At least the Queen was aware of both him and Tallis: she, indeed, had not much opportunity of forgetting either, for these two musicians of hers were quick to call her attention, in the proper obsequious manner of the period, whenever the shoe pinched.

The business of printing and selling music, including ruled music paper, was made a monopoly, and this monopoly granted to the partnership of Tallis and Byrd; no doubt they paid a suitable lease fee into the royal coffers. They appear not to have been members of any Guild, such as the Stationers, for the printing of music was something new. Musical quotations or rubrics in books, especially religious books, date from as early as Caxton's successor, Wynkyn de Worde and for the past hundred years there had been a whole stream of prayer books: Sarum Use missals under Queen Mary, and, during the reign of the Protestant Virgin, many printings of Sternhold's editions of the Psalms. This publishing work was given out elsewhere, leaving Tallis and Byrd to do as they wished within their limited field. Even when we remember that their licence enabled them to import and sell printed music from the Continent, it still was no obviously lucrative venture for them. There was nothing to stop composers ruling their own paper, and most music was supplied to choirs and places where they sang, to the houses of nobles and merchants, in manuscript parts. However, Tallis and Byrd printed and published at their own expense a volume of their own vocal compositions, one Thomas Vautrollier being the actual master printer on the job.

But before long Her Majesty had a petition for relief from Tallis, who was now over seventy, asking for a lease, and reminding his royal mistress that he was "now verie aged and hath served your majesty and your Royall ancestors these fortie yeres and hadd as yet never anie manner of preferment except onely one lease . . . which being now the best parte of his lyvinge is with in one yere of expiration", adding that the printing licence had involved him in a loss of 200 marks.

The "lease" for which Tallis asks was presumably the lease of some suitable Crown lands. It was not that he would wish to reside there himself, but leases were securities yielding dividends: they are used even to-day in this way, but were used much more so in the seventeenth century. The Crown parted with revenue for a term by handing over a lease, and the recipient could do as he wished, either enjoy the revenue, or part with the lease for a term for a lump sum. But he, the recipient, had to collect the rents and take full responsibilities, even to clearing up legal difficulties, and there were many, at his own cost.

Many of these leases were obtained by the Crown by confiscating the estates of Catholic traitors. A man's house and land was taken away, not so much from himself, as from his family, for he would be in circumstances in which he would be unlikely to make use of them.

Now Tallis had been brought up in the Latin Catholic liturgy, and it is a difficult thing to forget the beauties of any religious ceremonial experienced daily, as Tallis at Waltham would have experienced it. The Mass, to Tallis, and the Latin language, must have seemed inseparably connected with the practices of religion. However, he was no bigot. Neither was Byrd: both were loyal and law-abiding servants of the Queen. There was, it seems, a great deal of tolerance behind the vicious-sounding laws. Not only were Catholic musicians not persecuted, but they even gained Royal Household appointments and the grants of leases of land sequestered from their co-religionists, who were thought to be neither loyal nor law-abiding. The beginning of the modern conception of freedom of thought, whereby a man may think what he likes, say a great deal of what he thinks, but be very cautious before putting his words to action, was in being in Elizabethan England, and Tallis and Byrd gained thereby.

Tallis was given a lease, and then Byrd came forward, complaining that he, "being called to Her Majesty's service from Lincoln Cathedral, where he was well settled, is now, through great charge of wife and children, fallen into debt and great necessity. By reason of his daily attendance in the Queen's service he is letted from reaping such commodity by teaching as heretofore he did. Her grant two years ago of a licence for printing has fallen out to their loss and hindreance to the value of 200 marks at least".

Byrd was also granted a lease, in Essex, though it was not a pure case of bounty, for the composer had to pay for it, and even then it was somewhat of a gamble, for he could not enter in full possession until the death of the then occupier. Eventually the whole tangle, for there were powerful patrons, and unscrupulous speculators anxious to cheapen leases and then buy them for themselves, involved Byrd in a long and unsatisfactory lawsuit. During this time both Byrd and Tallis may be supposed to be living in the Royal Household at Greenwich, from the hill of which on clear days they could see the whole panorama of the river, the city of London with gothic St. Paul's and Westminster Abbey further to the west. They may also have had lodgings or apartments in noblemen's houses in the City itself. Both did private teaching, and we know from the legal documents connected in the lease difficulties that Byrd taught at least one daughter of a powerful nobleman: let us suppose he taught her the virginals.

But Byrd seems to have hankered after country life: from what we can read of his character through its litigious results, we may suppose him to have been of independent mind and strong, if not pugnacious, personality. The Byrds and their children, with musical instruments and furniture moved to a house in Harlington, supposed to have been near the still existing horse pond, and there they settled down for some years, such lawsuits as Byrd indulged in being about other leases: one in Gloucestershire, for instance. However, local matters troubled him, for the Bishop of London ordered his parish priests to render a return of all such as refuse to come to their parish churches within the diocese of London. Mrs. Byrd was cited, more than once. But nothing more than the standard fine of one shilling seems to have been imposed.

Harlington is now a featureless suburb on the Great West Road. Most of West Middlesex is now such a mass of red boxes hiding here and there an old grey church, that the imaginative effort to realize how it was in Byrd's day is a difficult one.

When Byrd saddled his horse and rode north-west, he soon would come to Uxbridge. If west, to Eton, and so across the Thames to Windsor. Uxbridge was also the main staging point after Charing Cross for Oxford. Riding to the east brings the travellers to Westminster and thence to London, and eventually to Greenwich. Cambridge is further off, nevertheless it was for St. John's College in that University that Byrd wrote short choruses for Legge's Latin play, Ricardus III, an interlude from which, it has been suggested, was the original of the virginal piece known as "The Ghost", to be found in the *Fitzwilliam Virginal Book*.

He would ride to London to teach, to Greenwich to undertake his duties as organist of the Chapel Royal, to Uxbridge as a market town, and to Windsor as organist, and perhaps to teach.

On Sundays Mr. Byrd seems sometimes to have absented himself from his "house at Harmousworth or Craneford", to have crossed the river at Windsor, and gone right into Berkshire; these journeys were quietly, if not secretly, made. A Roman Catholic priest, Father Weston, and a Mr. Bold, in the summer of 1586, visited a Berkshire house of the old faith and found "they had a chapel for the celebration of the Divine Mysteries, an organ likewise and other musical instruments, and, moreover, singers of both sexes belonging to the family, the master of the house being singularly experienced in the art. . . . We met there also Mr. Byrd, the most celebrated musician and organist of the English nation, who had been formerly in the Queen's Chapel, and held in the highest estimation; but for his religion he sacrificed everything, both his office and the Court and all those hopes which are nurtured by such persons as pretend to similar places in the dwellings of princes". It is, surely, unreasonable to deduce that Byrd himself said this or grumbled in some such strain to the priest: it was possibly Father Weston who was depressed and exaggerated the evils those of the Faith suffered under. In the absence of documentation, supposition is fatally easy and fatally attractive. For instance, when Byrd had played the organ during the Divine Mysteries before dinner, may we not suppose that he played the virginals to the company after dinner?

In spite of his baffled attempt, through litigation, to own an Essex lease, Byrd seems to have set his heart on that county, not, as we might first suppose, because of all the Home Counties it most resembled Lincolnshire, for that portion of Essex at which he made more than one attempt is quite hilly. The Byrd country lies, very roughly, between Chipping Ongar and Brentwood, in the Roding valley. Stondon Place itself, where he eventually settled, is nearly three hundred feet above sea-level, while the fields sloped higher still to the back, or south, of the house. The reason for his choice is beyond a plausible guess.

However, a time came when he was successful in that he did take possession of, and live in, Stondon Place, at the end of the village of Stondon Massey as a man rides in from Chipping Ongar, but unsuccessful in that he had a great deal of trouble to continue to live there. The constant litigation with a Mrs. Shelley, a lady of about Byrd's age, makes amusing and distracting reading, because all parties seem to exaggerate as much as possible. The Crown lease was in dispute, and Byrd was accused of many things. Of cutting down timber, of being rude to her—"and . . . before her sayd, that yf he could not hould it by right, he would holde it by might"—of not paying all the rent when he should, and "practized to disgrace her with divers her honorable friends". In return, he accused Mrs. Shelley: but we are not interested in Mrs. Shelley.

He also had trouble with a churchwarden of Stondon who had the right of occupying two or three rooms in Stondon Place, or so he said, but Byrd dispossessed him, and successfully maintained the inviolability of his house and his two hundred acres against all comers, both angry elderly widows and lodging churchwardens. Dr. Fellowes names a total of six lawsuits in which Byrd during his long life appeared a principal, and in four he was plaintiff and in only two defendant.

Tallis had died before his younger friend's removal into Essex. However much Byrd quarrelled with neighbours (or they with him, on sufficient or insufficient reason), there appears to have been no dispute between the two musicians. Tallis was godfather, we learn from his will, to Byrd's second son. Byrd and Tallis got rid of a potential source of trouble by allowing a printer named Easte, East or Este, to rent their monopoly on printed music. Some years after the death of Tallis, the monopoly passed altogether from Byrd, and became the business of Morley.

Morley had been a pupil of Byrd, was organist of one of the City churches, lived in his own house within the walls, and became organist of St. Paul's, and later became one of the Gentlemen of the Chapel Royal. He was a much younger man than Byrd, but died before him. There is no evidence that Byrd bore Morley any ill will because of the change of the monopoly, even if we were sure that it was an arbitrary decision of the Crown. Morley dedicated to Byrd his book, which is the first book of its sort in the English language, *Plaine and Easie Introduction to Practicall Musicke*, a volume not printed by the monopoly agent Easte (for Morley continued Byrd's connexion with this man) but by a well-known printer of madrigal books on Bread Street Hill. Morley, more than any other Elizabethan composer, was a Londoner: his work, his dwelling and both his printers lay within the city walls, out of which he need never stray into the barbaric lands beyond, except when he rode under the two gates of London Bridge and turned left, through the broad thoroughfare on the Surrey side

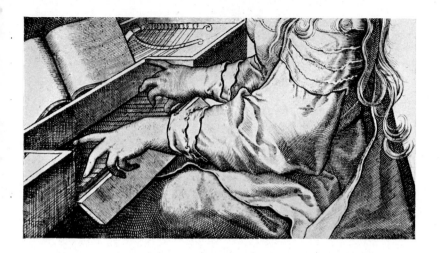

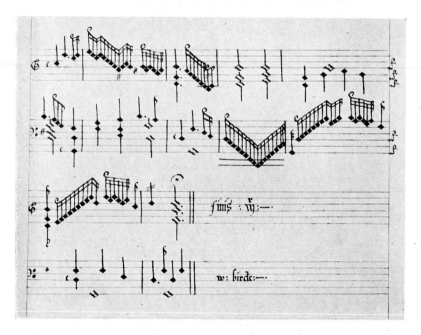

The upper illustration shows detail from the title page of *Parthenia*, and the lower, the last bars of the 2nd Pavan from a series of 9 pavans and galliards in the MS of *My Ladye Nevells Booke*.

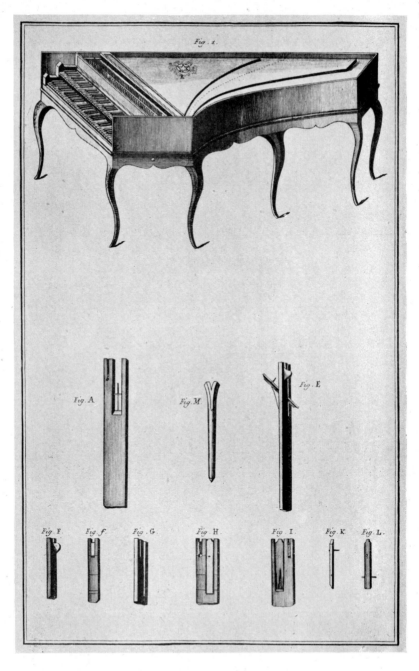

The clavecin according to Diderot (1774). A. Jack without plectrum.
E. Jack with plectrum. F. f. G. H. I. Jacks. K. L. Plectra. M. Pin.

known as Battle bridge, on his way to his Chapel Royal duties at Greenwich.

But there is something unpleasant, a sort of distasteful mystery, about Morley's friendship with the Dean of St. Paul's: he may even have been a sort of spy or *agent provocateur* among the Roman Catholics. An exile wrote of Morley, "he hath played the promoter and apprehendeth Catholickes" and a Government counter-espionage official wrote that he had "browght divers into danger". But Byrd was not "browght" into any trouble through Morley, and Byrd continued to be his friend. Perhaps both Byrd and Morley belonged to those who saw certain of the Roman Catholics as belonging to what we might nowadays call a Continental Roman Catholics Fifth Column. It must be remembered that the events in France, Spain and Germany were being enacted which led up to the Thirty Years War, and religion and politics were already inextricably intermingled.

Morley's life links not only with the greatest musician of his time, Byrd, but also with the greatest dramatist. Morley wrote song tunes for Shakespeare's plays, and lived in the parish of Little St. Helens, adjoining the parish of St. Helens, Bishopsgate, which has Shakespearian associations. Both men were assessed with goods to the value of £5 and taxed 13s. 4d. Both appealed. Christopher Marlowe is supposed by some scholars to have had a hand in the *King Henry VI* plays attributed to Shakespeare, and indeed there is little doubt but that Morley, Marlowe and Shakespeare were all acquaintances.

Our ignorance of the lives of the great Elizabethan musicians and dramatists is tantalizing. Consider this parallel. On the 1st of June, 1593, Christopher Marlowe was stabbed in an affray in a Deptford tavern. The Coroner's report alluded throughout to the deceased as Morley. From documents assembled by J. L. Hotson in his *The Death of Christopher Marlowe* it is plain that he was engaged in political and perhaps even religio-political espionage, like Thomas Morley, who, indeed, must have often passed through Deptford on his way to Greenwich, as we have seen. He was a Gentleman of the Chapel Royal at the time of Marlowe's death: he was sufficiently in favour at Court to be given the printing monopoly of music some years later. Marlowe's killer was pardoned. It seems therefore that, at the end, Marlowe and Morley were on opposite sides, though not necessarily drawn into the same web of intrigue. When Morley heard of Marlowe's death, he may have been afraid: afraid for his position in the Chapel Royal and at St. Paul's, perhaps even afraid for his life, and he determined, we

c

may suppose, to be completely loyal to the Court. When Byrd heard of Marlowe's death, he moved further away from London, and took up his residence at Stondon in Essex. This sequence of events is not necessarily cause and effect, but Byrd certainly managed well through aloofness, enjoying both the Old Religion and Royal favour.

Sir Thomas Gresham left much money in his Will for a series of music lectures among other educational benefits to be given in the City of London, and Bull became the first professor of music. He had been a cathedral organist in the West country, and had come to London to be one of the organists of the Chapel Royal. He was already known for his great skill as an executant, both upon the organ and the virginals and he, of all the composers of his time, most dedicated himself to the domestic keyboard instrument., A painting in the Music School of the University of Oxford shows him bearded—like Tallis and Byrd—sallow and serious, and with a pair of fine moustachios, while Byrd, though with moustachios, ran more to the beard we now call Naval, for Bull's was rather whispy. Behind Bull's magnificent collar stands a skull resting on an hour glass, and the picture is framed by these words:

> The Bull by force
> In field doth Raigne
> But Bull by Skill
> Good will doth Gayne

forming a somewhat empty quatrain, but attesting to his skill and popularity. Although Bull carried a Doctorship of Music away from Oxford, he knew no Latin, which, on the face of it, is rather surprising, especially as in that very Latin-speaking age not to know it meant one was not quite the gentleman: just as, according to Morley, not to be able to read your vocal part at sight made people ask how you were brought up. But Bull, who so far in his life appears to have enjoyed exceptional Court favour, was forgiven. Perhaps he added to his great manual dexterity and undoubted talent for composition (he was the Liszt of his age) considerable charm and personality. The executors of Sir Thomas Gresham made a special concession for him.

> . . . the solemn music lecture twice every week, in the manner following, viz. the theoretique part for one half-hour, or thereabouts, and the practique, by concert of voice or instruments, for the rest of the hour, whereof the first lecture should be in the Latin tongue and the second in English; but because at this time Mr Dr

Bull, who is recommended to the place by the Queen's Most Excellent Majesty, being not able to speak Latin, his lectures are permitted to be altogether in English, so long as he shall continue in the place of music lecturer there.

After attaining this post, Bull must have been one of the best known musicians of his time. He was given a gold medal by James I not, one supposes, for one hundred and fifty individual keyboard pieces (Byrd's output was a mere one hundred and twenty) but as one of the organists of the Chapel Royal. Stowe relates a visit of the King to London, and how he and Prince Henry dined in the Hall of the Merchant Taylors, where "John Bull, Docter of Musique, one of the organists of His Maiesties Chappell-Royall, and free of the Merchant-Taylors, being in a citizen's gowne, cappe, and hood, played most excellent melodie upon a small payre of Organes, placed there for that purpose onley". It is permissible to hope that Ben Jonson was among the King's followers on this occasion. There was to be a link between the poet and the musician in the future. More than three hundred years lies between this possibility of Jonson and Bull being in the same room, and Bull's music being quoted by Strauss in the score of an opera founded originally on Jonson's *Volpone*. Strauss quotes an *In Nomine* by Bull for the virginal during the pseudo legal scene which, in Jonson's original, was Act v. sc. vi.

Bull had to resign his Gresham Professorship on his marriage, but later somewhat replaced this work by entering the service of Prince Henry at a salary of £40 a year. He had, some years back, petitioned the Crown for one of those leases so popular with Gentlemen of the Chapel Royal, and had received one to the value of £20 per annum: as he retained (it is supposed) his position of organist he was comfortably off, indeed, Morley, Byrd, Bull and others were far better off materially than the composers of Vienna in the eighteenth century, where we have another city, rich and spacious, in the glow of a vigorous musical life, behaving far more parsimoniously and being far fuller of intrigue than a London under a Queen noted for avarice and a King from Scotland and a general political air of great unrest.

But then the blow fell. It has never been decided exactly why Bull fled to Flanders, but the Cheque Book of the Chapel Royal says "John Bull, Doctor of Musicke, went beyond the seas without licence, and was admitted into the Archduke's service, and entered into paie there about Michaelmas". The Archduke's capital was Brussels, and the English Minister there was of the opinion that Bull did not leave London

for any reason of disaffection or religion, but because of his fear of
"the hand of justice, for his incontinence, fornication, adultery, and
other grievous crimes". A later writer says that Bull left His Majesty's service "being possess'd with crotchets as many musicians are".

When Bull reached Flanders he went to Amsterdam, where Swee-
linck, called Swelling by one English writer, was the organist, a man
of much talent and virtuosity and who was to become an influence in
north Germany and therefore, indirectly, to help form the style of the
great Bach. Besides the man named Swelling, Bull would meet
fellow countrymen in exile: John Bolt, virginal player to the late
Queen, who suddenly had to escape as suspected of a plot; possibly
the Cornishman, Tregian, making manuscript copies of virginal music;
and Peter Phillips, whose virginal music in manuscript form was circu-
lated in the cities. Bull's name was well known, for many of his manuscripts, too, were passed from hand to hand, while his skill at the
virginals had become known across the Channel. So the instructed
and musical people of Antwerp, Brussels, Amsterdam, The Hague,
Delft and other cities were acquainted with English composers. It
became natural that Bull should, in a few years, become organist of
Antwerp Cathedral. In these last years of his life he composed one of
his best known pieces. "Het Juweel van Doctor Jan Bull quod fecit
anno 1621 December" is written on one of the manuscript copies of
what is now called "Dr. Bull's Jewel". And so we leave Bull, who
died a few years later, and quote the plaintive question of an humble
aspirant of an amateur composer, a minor canon of Chester Cathedral.

> . . . and must the matchless excellencies
> Of Bird, Bull, Dowland, Morley, and the rest
> Of our rare artists (who now dim the light
> Of other lands) be only in Request?

And the answer must be, yes, we are afraid so.

Of the four composers named by the Chester poet, we have dealt
with three. Of Dowland, not much need be said here, for his great
work was the composition of songs with lute accompaniment, and
he wrote little virginal music. As the poet Barnfield says, "Dowland
to thee is deare, whose heavenly touch Upon the lute doth ravish
humaine sense." He was perhaps an Irishman, and was a lutenist
in the service of English ambassadors abroad, in France and Italy
and in the Holy Roman Empire, while he later took service as

lutenist in the Court of the King of Denmark, ending his career, however, "in our Palace of Whitehall".

Farnaby, one of the most delightful of the group of virginal composers, is a man of whom we seem to know little. He was possibly a Cornishman, and may, from the omission of his name from the collection of madrigals published in 1600 in honour of Queen Elizabeth, *The Triumphs of Oriana*, have died before this date.

Orlando Gibbons belongs to a slightly later generation. The others are usually, and loosely, called Elizabethans, although two of the greatest of them, Bull and Byrd, lived on to be subjects of James. But Gibbons is Jacobean and even Caroline. He was born in Cambridge but baptized in Oxford: this amazing oscillation was ended by his entering King's, a college which may prove, to the assiduous drawer-up of teams of musicians, to rival Christ Church itself as a nurse of heroes. Gibbons had a brilliant and unchecked career. Coming down from Cambridge he became organist of the Chapel Royal, and then preceded Purcell as organist at Westminster Abbey. Gibbons lived in Woolstaple, in Westminster, which is where Bridge Street now stands.

Musical life lay mostly in and around Westminster, around the Court, its Chapel, and the Royal Peculiar of the Collegiate Church of Saint Peter, and this life, with its royal, military, scholastic, religious and musical element has no counterpart to-day.

The King, with his whole Household, travelled towards Dover to meet Henrietta Maria, who was to come over to him from Paris. With him in his place among the Gentlemen of the Chapel Royal moved its organist, Mr. Orlando Gibbons. At Canterbury, barely middle-aged, he was attacked, it is said, by apoplexy, and died: there is a memorial in the Cathedral.

In English musical history, there was a diminution, almost a gap, during the reign of Charles I and the ensuing Commonwealth. There was no important keyboard composer from the death of Gibbons to the Restoration, and in Purcell we have a man who adorned the harpsichord rather than the virginals: a man who was the precursor of Handel rather than the successor of Byrd.

3. The Music

Anyone interested in this book will very likely have seen, or owned, a modern reprint of virginal music, published by Augeners or Novellos, or some foreign House such as Breitkopf and Hartel. There will be perhaps a dozen pieces, with an editorial introduction. The pieces themselves will be printed in the same notation, and usually with the same phrasing marks and bars, and time and key signatures, as for Bach or Mozart. Played straight away on the modern upright pianoforte, sometimes the music will seem effective, sometimes curious, more often dull and lumpy. The metric impulse will often elude the player, and sudden intrusions of demi-semi-quavers will baffle him.

It is necessary and interesting to go behind these modern reprints, which will again be alluded to at the end of this section, and to examine the sources from which they come. Most music, like most books, of a standard nature, have a long bibliography behind them. Manuscript, first edition, second edition, collected edition, edited edition with notes, popular edition, and so on. Sometimes this sequence shows a deterioration of text, sometimes a clarification. The poetic drama contemporary to the virginal composers may be examined in any good library in almost all texts: photographic facsimiles of first editions, bowdlerized editions, "for the young", and scholarly volumes so overrun with comment that the words of Shakespeare or Marlowe are next to impossible to discern.

None of this is the case with Byrd, Bull, Farnaby and their fellows. Only one volume of virginal pieces was published in their lifetimes, and except for such quotations as Hawkins and Burney in their ignorance and pride deemed it proper to make, nearly three centuries elapsed, while the bulk of this music remained in manuscript, some of it hidden and unregarded in private libraries. Some of it is still unprinted, and the field is still an open one for scholarship. Not that this book can presume, considering the largeness of its subject, to enter into these august pastures. Nor can this author, considering the crashing errors made by the most notable authors, dare hope that he himself is free from error. The same pieces have been supposed to be different pieces: different pieces have been supposed to be the same pieces. Writers of books have copied errors from earlier books. Some day someone should do for the virginal composers what Skeat has done for the more remote Chaucer.

One of the earliest manuscripts dates, it is supposed, from 1565, and is known as Thomas Mullinar's manuscript. He was the scribe, and the music he transcribed was, it seems to me, organ music and not virginal music. It is modal polyphony, unornamented, non-metrical, and sustained. Its composers are Redman, Blitheman—the teacher, perhaps, of Bull—Tallis himself, and Farrant, who is probably the same man as the stormy organist of Salisbury Cathedral. Mullinar was Master of the Choristers at St. Paul's Cathedral. His manuscript collection has not been printed, nor has any selection from it been offered for sale. Of Blitheman's dozen or more pieces one is quoted in full by Hawkins in his history, while J. E. West includes two pieces from this manuscript collection in his Novello edition named *Old English Organ Music*.

Brief mention must here be made of Hugh Ashton, whose "Hornepipe" is usually considered important. His identity is not certain, and the dates of his virginal compositions present difficulties it is unreasonable to go into here. His music, in my opinion, has little aesthetic appeal, though in the piece named at least he shows a movement away from the organ style to a definite keyboard texture.

The fingering of this music was possibly, some say probably and even certainly, confined to the middle fingers only. This middle finger tradition is held to have obtained on the virginals and a most ingenious theory regarding it is put forward by Dr. Hans Hickman in his book *Das Portativ*. He draws attention to the angels and other musicians shown in Gothic church architectural sculptures and panels, and in pictures. They have a small organ, complete with pipes, strapped across their back with the instrument itself on their chests. If this was the common posture of the mere mortal playing a portable (hence the word portative) organ, the keyboard would be at right angles to himself and the right hand would play in that posture. A simple experiment will convince anyone that the middle fingers, crawling near and far, are the only ones it is practicable to use. While the right hand is engaging its fingers thus, the left hand pumps.

As construction and invention progress, technique and names often lag behind. The middle fingers were used in the old organs, and therefore should be used in the new virginals, although very different in every way, including position. A theory, but a plausible and a human one.

The next manuscript of importance is very important indeed: it is a manuscript with the title *My Ladye Nevell's Booke* found, according

to its most recent and truly scholarly editor, Miss Hilda Andrews, in
Eridge Castle in Sussex, the seat of the Marquess of Abergavenny.
Its history may reasonably be deduced thus. Byrd numbered among
his pupils a Lady Nevell, and wished to give her a volume of his virginal
music. He rode over to Windsor from his Middlesex home and
encouraged one of the musicians on the establishment of St. George's
Chapel to transcribe his music for him. This scribe, Baldwin by name,
was a great admirer of the Master, and wrote a really beautiful musical
hand. His lozenge-shaped notes, running up and down in the scale
passages, seem to make a design as attractive and ornamental as the
music itself. He was surely extremely careful, and it was to be very
many decades before English printing could turn out anything so
clear and neat, and it has never (though never is a big word) done
anything so charming. So much for manual labour. Baldwin
usually wrote at the end of each piece a note giving the composer's
name, in every case Byrd, of course, and sometimes his office, such as
that he was of the Royal Chapel. All subsequent commentators on
this noble volume of manuscript have pointed out the sudden enthusiasm of one of these ascriptions "mr w birde homo memorabilis",
though there is also a "mr w birde laudes deo". Baldwin, in a poem
of some strength if of unusual form, preceding a motet collection he
made, says:

> For they [i.e. all the composers he has previously eulogized]
> May now give place and sett themselves behynde,
> An Englishman, by name, William Birde for his skill.
> Famous men be abroad, and skilful in the arte
> I do confess the fame and not from it starte:
> But in Europpe is none like to our English man.

When Baldwin had finished the volume, Byrd presented it to his
virginal pupil, the Lady Nevell. This was in 1591. Her husband,
who was later Lord Edward Abergevenny, gave it to Queen Elizabeth,
perhaps for her to play from. Equally, perhaps, she found it too difficult, and gave it into the keeping of a Mr. North, a relation, it is said,
of Lord North. He bequeathed it to his son, who gave it to an attorney at Clifford's Inn, who gave it to a member of the Abergevenny
family, and it is due to this member, who wrote a useful note in the
volume, that we can trace the book thus far. Somehow it later came
into the possession of Dr. Burney, who certainly thought it interesting,
if a little too gothic, and who retained it throughout his life. At the

sale of his library in 1814, it was purchased by a private gentleman of London, and in 1826 bought by a bookseller of St. James's and by him sold to Lord Abergavenny at some date before 1833.

Its modern publication is a model of how this sort of thing should be done. The engraving (it seems not to have been set up from type) is almost as marvellously clear and attractive as Baldwin's own script. Miss Hilda Andrews approached her task with respect and care, and only those alterations have been made which modern notation (Baldwin wrote for six staves) demands.[1]

Many of the pieces were copied or printed into later collections; among the unique pieces are some pavans and galliards. We also have the full title of the song on which Byrd wrote one of his most famous sets of variations, a set copied into another and later collection, and more than once the subject of a modern reprint, "Will Yow Walke The Woods Soe Wylde." If we think of the tune, and pronounce the "you" as written by Baldwin, the second note of the tune receives added colour.

The third volume was as different from the manuscript book of Lady Nevell, as hers was from the collection of Mullingar: for *Parthenia* was a printed book, and its pirating has saved the time of more than one unscrupulous editor. Heffer of Cambridge have recently issued a photographic reproduction in their Harrow Replica series, but intending hunters after this slim folio should be warned they will find it difficult to play from. This is no fault of the modern publishers, whose reproduction is perfect, but partly of the six stave convention of the time, partly because the 1611 engraver did not place his left- and right-hand notes in relation to each other, and partly because this printing is far inferior in clarity (let alone in beauty) to the painstaking and artistic work of Baldwin of Windsor.

As this volume is not scarce, only a short description should be necessary. The title-page declares that it is "the first musicke that ever was printed for the Virginalls", and goes on to say "Composed By three famous Masters, William Byrd, Dr John Bull and Orlando Gibbons Gentilmen of his Ma(jesties) most Illustrious Chappell". His Majesty was James I.

Underneath the wording which has just been given is the engraving of a virgin with long tresses, severe of aspect and with podgy hands, playing a virginalls with the lid, of course, open. It is not a curiosity

---

[1] Published by Curwen & Sons, 1926.

that she does not care to look at the open score before her, for few musicians as portrayed by artists take their work seriously. Is it a curiosity that her left hand makes great play with the middle finger, but that she does appear to be using the thumb of her right hand? It is probably only William Hole, the artist, and his ideas of keyboard playing.

From the imprint itself and from a note by Dr. Deutsch it is permissible to give the following narrative of *Parthenia*. Bull had the Princess Elizabeth among his pupils, who had, as one of her ladies, a Dorethie Evans. On the behalf of the Princess, this Miss or Mrs. Evans occasioned Dr. Bull, not then in disgrace, to collect, and the holders of the music-printing monopoly to print, a book of twenty-one pieces for the virginal. Now Byrd had long ago resigned his monopoly to Morley, and Morley had in turn handed it to a printer named G. Lowe, and so we have the full imprint: "Lond: print: for M Dor: Evans, Cum privilegio. Are to be sould by G. Lowe print(er) in Loathberry."

The published volume was very successful, and several reprints kept the enlightened virginal player interested for nearly a hundred years afterwards. Then it faded from sight, and only about a dozen copies of these seventeenth-century printings are known. But this number was at least twelve times as many as the greater manuscript collections, so the pieces from *Parthenia* were the most common to be resurrected by the Victorian and Edwardian editors.

The above narrative has not the documented authenticity of that concerning the Lady Nevell volume, but is a plausible fitting together of the known facts.

The largest and most important of all the virginal collections soon followed after *Parthenia*, for its last probable date is 1619, while *Parthenia* is 1611. Here again we are in the realms of imaginative reconstruction, but it is generally supposed that a gentleman named Tregian of Cornish family, imprisoned in the Fleet for his religious activities, copied out a huge collection of virginal music while so imprisoned. Another theory is, that he transcribed later, while in exile. He died in 1619, and his sister had some difficulty in taking his manuscript away from the Fleet authorities. Tregian, being a Roman Catholic, may have brought a certain anti-Protestant bias into his copying. So thinks Miss M. H. Glynn in her volume devoted to virginal music, with the result that while the music of Byrd was reasonably presented, Bull was often mutilated, and inferior readings of his pieces inserted, and superior pieces rejected. When Tregian's sister secured the manuscript, she had it carefully and beautifully bound, and then we know nothing until we learn that Mrs. Pepusch, wife of the compiler of the music for *The Beggar's Opera* of 1727, was in possession of the book, sat down at her harpsichord, opened it at page one and quite failing to play the first piece, shut the book up again. As the first piece, Bull's variations on the tune called Walsingham, is the most remarkable, most difficult and longest in the book, Mrs. Pepusch must have been a curious sort of woman, for later on there are several short, easy and melodious pieces, which one supposes even she could have managed. A quite different story is, that Dr. Pepusch became quite a Tudor enthusiast, and played from the virginal book to large circles of friends. In 1762, at the sale of the library of the deceased Doctor, it was bought for ten guineas and passed to Viscount Fitzwilliam (no apparent relation of Pitt's President of the Council). Dying in 1816, he left his library, including Tregian's virginal manuscript, to the University of Cambridge, who built a house to receive his gift: hence the Fitzwilliam Museum, and hence the title given to the manuscript, *The Fitzwilliam Virginal Book*, the greatest single name in all virginal literature. In 1899 the whole MS. was published, in two volumes.[1] These two volumes contain the heart of virginal literature. More pieces of more different forms by more composers are represented than in any rival book or manuscript. Consequently, our interest in the sources of virginal collections compiled after 1619, the last likely date for the *Fitzwilliam Virginal Book*, ceases.

Perhaps Cosyn's virginal book is the most remarkable of the others. His contains music by Byrd, Gibbons, Bull and himself, among others, and it has been remarked how poor the Bull pieces are and how good the Cosyn. Some think that Cosyn stole Bull's pieces, but others, and with them the pro-Bull Miss Glyn, feel that Cosyn ascribed his own pieces to Bull. Certainly the pieces ascribed here and elsewhere to Bull show him as a most unequal composer. Benjamin Cosyn was organist of the Charterhouse, then of course in London, where some of the building still stands, to the north-east of Smithfield Market. It is a curious coincidence that Dr. Pepusch, one-time owner of the Fitzwilliam manuscript, was also a holder of that office. The list of contents reads "A Table of these Lessons followinge made and sett forth

---

[1] Published by Breitkopf & Hartel. Edited by J. A. Fuller-Maitland and W. Barclay Squire.

by Ben Cos", and continues to mention Lessons by "Mr. Doctor Bull" and "Mr. Or. Gibbons", Tallis and Byrd, and "six services for the Kings Royall Chappell" and, finally, "A Table of all these Lessons generally contained in this Booke are in Number: 96. By me Benjamin Cosyn Right owner of this Booke."

There are other virginal collections, Foster's, for instance, and that of Elizabeth Rogers. There are shorter collections, too, but not much new material. Favourite pieces would appear in collection after collection. Some smaller manuscripts are now to be found outside England: a holograph of Thomas Tomkins is in *Bibliotheque du Conservatoire* in Paris, and the New York Public Library has been a purchaser when opportunity offered.

So we are faced with this large accumulation of music, mainly manuscript at the time, with about half or rather more in print now. What does it amount to?

First of all, the virginals for which it was all written. The instruments have been described physically in section one of this chapter, and here we need do no more than emphasize the short compass. Byrd in *Parthenia* never exceeded

Gibbons, however, goes a third below Byrd. In the *Fitzwilliam Virginal Book* Farnaby goes a third above Byrd, so that Byrd's compass was extended by a fifth, but there the matter ended.

At the left-hand end of the virginal keyboard there would sometimes be a white note on the left of the ending F key. This left-hand note would sound C, the D and E sounding on the black notes usually F sharp and G sharp, the F♯ and G♯ sounds being altogether omitted. This arrangement not only gave a low C in the bass without enlarging the keyboard of the instrument more than if the compass had merely extended to low E, but allowed for a tenth to be stretched with great ease, from C to tenor E, both because of this "faked" left-hand end, and because virginal keys are narrower than are modern pianoforte keys.

When we come to discuss the music itself, and arrive at the pieces which are fugued, we will find, sometimes, an abundance of sharps and flats producing harmonies on the modern keyboard unfamiliar to those whose knowledge of music does not extend before or after the Haydn-Brahms period; many amateurs and some professionals live all their lives cosily within this great period. It is usually supposed that the virginals, like all keyboard instruments, were tuned exactly and not in equalized temperament (whereby the vibrations are allotted to each note by arithmetic rather than by ear), but this aural tuning produces an increasing maladjustment between the more remote sharp and flat keys. As composers avoided the keys more remote from C major, and usually modulated, or started their movements, in keys closely related to C major, the "wolf" was not heard. And, finally, it is usually supposed by the more popular historians that J. S. Bach, in his *Well Tempered Clavier*, showed how the keyboard could be adjusted by equal tuning to enable pieces in keys remote from C like C sharp major or B flat minor to be performed.

Now we have the problem. If the virginals were not tuned in Bach's way, some of these fugued pieces which modulate quite alarmingly would be pleasant on the ear. If, however, they were not tuned as the voice sings, some of the pieces would have sounded as harsh to the virginalists as they do to us. My own preferred solution is, that the virginals, which, owing to the plucking action of the plectrum, would often require tuning, were usually tuned by the performer before playing, and that he tuned according to the nature of the piece to be played. There is no written evidence I know of to bear me witness, but we can marshal the following three pieces of data:

(1) The age was not a specialized one, and the human voice was the chief and most admired musical instrument. Here one inevitably quotes Byrd, "there is not any Musicke of Instruments whatsoever, comparable to that which is made of the voyces of Men . . ." and the human ear would have been proportionally delicate.

(2) Instruction was given verbally and not in "tutors".

(3) The virginals often went out of tune and it was easy for the player to tune them again. We may presume that experiments in tuning were tried.

In our specialized and instrumental age the performer takes the sounds of a pianoforte for granted, and if the parts jar, blames the music, while the Elizabethan may have blamed the tuning of the instrument.

The music carries many marks of ornamentation to each piece; almost, one could say, to each bar. These ornaments, trills, and turns, are denoted by one or two strokes, as the case may be, through the stem of the note to be treated.   Opinion differs both as to the meaning of these marks, and their desirability when the music has to be performed on the modern pianoforte.   It is usually thought that the more common of the two marks, the two-stroked stem, means a mordent, and perhaps the one stroke means a short appoggiatura.   Landowska takes the view that very decidedly the ornaments must be played, but then she writes with the harpsichord in the back of her mind, and the pianists differ.   Harriet Cohen writes, for instance, "I personally think that the very early keyboard music is complete without ornaments, but that the later period needs them," and the context of this remark in her book *Music's Handmaid*[1] shows that by the "very early" music she means Byrd, Bull and Gibbons.   Dr. Fellows says "On a pianoforte they should be sparingly observed."

The editors agree with the pianists.   Miss Hilda Andrews, the editor of *My Ladye Nevell's Booke* says "much of the florid figuration is better omitted altogether", and Sir Granville Bantock does not even discuss the matter, but prints his scores without any marks of ornaments, printing out the trills he wishes performed, and these are not very many.   Mr. van den Borren brings the scholars to reinforce the pianists and editors: in his invaluable *The Sources of Keyboard Music in England*[2] he declares he considers virginal music sounds completely adequate on the pianoforte without ornamentation, and that he feels the manuscripts and *Parthenia* show ornamentation to excess, possibly due to the zeal of a scribe, and that "the distribution of these little ornaments is often very arbitary".

The matter would appear settled: play the music without ornaments.   But my own opinion is, that the ornamentation often shows the rhythm, as in this by Byrd from *Parthenia*

here the ornament on the F gives a slight accent to the weak part of the bar, suggesting duple time and contradicting the triple time signature, which is, however, marked in a pronounced way in the third and fourth bars.   The tenor line in the second bar helps this metrical illusion.   I need hardly add that such playings

---

[1] Faber, 1936.

[2] Novello's *Handbooks for Musicians*.

with time were as much in Byrd's line as playings with key in Beethoven's.

The same melodic phrase occurs elsewhere. This is how Bantock starts his transcription of No. 262 from the *Fitzwilliam Virginal Book*, a Toye by Bull.

But if I copy the start as in the manuscript

surely the delight of the melody is much enhanced.

A third reason for the retention of ornaments is when parts enter in imitation, and ornaments help to fix the fugal line and make it easily recognizable as it recurs. This argument is only a slight one, for quite often the manuscripts themselves do not indicate ornamentation in all the imitative parts. Here, for instance, are the first two bars of an "Ut, mi, re" by Byrd, No. 102 in the *Fitzwilliam Virginal Book*.

Ornamentation here merely makes for confusion. But in these two bars from the eighth variations of Byrd's set on "The Woods so Wild", No. 67 in the *Fitzwilliam*,

we may surely see careless transcribing. If the copyist put in the ornaments after writing the text, he omitted to cross the D in the tenor of the first bar, and crossed instead the last C in the alto of the same bar. If we make this little correction for him, we have a perfectly clear passage in *stretto*, whose clarity is helped by the ornamentation.

Therefore I should like to enlarge the rather negative views quoted from others, by adding that ornamentation often helps with rhythmic subtlety, enhances the charm of melody, and helps to clarity in fugued passages, but that it should be omitted when it does not one of these three things, which is, perhaps, most often of all.

As for the technical difficulty of playing virginal music on the piano-forte, opinion has varied from the extreme view that the music is so difficult that the players of those days must have been very highly skilled, to the moderate one that most of the pieces may be mastered after a little practice. But the truth surely is, that no broad opinion can be laid down at all. What we are considering is a whole school or manner. How difficult is Romantic pianoforte music? What a question! Some Mendelssohn is quite simple, some Chopin most difficult. In the same way, the answer to the parallel virginal question is, some Farnaby is quite simple, some Bull most difficult. The tremendous range and extent of the virginal school is simply not appreciated by some writers: from Bull's variations on the tune called "Walsingham" to one of the short anonymous dances of the *Fitzwilliam* is all the difference between the "Goldberg Variations" and the D minor minuet from the *Little Book of Anna Magdalena Bach*.

Every sort of technique is called into play. We even have cross hands in the 28th variation of "Walsingham": Bull is usually the most difficult and technically adventurous master, though it was Farnaby who wrote a short piece for two virginals. Bull is thought by some possibly to have been virginal tutor to Queen Elizabeth, and her degree of technique has often been speculated upon. But her attainments would depend less upon the mastery of her teacher than her own seriousness of application while practising, and how do we estimate that? That particular Queen had many more exciting things to do than to apply herself to the virginal keyboard by the hour.

In examining this great mass of music, we may distinguish not only many forms, variations, ecclesiastical counterpoints, dances and programme music, but also different textures and moods amounting to different genres. Some of Farnaby's pieces might almost be called Mozartian in their grace, directness and simplicity, while whole passages by the same master, or by Bull, seem on paper like passages from the more florid and contrapuntal pages of the *Well Tempered Clavier*. But in making our survey, it will be simpler to keep to the avowed forms.

We consider first the dances, and, of these, the Pavans.

. . . a kind of staide musicke (says Morley, in a much-quoted passage from his *Plaine and Easie Introduction to Musick*) ordained for grave dauncing, and most commonlie made of three straines, whereof everie straine is plaid or sung twice, a straine they make to containe 8. 12. or 16. semibreves as they list.

The most popular single piece of virginal music current to-day is a Pavan by Byrd, for the Earl of Salisbury, while Gibbons wrote a dance to the same dedication which is nearly as popular. Both these are in *Parthenia*, while the Gibbons is in the *Fitzwilliam* too. There is another grave and beautiful Pavan, called after Sir William Petre, also in *Parthenia* and also by Byrd. Perhaps the most beautiful melody for the Pavan is by Dowland, and originally appeared in *Lachrymae, or Seven Teares, figured in seaven passionate Pavans*, which Byrd transcribed for keyboard. But Morley's arrangement for virginals (*Fitzwilliam* No. 153) forms one of the strongest and most memorable of all the pieces in this dance form. The simpler and graver music, which suited Byrd so well, is best in these Pavans: Bull, in such Pavans as *Fitzwilliam* No. 34, with his spread chords and variation form, is dull and prolix.

The Galliard was joined to the Pavan. Says Morley, "After each Pavan we usually set a galliard . . . a lighter and more stirring kinde of dauncing then the pavane. . ." The Galliard in *Parthenia* by Byrd printed after the Petre Pavan is a notable example of this dance, and so is also Byrd's Galliard called "Sir Jhon Graye" in the *Fitzwilliam* (No. 191). In her *Music's Handmaid* Miss Harriet Cohen gives space to a third Byrd Galliard, that in *Parthenia* which comes after the "Salisbury" Pavan. But on the whole the Galliards which have come down to us seem slightly less interesting than "the staide musicke ordained for grave dauncing". The La Volta is supposed to be a Galliard with a caper, and in No. 155 of the *Fitzwilliam* Byrd has a specimen with a lovely melody used, or similar to a melody used, by his contemporary Italian lute composers.

The Coranto kept in musical fashion longer than the Pavans and Galliards. Well known to the eighteenth-century harpsichordists, it has had two forms, one, the French, the Courante, in which three-four and six-eight time is confused at the cadence, and the other, the Italian, the Corrento, in which the time is plain triple throughout. "Dr. Bull's Juell", in *Fitzwilliam* and in Cosyn, gives examples, as we may expect, in mixed rhythm, mostly however in six-eight.

The Alman, too, like the Coranto, was the beginning of a mighty

D

tribe.   Perhaps the most attractive, and certainly the most interesting
with its quadruply repeated notes, is Bull's Alman which carries the
name of the Duke of Brunswick: a charming piece, and quite un-
Bullish in its direct simplicity.   But it is very different from the even
semiquaver flow of the Allemandes of Bach and Handel.

The Jiggs are usually short and simple: English unsubtle and reasonably non-contrapuntal, with none of the inverted counterpoint of
Bach.   Byrd's dance *Fitzwilliam* No. 181, has a catchy syncopated
melody: Bull's "My Selfe" No. 189 in the same collection is particularly fresh and breezy.

The Round is also a dance in virginal music, and not a sort of
Englishing of "Rondo"; it is not very frequent, but Byrd's setting
of the well-known (to country dancers) "Sellenger's Round" (*Fitzwilliam* No. 64), has been reprinted in one of Sir Granville Bantock's
editions: it is unusually difficult for a Byrd dance, if the pace of the
original is to be maintained in the variations.

The Toye was also a dance, and there are two simple and most
charming specimens.   One is by Farnaby, *Fitzwilliam* No. 270, and
the other by Bull, named after the Duchess of Brunswick, *Fitzwilliam*
No. 262.   Both are so clear and easy to play that they may be recommended to those who have not hitherto tried virginal music: no
better introductions to the whole *corpus* could be imagined.

The Barley Break was also a country dance, and there is a good
specimen by Byrd in *My Ladye Nevell's Booke*, No. 6.

This brings us to the end of our rapid survey of the dance forms.
In the more popular and obvious pieces which we have noted the
music can make an instantaneous appeal: it is rhythmical rather than
contrapuntal, and anyone able to play and to appreciate the country
dances gathered and arranged by Cecil Sharp will take even more
pleasure in these fresh and beautiful compositions.

And so we come naturally to the variations on the popular secular
songs of the day, naturally, because some of the dances are in variation form, and most of them were danced and perhaps sung at the
time the composers made their arrangements.   There is no infinite
step between Byrd's "Sellinger's Round" and his "O Mistris
Mine".

This tune of "O Mistris Mine" does not scan with the song from
Twelfth Night, and must be taken as an air independent of, and perhaps
before, Shakespeare's play.   Byrd's variations are justly famous and
occur in *Fitzwilliam* No. 66.   It was a form in which Byrd seemed

particularly at home, and he wrote more successful sets of variations than all the other virginal composers put together. Keenly beautiful is "Callino Casturame", the mysterious name of a tune alluded to in the soldiers' musings scene in *Henry V*: according to Fellowes the title is a corruption of the Irish "Colleen oge asthore", not that this elucidation takes most of us much further. This Irish tune is treated in *Fitzwilliam* No. 158. "Jhon come kisse me now" *Fitzwilliam* 10 , "All in a garden grine" 104 , and the really great "Will Yow Rome the Woods so Wild", which appears both in *My Ladye Nevell's Booke* and in *Fitzwilliam* No. 36), are other sets of variations by Byrd. The opening of this set of variations, with its rolling left hand and consecutive open fifths, is both mysterious and effective on the pianoforte, an effect which may be accidental, and a sort of dividend on the years between. Byrd's development is unusually interesting. The tune between upper and lower pedal points, or broken up by imitative figures, or below even semiquavers, gives continual interest throughout the fourteen variations, and there is no finer set in all virginal music. Might one not say, and having in mind that sort of variation which did not depart too far from the melody (i.e. excluding such treatment as is meted out in the "Goldberg", which is a harmonic set) that Byrd shows us as interesting music in the variation form as we will find until we reach Mozart?

"The Carmens Whistle", a cheery quick tune, is the subject of *Fitzwilliam* No. 58, and appears as well in *My Ladye Nevell* and in the *Forster* collection. To make the variations reasonably playable, and even intelligible, the tune has to be slowed down considerably. "Rowland, or Lord Willobies Welcome home" is in *Nevell*, *Forster*, *Fitzwilliam* No. 160, and in some of the other smaller manuscripts, and is a short and unusually simple set of variations, while with "Wolsey's Wilde" *Fitzwilliam* 157 Byrd has reached the large gramophone and Landowska public. This harpsichordist plays the piece with great dignity and leisure, using, or so it sounds, all the resources of her instrument, a machine identical in essence, it is true, with the virginals, but very different in effect, with its two manuals and octave-doubling stops.

Apart from these often great and always interesting examples by Byrd of variations on popular songs of his day, Bull produced, in his "King's Hunt", a piece so popular to-day as almost to be hackneyed. It is a rather dull and obvious piece of programme music, and that Bull enthusiast, Miss Margaret Glyn, even goes so far as to suggest that this is one of the examples of Tregian, the transcriber, putting Bull's name to a poor work out of religious hostility.

Farnaby's most interesting setting of a popular song is, typically with this composer, a short and simple setting of "Tower Hill", followed by a melodic variation of considerable originality, ending with a third set of eight bars bringing the piece to a melodious close (*Fitzwilliam* No. 245). The whole is in strongly-marked duple time, reminiscent to some of the metre of the Alman.

One of the two most difficult virginal forms to apprehend is counterpoint upon an ecclesiastical *cantus fermus*, the other form being the Fantasia. My own idea as to how best to approach this music is first to listen to choral polyphonic singing, say, Byrd's *Ave Verum*, then try to reproduce this vocal score on the piano. Failure is inevitable, but at least the difficulties of success will be apparent, and on tackling the same composer's *Miserere* of four parts Fitzwilliam No. 177 the player will perhaps be in a position to glimpse the spirit behind the notes. Sir Granville Bantock, in editing this *Miserere* for his Byrd album published by Novello has marked the *cantus fermus* as to be clearly brought out in playing, but this surely is a mistake, like that of players who bring out a fugue subject, however conventional it may be. The interest does not lie in the bald succession of notes which forms the skeleton of the piece, but it does lie in the counterpoints, which in this *Miserere* are of great expressive beauty. Bull, however, in his pieces like the *Salvator Mundi* Fitzwilliam 45 becomes baroque in his texture, and we have this sort of thing: jolly and melodious in short stretches, but making the whole piece, which starts off in dull counterpoint of *cantus fermus* above even quavers, too episodic.

The earliest keyboard music, that in the Mulliner manuscript, was largely devoted to counterpoints on *canti fermi*, and Tallis, the oldest of the forced contributors to the Fitzwilliam collection, carries on the Mullinar tradition but tries for a little instrumental variety by repeating the notes of the *cantus fermus* in his *Felix Namque*, while Bull, as we might expect, makes little metrical patterns from his theme. But it is too much to suggest that the virginal composers became more and more bored with this method of composition, but did not drop it altogether as not being certain what to put in its place.

If Byrd used *canti fermi*[1] it was for a very good reason, even if we cannot guess the reason now. I think we should be humble in the presence of one of the very greatest of all composers, even if we allow ourselves a few gibes at the more flashy Dr. Bull. It is indeed difficult to put ourselves into the mind of Byrd: but suppose we had never heard any music except solo or concerted voices, unaccompanied or accompanied by viols or lutes or virginals, or, possibly, an elementary type of organ; had never heard an opera, or what we call an oratorio, or a modern symphony orchestra, or a noisy pianist playing the noisy music of a noisy composer; had heard no loud noises of any mechanical sort except a cart going over cobble stones, we will see what an imaginative effort is required to put ourselves in A.D. 1600. Further, we have to add and to subtract all sorts of theological and political assumptions, and if the effort is indeed too much, let us admit that perhaps we should not glibly judge what appears to us to be a somewhat dull piece of virginal music. Sir Granville Bantock, in his Note to his collection named *Old English Suite*,[2] writes "While he (i.e. the editor) has the greatest respect for the composers (i.e. Byrd, Gibbons, Farnaby, Dowland and Bull) he holds it undeniable that many things which sounded well in their day have now become so obsolete as to be positively unpleasant . . . he has not scrupled here and there to alter a harmony, or a note or two. . . ." This is quite the wrong way to approach virginal music and arises from modern complaisance amounting to absurdity. Literature escaped from this fatuous complaisance two hundred years or more ago, and editors who would

---

[1]When this book was in proof there appeared the second edition of Edmund Fellowes' life of Byrd (Oxford Press 1948), with much new information in the chapter about his music for the virginals. Two points here may be made: interesting harmonies result from the impingement of the *cantus fermus* on the other parts; Byrd's resourceful and prophetic figuration, which makes his music to some extent a forerunner of Bach— compare this with the C major fugue from Book 2 of the "48 ". It is from a Pavan in a MS. collection in New York.

[2] Published by Novello.

"not scruple" to alter a word or a rhyme here and there in Spenser would hardly find employment.

In spite of one's own homily, and faced with all the pieces, wandering Dorian scales and the like, named Preludes, it is better to pass hurriedly and humbly on.

Now we come to the most important and yet most baffling of forms, the numbers called Fantasias, of which by far the best known is the example by Gibbons printed in *Parthenia*. Morley can again help us, in his *Plaine and Easie Introduction to Practicall Musicke*.

> The most principall and chiefest kind of musicke which is made without a dittie is the fantasie, that is, when a musician taketh a point at his pleasure, and wresteth and turneth it as he list. . . . In this may more art be showne than in any other musicke, because the composer is tide to nothing but that he may adde, deminish, and alter at his pleasure.

Roger North, writing his manuscript notes towards the end of the century (I quote from the Oxford University Press printing of them) said: "The method of the old fancys was to begin with a solemn fugue, and all the parts entered with it one after another, and often in different keys, which is the best garniture of fugues, and then followed divers repeats, retorts and reverts, of which art the audience was little sensible, and being but labour in vain must be passed upon account of Industry and striving to doe well," and so Roger North takes the usual Philistine view of old music whose drift is not clear. The Morley word "point" and the North word "fugue" mean the same thing, we might call it just a theme of a type useful in polyphony.

As approachable as the Fantasia by Gibbons in *Parthenia*, indeed with a little imaginative licence, perhaps more so, is the piece called "The Bells" by Byrd (No. 69 in the *Fitzwilliam*). The point or fugue here is just two notes in the bass, C and the D above it in trochaic metre, and this point is used as a ground throughout. The imaginative licence to which I have just referred alludes to my idea that Byrd was riding into Whitehall from his house in Middlesex and heard the Abbey bells; as they are wafted on the wind they increase and diminish in strength. When he rides through Tothill Street into the Abbey Church Yard the light east wind (it is summer) positively pours the sound about his ears. The bells seem to suggest a folk tune above the ground bell as he gives up his horse to a boy, and the descending semiquavers clang above him as he enters by the old west door.

The fantasia which has perhaps produced the most argument and technical interest is No. 51 in the *Fitzwilliam Virginal Book*, a fantasia whose point is a scale, and which is therefore called "Et, re, mi, fa, sol, la": it is by Bull. The modulations are so rapid and extreme that on the first page the treble line has

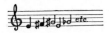

It is this sort of thing which has made people wonder whether the equal tuning of virginals was practised: certainly this piece is full of satisfying harmonic interest when played upon a normally tuned pianoforte.

To pass from these great if to me partly mysterious fantasias to the little pieces called "Dreame", "Rest", "Conceit" and "Humour" by Farnaby is play after work. There is nothing so simply appealing in all the realm of virginal music as *Fitzwilliam* 194-6 and 273. "Humour" does not mean, as at least one editor seems to think, Mr. Giles Farnaby's fun but, rather in the Jonsonian sense, the sort of man he is, and the upward and downward scale passage in semibreves may allude, if it alludes to anything, to his solemn exercises in the fantasia.

There is a certain amount of programme music in the *corpus*, and this music has received far more attention than its intrinsic merits warrant, for it is much easier to write about early attempts at storm or battle music than about the abstract fantasias. As one may without arrogance say that Beethoven's "Vittoria" is a poor thing, so perhaps the same verdict may be advanced about Mr. Byrd's "Battell" and Mr. Munday's "Faire Wether". "The Ghost" by Byrd is of much greater interest, and is thought by Dr. Fellowes, following Dr. Naylor, to have originally, before Tregian copied it as piece No. 162, acted as a Prelude before the entry of the ghost of Edward IV in the Latin play on Richard II given at Cambridge by the Master of Caius in St. John's College.

Less interesting, or so it seems, are the transcriptions by Peter Phillips, another exile in the Low Countries with Bull, of madrigals by mainly Italian composers: the vocal lines are much ornamented and the spirit of the original seems as wholly lost as it is when Listz operates upon Mozart. Lastly, *Fitzwilliam* No. 55 is the earliest known piece for two keyboards and four hands. We see Farnaby, who wrote it, making the very most of the simplest cadences:

The chief modern re-issues of this music, apart from the noble, but to the amateur mostly unobtainable, Fuller Maitland and Barclay Squire *Fitzwilliam Virginal Book* (Breitkopf & Hartel, 1899) and Hilda Andrews *My Ladye Nevell's Booke* (J. Curwen & Sons), are from Novello and from Augener. Novello, whose editor is the abused Sir Granville Bantock of these pages, is however preferable to the Augener series, for between Pauer and Barrett sad havoc has been done, without even acknowledgment, apology or a note of the sources. The Novello-Bantock set is made up of single volumes containing the music of Byrd, Bull, Farnaby and Gibbons and individually named *Album of Selected Pieces.* The Augener is called *Old English Composers for the Virginal and Harpsichord* and contains music by Byrd, Bull and Gibbons, besides the later Blow, Purcell and Arne. The whole used to be obtainable in one single cloth-bound volume. Of foreign publishers, Breitkopf issued in two of their familiar thin paper wrapped volumes a selection of pieces from the *Fitzwilliam*, while Ricordi published a textually quite fair but a wickedly editorially-noted volume in their series whose generic name appears to be *Tagliapietra:* a beautiful word like a form of macaroni.

SHORT BIBLIOGRAPHY TO CHAPTER I

Charles van den Borren: *The Sources of Keyboard Music in England* (Novello's Handbooks for Musicians) translated by J. E. Matthew.
Margaret H. Glyn: *Elizabethan Virginal Music* (Reeves). This is a modernized edition of her *About Elizabethan Virginal Music and its Composers* (Reeves 1924).

[Miss Glyn makes the point that her book covers the whole field, while Borren's deals mainly with the *Fitzwilliam* book. This is not quite fair, for Borren ranges widely, though his main attention is concentrated upon the largest collection, that is to say, on the *Fitzwilliam*.]

These two books rather supersede:

E. W. Naylor: *An Elizabethan Virginal Book* (London, Dent: New York, Dutton 1905).

The two biographies of importance and illumination, setting a new high standard in biographies of musicians of this period, are:

Edmund H. Fellowes: *William Byrd* 2nd edition (Oxford University Press 1948). Supersedes entirely the same author's book of the same title issued in 1923.

Orlando Gibbons (Oxford University Press 1925).

This is a short book list indeed, only four titles, but the books are packed with information. One or two other books are mentioned on pp. 199 and 237.

CHAPTER II

THE CLAVECIN IN FRANCE

1. The Instruments in Society

VOLTAIRE, in his introduction to his study of the age of Louis XIV, says that until the age of the great monarch, the Italian view of the French, that they were barbaric, was an insult almost deserved. He goes on to say that the fine arts were not practised, which, he adds, proves that the applied arts were not practised either, for it is only when life has reached a reasonable state of practical refinement that people have time for poetry, music and painting. This is not a view which would be shared by all, certainly not the Dutch during their fight for their republic, or by the modern English who practised all the arts while under bombardment from the Germans. That Voltaire should say it of the French tells us something of the nature of French art: it is a civilized addition to life, not an escape from pain and difficulties, nor a means of justifying God to Man.

To translate ourselves into French terms, we must imagine that England, divided and turbulent, had enjoyed no Elizabethan age, had produced neither Shakespeare nor Byrd, but that a monarch with the charm of Charles II, with all the power to which Charles I aspired and with a life as long as Charles II, James II, and William and Anne put together, was the centre of a civilization which produced its own Purcell, its own Dryden and Congreve, together with many earlier Horace Walpoles, and did everything on such a scale and with such glamour that London, though not eclipsed, was overshadowed by Paris, while much of the rest of Europe was not only eclipsed but was sent mad. Such was the power of the great sun of France when at last it rose.

In this barbaric pre-Louis XIV age the virginals in France were called *épinettes*, and had no music composed specially for them because the lute was much more popular and because the composers were not available.   So the music for the epinettes consisted of what we might perhaps call folk dances: *Quatorze Gaillardes, neuf Pavannes, sept Bransles et deux Basses-Dances, le tout reduict de musique en la tablature de ieu Dorgues, Espinettes, Manichordions et tel semblabes instruments musicaux, imprimees a Paris par Pierre Attaignant, MDXXIX*, was one of the first of these collections.   In this title we note the early mating of the Pavan and Gailliard, though Attaignant's Galliards precede his Pavans in the book as well as exceeding them in number.   Dorgues stands for D'orgues, or organs.   The word Espinette is that from which our own name Spinet derives: the French for thorn, one remembers, is *l'epine*, and alludes to the thorn which plucks the string actuated, in the first instance, by the finger which presses the key.

Manichordion, in Attaignant's title-page could have been an instrument with only one string, but was more probably an instrument with several strings sounded on the principle of many notes to each string.   This instrument was possibly a short clavichord.   There is a definite reason why it could not have been a species of espinette, for the principle of one string sounding several notes depends upon it being struck at different intervals and one end always damped.   Now if the thorn dropped back into place the damping would at once effect the whole string, which would cease to vibrate upon the instant.   If the striking head remains on the string, holding it up, that undamped portion will vibrate and give off the note.   But the essential quality of the whole virginal, espinette and clavecin family is that the vibrating quill plucks the string and falls immediately back into place.

It was the clavecin for which all the great French composers wrote, and the word perhaps derives from the Latin *clavicymbalum*.

From the name to the thing.   If you take a piece of string and stretch it against wood, say against both arms of a wooden chair, it will twang when plucked at a definite pitch.   If you now stretch the string tighter, it will vibrate at a higher pitch and with a clearer tone, and so higher and clearer until the string (or the chair arm) breaks.

The virginals in England and their French equivalents, the spinets, could not take much tension, nor was the art of stringing sufficiently advanced for the strings to take this tension.   To get a really good pure and deep bass note a long strong string is necessary which, when subjected to great tension, will rise in pitch from the inaudible to, say, the

C two octaves below middle C. But the box-like spinet or virginal cases were not long enough to accommodate such bass strings. Had the box been lengthened a difficulty would have arisen with regard to that part of each high treble or low bass key which actuated the jacks. Before the more intricate modern pianoforte mechanism was invented, the jack-striking and string-plucking mechanism was very simple and required that the keys should be near the strings. This they were in the small virginal, but could not be in a six-foot instrument, unless the keyboard was turned right round, so that instead of lying parallel to the strings, it lay like the platforms of a terminal railway station, at the end of the strings. It would not then matter at all to the jacks how long the strings were. The tuning pins and the jack bridge (a bridge over the strings was necessary to prevent the jacks jumping too high and out of control) were parallel with the keyboard and near to the player: the strings then stretched away for as long as the two opposing forces could endure without something breaking. The longer the string, the lower the pitch: the greater the tension, the higher the pitch. Longer and longer strings subjected to higher and higher tensions: in the days of this noble long instrument, called the clavecin in France and the harpsichord in England, wood only was used and the strings lay parallel and flat, like (beautiful phrase) a "couched harp". When iron and then steel and specially manufactured pianoforte wire with a hammer action is used in a case very similar to a harpsichord case, you get the modern grand pianoforte, with long thick bass strings subjected to a tension to be measured in tons.

But the harpsichord length and tension, though less than that of a modern pianoforte, was considerable, and the all-wooden case with its soundboard helped to give a strong and masculine tone. When people talk of the tinkle of a harpsichord, they often mean they have been listening to a spinet or virginal. Harpsichords do not tinkle: their peculiar sound is a sort of thud plus rustle. Quietly played it is a whisper, strongly and quickly played it is a rush.

Spinets tinkle: they have short strings and little tension. But here must be put down the difference between the instruments. If you see a box, quite rectangular, the instrument is a virginal or a square pianoforte or a clavichord. If you see a triangular instrument with a wing flap which can open and the keys at an angle of about forty-five degrees with the strings, it is a spinet. The spinet obviously grew out of the virginal. If you see a long lean instrument with a keyboard at the end, it is a clavecin if made in France, a harpsichord if made in England, or a grand pianoforte. As for the difference between the square pianoforte and the virginal, and the grand pianoforte and the harpsichord, it is in the method of vibrating the string. The virginal and harpsichord both pluck it, while the pianoforte hits it. It is interesting to remember this, and then to note errors in exhibition catalogues, or in auction sales. The most common errors are to call old square pianofortes spinets, and to call real spinets harpsichords. Or even, "this instrument is almost a spinet", meaning it is an old piano. In this case there is no "almost": "almost a spinet" could only mean a virginal in which there was a definite angle between the keyboard and the strings and for which the accommodating case had been made out of the rectangular. Virginal, spinet, harpsichord are different sorts of dogs, small, medium, large, with corresponding tones of bark: square pianofortes and grand pianofortes and cottage pianofortes are different sorts of cats. There is no cat "almost a dog".

But there are two complications to an otherwise unadorned piece of verisimilitude. Firstly, the French called virginals spinets, so a French spinet is any small instrument plucked whose keyboard is not end-on to the strings. Secondly, the clavichord is also a rectangular box with a keyboard parallel to the strings, but in a clavichord the strings are hit and held by tangents from below, not plucked.

The French, to make it quite plain what they meant when they said, as for instance did the composer d'Anglebert in 1689, "Piéces de clavessin avec la manière de les jouer; diverses chaconnes, ouvertures et autres airs de M. de Lully, mis sur cet instrument," usually added to *clavessin* the words *à queue*, calling the true spinet just *l'épinette*, and the true virginal, *clavessin carré* or *clavessin rectangulaire*. All of which is quite clear. But as the clavecin in France was essentially an aristocratic or upper bourgeois instrument, we do not have to consider small houses, small instruments and humble people. In fact, the structure of French society was such that there was very little of a cultured lower middle class or small landed gentry. The impoverished nobleman would rather have a useless and decayed clavecin in his useless and decayed and much mortgaged mansion, than a neat spinet in a neat cottage. The neat spinet in the neat cottage conception was essentially an English ideal and did not enter French thought until the years immediately preceding the revolution, when the richest courtiers played at simplicity. It was never an esteemed mode of life for people who were gentry and cultured, but undeniably hard up. It would be interesting to trace the reasons why in England and Spain (think of Don Quixote) the impoverished gentleman who nevertheless paid his way and lived modestly was esteemed, but why in France, Italy and in the Empire he had either to sink to the gutter or put up a show of wealth. In England debts were dishonourable: in France, honourable. Too succinct? Yes, but at any rate the modest spinet played no part in French music.

We must deal with a problem of tuning which did not occur with the virginals in England, because their music was more varied in the ecclesiastical modes and less varied in the keys of the major and minor modes than the later clavecin music in France.

First the scientific explanation which is generally given like this: if you tune a keyboard instrument in fifths, making each string exactly a fifth above its predecessor (or a fourth below, which is the same thing), when, after twelve such tunings you arrive back at the string you started with, you will find it does not sound the same note: it is slightly higher. This degree of sharpness is known as a "comma".

If we approach the problem from a more interesting if less scientific point of view, we must first make the point that the voice in singing knows nothing of vibrations per second or of tuning forks. It is the traditional ear alone which arbitrates: traditional, because no one knows how a being would sing if he was original: children begin to sing by copying. Thus different civilizations carry different scales from generation to generation. But it has been found that the voice tends to make the leading note in the modern major and minor modes a little sharper and the passage from the subdominant to the mediant at a cadence a little less than a semitone by slightly flattening the subdominant. Thus in D minor the C sharp ascending is a little more than sharp, while B flat in the key of F major is a little flat.

This applies to all notes: D flat is, so to say, to the left of C sharp, E flat to D sharp, and so forth.

There are three ways of solving this problem of tuning on the keyboard. It can be supposed that in the music to be played on the instrument all F's will be sharp, and all B's flat and that all C's will be sharp and all E's flat. This will do well for music written in such keys as D minor, C major or G major, provided that the modulations are direct and that there are no episodes in remote keys, and that, in the case of such keys as B flat, the tonic minor is never touched upon. When composers forsook the lands of the modes for the wild enharmonic and unexplored geography around the modern key system, it may be taken that they made a great advance. And so they did, but they could not take the lovely garden they had hitherto inhabited with them. Byrd writing in apparently D minor but really in the Dorian mode had one set of effects, Rameau in his sequential adventures from G minor in his *L'Enharmonique* had another set, and had the theoretical knowledge to use Byrd's set too. But only the theoretical knowledge: composers cannot write creatively out of their own particular harmonic idiom, so apparent progress is but change.

Nevertheless, to accommodate the growing interest in what the academics have always called "extravagant" modulation, and to allow at least the comparatively neutral ground of A flat to be also G sharp (which is about as far as Rameau goes) tuning by semitones became the custom. Each semitone was place equidistant from its neighbours within the octave, which are mathematically determined by the vibrations at one end being twice as fast as at the other. This method, usually called equal temperament, is now universal on all pianofortes, and may or may not have been universal on French clavecins of the seventeenth and eighteenth centuries. As these instruments had very frequently to be tuned owing to their comparatively slack tension and the pull exercised by each pluck of the quill, and as the musician himself often tuned his own instrument, it is clear that there need have been no hard and fast rule as to the tuning of any given clavecin.

The third way was to provide extra strings and a keyboard in which each black note was divided so as to allow each sharp a slightly higher tone than each flat, like this

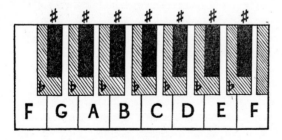

"Pour parvenir à rendre le Clavecin," writes Jean Benjamin de la Borde in 1780, "un instrument tout-à-fait musical, il est nécessaire que le clavier porte autant de touche qu'il en faut pour executer les vingt-un sons differens contenus dans l'intervalle d'une octave," and gives the keyboard diagram reproduced above, saying that a clavecin to that pattern had been made by M. Chiqulier, *Garde des Instruments de la Musique du Roi*, a position which was taken over the following year by the greater Taskin, and an employment which was similar to that given to the boy Purcell when he was asked to look after the instruments of Charles II.

The French were great importers of instruments from Italy or the Netherlands. Sometimes the cases were repainted in France: Charles Burney during his expedition of 1770 saw a Ruckers clavecin made in the previous century belonging to M. Balbastre, one of the organists of Notre Dame who had announced his ownership by having had painted on the inside of the front flap above the keys a short piece of music: "Pastorale par M Balbastre, le 6 Aoust 1767," and had otherwise "painted inside and out," as says Burney, "with as much delicacy as the finest coach or even snuff box I ever saw in Paris. On the outside is the birth of Venus; and on the inside of the cover the story of Rameau's most famous opera, Castor and Pollux; earth, hell, and Elysium are there represented: in Elysium, sitting on a bank, with a lyre in his hand, is that celebrated composer himself: the portrait is very like, for I saw Rameau in 1764."

Although the French were slower than the Belgians, as they would now be called, or the Italians, to make clavecins, and although their output was perhaps never so great as that of the London manufacturers, yet they had one firm of particular importance, founded by F. E. Blanchet who is known to have lived in Paris after 1650. One of his daughters married one of the Couperins, a long continued family of organists who were usually attached in their professional capacity to the Church of St. Gervais, a typical match in the times when the makers of instruments and the makers of music were all part of the same large family, and even sometimes the selfsame man. It was a Belgian, Pascal Taskin, born at Liege in 1730, who carried on the Blanchet tradition, coming to Paris and learning from what must then have been the very aged François Etienne Blanchet. It is strange that the Belgians have excelled so much in the manufacture of clavecins, and that the native French had not their equals. London was as much at fault, her great harpsichord makers coming from foreign countries, from Switzerland, or from Scotland.

In due course Pascal Taskin obtained the Royal appointment of *Facteur de Clavecins de la Cour, et Garde des Instruments de Musique de la Chambre du Roi.* His shop and warehouse was in the Rue de la Verrerie, a street which leads, just by crossing the Rue de Rivoli, to the Church of St. Gervais. One may be quite certain that all the Couperins, including the great François himself, knew the Blanchet-Taskin establishment very well.

In 1768 Taskin made a great invention, or so say all the French writers on the subject, by introducing leather plectra as an alternative to quills, and thus giving a buff registration at will. This was not an entirely new thing, for it was a device sometimes adopted in the sixteenth and seventeenth centuries. The leather had the added advantage that, as it imposed less strain on the strings, the instrument did not require tuning quite so often if this stop was frequently used.

Taskin was himself succeeded by another Blanchet, a grandson, and a great-grandson was the last of the line, realizing the family fortune and retiring to Italy to spend it. The modern firm of Erard continue the tradition with new-built clavecins modelled on those of Taskin, buff stop and all. A peculiarity of French clavecins is that they usually have two sets of strings, instead of only one set. This fact is of some importance in French clavecin music. For instance, in this passage from Couperin's *Les tours de passe-passe*

the two G's on the first beat of the last bar is unplayable on a one-manualled instrument, and would only sound as a single G on a two-manualled instrument with only one set of strings. But with a different set of strings for each manual, and with, let us say, a buff stop for the right hand and a lute for the left, the syncopated tune with its detached note accompaniment would be perfectly clear.

French musical activities, and therefore French musical instruments, were very much centralized in two places; one was Paris, and the other moved with the Court, but usually was at Versailles. Paris was the sole residence of those nobles not at Court, of the financiers and the wealthy bourgeois, and provincial life suffered in consequence. England has no parallel; for a British equivalent we must consider eighteenth-century Ireland, with its four provinces depopulated of wealth and genius, to enrich Dublin and London. Paris became a large and stately city, and travellers from London invariably speculated as to which was the larger metropolis. Voltaire considered that while the two cities were of about equal size, the wealthy private houses of

Paris contained much richer furniture, and the medical adviser to an English Ambassador in Paris tells us about the hangings of rich tapestry with gold and silver threads, the velvet beds, the cabinets and bureaux of ivory inlaid with tortoiseshell and the gold and silver plate. In such surroundings would be the domestic clavecin.

Travelling tutors are the source of much information: the clergyman who accompanied on tour a son of the Marquis of Bath, for instance, says in his journal, printed in the "Select Works" of John Douglas in Salisbury in 1820, of which diocese he became bishop:

> Most of the streets of Paris are as little frequented on week days as those of London on Sundays [and goes on]: It is the utmost ambition of a Frenchman of rank to have a grand *hôtel* in Paris; for the French nobility seldom possess houses on their estates in the country fit for their residence. . . . No wonder, then, that Paris abounds with fine houses, since the nobility seldom possess fine houses elsewhere. In London, on the contrary, our nobility regard themselves as mere visitors, to attend the parliament in winter, and return to their country seats in summer. Hence all their grandeur is reserved for their permanent residence. . . . [In London] there is scarcely any difference between the habitation of the nobleman and the trader. Whereas at Paris, each *hôtel* has a courtyard in front, bounded by high walls . . . entirely hid from the passenger . . . streets containing the most of these noble houses were less gay than those where there were none.

In these gloomy shut-off mansions "it costs some trouble . . . to discover who is the mistress . . . everyone lives according to his or her fancy," as Leopold Mozart complained, adding, "Pomp and splendour are still extravagantly admired and pursued by the French. . . . The greatest riches are possessed by . . . several bankers and *fermiers generaux*, and their money is chiefly spent on Lucretias, who, however, do not stab themselves."

Voltaire in his *Princesse de Babylone* says that in Paris (the date is 1768) there were about one hundred thousand people with nothing to do but amuse themselves, and much of this amusement consisted in criticizing the arts which other people created. The Court at Versailles, though not far off, might have been in a remote Province for all the effect it had on the artistic life of the Parisians. When the possibility of Mozart becoming organist at Versailles arose, the composer remarked that he who accepts a position at Court is forgotten in Paris.

Thus the clavecin in Paris tended to become the instrument of the dilettante, of people who liked to have a handsome and expensive instrument in their house, who would pay well to have their daughters taught how to play it, and who would expect to be provided with music which was refined but not too passionate or thoughtful. The great difference between Paris and London was, that in Paris there were the wealthy hundred thousand and perhaps a million poor: London society had far less marked gradations, and music was a more private and individual art, practised equally by a suburban coalman, a snobbish attorney and a wealthy duke. The harpsichord in one English household was there to enable its owner to slumber after dinner, and in another to "excite the passions". But the clavecin was always expected to be polished and suave, as one accustomed to moving in the best bourgeois circles.

At the French Court music had little place. Some writers make much of the Court appointments given to musicians and such institutions as the *Musique pour les soupers du Roi*, but as far as I can see it only amounted to Louis XIV or XV having the wireless on in the Oeil-de-Beouf or in the Galerie des Glaces adjoining. There is no evidence that either monarch ever listened, and music had no part in the intellectual life of the Court as it had in that of Elizabeth of England. There was the ballet, indeed, and the opera, but even in these, music appears not to have been the predominant art.

There must have been clavecins in the Queen's apartments at Versailles into which the mob burst during the preliminary boilings of the Revolution, but historians do not mention them. Neither the diarists nor the letter-writers have the consciousness of the clavecin that Pepys had for the "harpsicon", even Madame d'Epinay the friend (so close, for a while) of Rousseau, barely mentions them. Rousseau himself has a typical anecdote, typical because it shows him, as usual, in a despicable position, a position in which he seems to have enjoyed finding himself discovered. While his little so-called opera *Le Devin du village* was running for the benefit of the Court while at Fontainebleu, he visited the Baron Grimm, a German long settled in France who had gained considerable eminence as a connoisseur of the arts and as a savant in general.

I found a numerous throng round the clavecin, from which Grimm quickly got up as I entered the salon. On the clavecin stand I saw a volume which I recognized, open at a piece which the Baron d'Holbach had suggested I should use, while assuring me that he would never allow the volume to leave his own hands.

Some time afterwards, I saw the volume again, this time on the clavecin stand of Madame d'Epinay. . . . No one spoke to me directly on the subject, but it became the gossip that I had plagiarized in my *Devin*.

Indeed he had, pretending that he only did it out of good humour to the eager suggestions of the Baron d'Holbach. A scandal such as this was very pleasing to Parisian society, and the conferences round the clavecin must have had added piquancy when it was likely that the plagiarizing composer might find them at it.

A painting of the time shows a concert in the house of the Comtesse de Saint-Brison. The clavecin is prominent in the large semicircular room: it is played by a woman, and as is usual in these contemporary pictures, the cellist is looking over her shoulder to find his bass part. In the background is a flautist standing near a fiddler—their parts would not have been written out for them in the modern way. It would appear therefore to be music for two treble solo instruments, say flute and violin, or two flutes, or two violins, as you please (such was the easygoing eighteenth-century custom), with the figured bass for cello and the left hand of the clavecin player, while her right hand filled in the harmonies. Rameau and Couperin wrote for just such combinations.

Chief among the patrons of the clavecin and its players was one of the *fermiers generaux*, which term should probably be explained. The very high cost of maintaining the Court resulted in spending money in advance of revenue, and financiers were approached for advances. They had to recoup themselves by collecting the whole tax and making what margin of profit was possible. These financiers were called the farmers of such-and-such taxes, the derivation coming first from those who rent ground for agricultural farming, then the act of letting ground for any purpose, as Richard II said, according to Shakespeare, "We are enforc'd to farm our royal realm," and so lastly to anyone who takes over any revenue-creating property, and for a fixed sum does what he can with it. Needless to say, this musical farmer, La Poplinière, had only handled a spade when acting the part of a peasant in an opera.

His first home for music was in his house in the rue Petits-Champs and then in the rue de Richelieu, both in the Palais Royal neighbourhood; in the days of his greatest wealth and grandeur he had a palace at Passy adjoining the Bois de Boulogne. His clavecin player was Madame Gossec, the wife of the leader, or chief first violinist, of the orchestra. As we noticed in the picture of the music-making at the

Comtesse de Saint-Brisson's home, it was by no means unusual to have a *claveciniste*. Rameau, La Poplinière's first orchestral director and chief protégé, may have been annoyed (he has the reputation of having been "difficult") by elderly Madame de la Guerre, who had all her life been *claveciniste*, having started on that decorative career at the age of five, when as Elisabeth Jacquet she was taken up by Louis XIV himself. When older, she married an organist, de la Guerre, later to become the official of the Chapel Royal, possibly the post that Mozart was offered a generation later.

Another great *claveciniste* was Marguerite Antoinette Couperin, the daughter of François Couperin himself, who deputized at Court for her father in his old age. The feminine tradition is still with us, the names of Wanda Landowska and Lucille Wallace coming at once into the mind.

Among the foreigners in Paris it was perhaps the Swedish Embassy which offered the best home to clavecin music when the Comte de Creutz represented his King at the Court of St. Louis. Gretry was often to be heard playing the clavecin at Embassy parties. The Baron Grimm, already mentioned, born at Ratisbon, was another influential foreigner, but he was not so much a patron himself as a stimulant to patronage in others. A character thus engaged tends to become misunderstood and perhaps even warped, and both Rousseau and Mozart have written unkind things about this figure who continually crops up in French eighteenth-century artistic history.

The clavecin had an important role in the opera, but in the opera of the Empire and of London it had not a merely important, but a commanding, role. Here in Paris conducting had been done by a stick rapping the ground, and Lully died through blood poisoning occasioned by the staff, wielded by himself indeed, wounding his own foot. Sometimes a roll of paper would be used much as a baton is now. Sometimes the orchestra would take their beat from their leader, the first violinist.

Opera had come into France in the middle of the seventeenth century from Italy, and had found a home in the theatre of the Palais Royal, a place made for the few rather than for the many, and with boxes usually leased by the year by the wealthy and a pit reserved for Court officials who had free admission. As time went on the theatre was enlarged until about the period of popularity of Gluck it was possible to hear his music for about half a franc. The opera house itself adjoined the garden of the Palais Royal, and as the performances started early and were over before nine, the audience, mostly people of rank, would walk in the gardens for a while before dispersing, the ladies carrying bouquets whose perfume, mingling with that of the powder on their hair, scented the air.   They did not always disperse, for sometimes alfresco music would keep them under the moon for hours.   Inside the opera house would be one or two clavecins according to whether the conductor used a keyboard instrument, or literally beat the time with a stick, a frequent but most irritating method, as the raps could be heard throughout the performance.   Rousseau, in his *Dictionary of Music*, says this of the clavecin player:

> The accompanist sustains the pitch of the voices and beats the time for the orchestra.   The first of these functions means that he always has under a finger the next note of the singer, so as to sound it in case of need and sustain or guide the voice if it falters or strays from the note.   The second demands that he marks the bass and his harmonies with strong, equal, detached and in every way well regulated strokes, so as clearly to mark the time for the other players, above all at the beginning of arias.

This is not at all clear, like much by this author.   The clavecinist who marked the time with chords on the figured bass was the conductor, while a second clavecinist, at the side of the orchestra, would accompany and guide the soloists.   The metrically beating stick is the equivalent of the metrically beating clavecin: the conductor with the stick could replace the conductor with the clavecin.   But both would equally need the services of the clavecinist whose work was more musical, and who acted as the filler-up of the harmony and as prompter and sustainer of soloists in one.   If the composer himself was present, and there was a stick time-beater, it is supposed the composer did not choose this noisy office, but rather that of the strictly accompanying clavecin player.

While a Rameau might thus be seated at the clavecin plenty of inattention to his work might be going forward among the audience. The Duc de Luynes records that "Madame de Duras came into the King's Little Gallery before the start of the Opera.   The Dauphin and Madame Adelaide sat down on her train, and the twenty year old Dauphin attempted to upset Madame Adelaide by tugging at her skirt. As a result Madame Adelaide at last fell, though she was not hurt, but she brought down Madame de Duras, who broke her ankle.   Fortunately she lay where she fell, had she attempted to stand the fractured bone might have pierced her skin. She was in great pain all night and was bled three times." The Duke does not allude at all to any inconvenience the rest of the audience might have been put to.

Gluck must have conducted from the clavecin in the manner he was used to in Prague, Vienna and London. On the day of the dress rehearsal of the dances in his *Iphigénie en Tauride* in Paris in 1779 a dishevelled young man named Mehul disclosed himself from a hiding place, proferring the naïve explanation that he had hoped to remain hidden until the performance itself but became too hungry. This began an acquaintance between Gluck and the then unknown Belgian composer, and it was arranged that Mehul should take lessons from Edelmann and for a time at least Mehul became a clavecinist, writing two or three sonatas on the Italian model.

At concerts, the *Concerts spirituels*, for instance, conducting by means of a roll of paper was the rule. These concerts were formed for the giving of music at times when the Opera was closed, during Lent, for instance, and hence even possibly the name. They were held in a salon in the Tuileries, a palace rarely used by either of the two long-reigned Louis, and it is more than likely that the clavecin in the Salle des Suisses was the only one in tune in the building.

To illustrate the universality of the roll of paper when the conductor was not at the clavecin (the stick beating seems to have been peculiar to the Opera), we may quote Rousseau again: he had just finished one of his "compositions".

> The musicians gathered to play my music. I had to explain to them the beat, the *piano* and *forte*, and the repetitions at the double bars. I was full of it. This went on for five or six minutes, all the time that they tuned: five or six minutes! It seemed more like five or six centuries. Eventually we could begin; I gave several raps with a beautiful roll of paper on my conductor's desk. All was silent: I began to beat time: the musicians began to play. . . .

This sort of thing, though amateurish enough, was however symptomatic, and was the beginning of the downfall of the clavecin. It was probably not however the roll of paper which turned into a baton, but rather the fiddle stick of the leader who, when acting as conductor, would wave it as though it were a roll of paper, that became in time the conductor's baton. Thus one clavecin, the time-beating clavecin, became no longer necessary, and the other, the filler-up of figured basses, passed away also when composers, writing in the symphonic idiom, ceased to compose from the bass, but composed from the melody or composed the whole texture as they progressed. The clavecin gave place to Erard's new pianofortes when the symphonic style became usual both for opera as in later Gluck, in Mozart and in the favourites of the Paris public Cherubini and Gretry, and for solo clavecin music, as in the sonatas of Mehul, rather dull and very thin as they are. In the *Concerts spirituels* themselves the symphonists, Gossec, Haydn, Mozart, Schobert and others early ceased or never began the *concerto grosso* style of writing, and as instruments were added and the players became better musicians, the clavecin gradually faded away. What it did during the process of fading, during, for instance, the *premier coup d'archet* of Mozart's "Paris" symphony, we do not know: possibly the clavecinist shrugged his shoulders, looked important, and folded his arms.

2. *The Composers*

There were numerous clavecin composers, quite as many as English virginal composers. Some tidiness may be brought into the English pattern by the natural pre-eminence of Byrd, Bull and Farnaby, with Orlando Gibbons the best known of the composers of the tail, for it is hardly fair to say, of the decadence. Similar tidiness may be brought into the French picture by the continued presence of the Couperin genealogical tree, with François Couperin himself not only the greatest Couperin, but the greatest native-born domestic keyboard composer in the whole history of French music until Debussy, with whom certain affinities may be noticed. Second to François Couperin stands Rameau, slightly younger, a greater man all in all, but not greater in his clavecin music, which tends either to be harmonic exercises appropriate to a writer on that science, or chips from his operatic work table, as in the charming Minuet in G from *Castor and Pollux* which appeared in his 1741 collection. The other composers had little individuality, and their pieces can only be recognized by period rather than by composer. The early ones wrote from the bass, like Handel, and the later ones from the melody. For some reason the second method seems childish, and one hesitates to say like whom. Charles

Burney would quite boldly have said "like Haydn". Musical writing nowadays shies from words like tune and melody and harmony, and prefers words like texture, fabric and pattern.

The important names before François Couperin's life work started were, especially, Chambonnières, a surname which hides a whole family of organists, also d'Anglebert and Begue. Contemporaries of François Couperin were Marchand, known popularly as J. S. Bach's Dresden competitor, Clerambault, Dagincourt, Rameau himself, Daquin popular still for his delightful "Le Coucou", and Dornal Duphly and Corrette, two *petits maîtres* of the decadence, for this music, unlike that of the English virginal school, had a decadence, soft, full and meaningless.

Before we turn to these composers, a word must be said about Lully. This man, from Italy, and promoted from the kitchen, had great skill in writing the sort of ballet music which Louis XIV enjoyed: the king himself danced in the ballet when he was young, and before he considered even the grave allegorical dances unsuitable for a monarch. The fat little Italian, with his small eyes, meanness, powers of intrigue, and great musical gifts, was essentially a courtier. He was not a Parisian and not a teacher, and his solitary Suite for the clavecin does not rank him as the first of the clavecinists. Nor can his colleague Lalande be so ranked either, and for similar reasons. Lully pleased the royal ear in the ballet, Lalande in the chapel, though Michel Richard de Lalande was nearer the Couperin tradition as he may have taught the clavecin to the daughter of Louis XIV, and he wrote some chamber music for the king to flirt through, *Musique pour les soupers du Roy*.

The early clavecinists seemed to have come from country organ lofts to Paris: thus two brothers named Champion, whose father and grandfather had been organists, became successful players and teachers of the clavecin, the more famous of the two, Jacques, changing his name to Chambonnières after an estate owned by his wife. The Couperins also originally came from the country, and owed much to the help and patronage of the Chambonnières.

François Couperin, born in Paris in 1668, was a member of the third generation and not part of the main stem of the family which branched from his uncle, also named François. His cousins were mainly born in Paris or at Versailles, and as they themselves married, the generations carry down boys with a Louis or a François in their names, until a spinster, supposed to have been an indifferent musician, brings the line to an end as late as 1860.

The Church of St. Gervais is on the right bank, to the east of the Palais Royal, and was therefore near the Opera and not very far from the *Concerts spirituels.* Organists were Couperins, and Couperins were organists, and there was an apartment, just like a London flat, at the back where some at least of them when their turn came used to live: the Church could be seen from some of the windows. An unpretentious apartment, just three or four rooms on one floor, showing that Paris had, after all, an ordinary middle-class life, if its components were not very numerous. François himself was organist at St. Gervais, but he appears to have spent most of his time visiting his pupils in their luxurious houses shut away from the streets in their own courtyards. He would attend at Versailles regularly, I suppose on horseback unless a coach was sent in for him, an easier but a slower method of covering a distance similar to that from Charing Cross to Hampton Court. One imagines that Couperin, like Byrd, was a good horseman, the reins held in strong but gentle fingers. "Salut Francois Couperin, Compositeur, Organiste de notre Chapelle et cy-devant Maistre de Clavecin de notre tres Cher et bien ame petit fils le d'Auphin Duc de Bourgogne" as the royal "Privilege General" reads to his book *L'Art de toucher Le Clavecin* which was dedicated to the King.

Couperin himself gives us more information in his old French in his Preface to the 1713 *Pieces de Clavecin*, saying that he would have printed this volume before had his time not been fully occupied by something "trop glorieuses pour moy pour m'en plaindre; il y a vingt-ans que jay l'honneur d'estre au Roy, et d'enseigner presqu'en même temps a Monseigneur le Dauphin Duc de Bourgogne, et a six Princes ou Princesses de la Maison Royale: ces occupations, celles de Paris, et plusieurs maladies. . . ."

As in the cases of Byrd and Bull, little is known of Couperin's life: what these illnesses were, for instance, to which he alludes. He lived to reach his sixty-sixth year in what must have been a most unwholesome city.

Rameau also came from the provinces, but he had a much harder struggle, though in his case too there are blanks of many years during which there is no definite news of him. His life divides into two: until he was past forty he was unknown and must have often been bitterly poor. He did not come to Paris and settle down like the Chambonnières and the Couperins. His native city, Dijon, seems intermittently to have called to him, while he took work as organist in other provincial churches. He ran quite true to type however in having an organist for a father. In his later 'teens he walked to Italy and back, not perhaps so formidable a journey as it sounds, for Dijon is about as far from Milan, Rameau's furthest Italian point, as Manchester is from London. Much of the journey would be mountainous, but Rameau was a fiddler and perhaps entertainment at the inns earned his supper and bed.

He soon returned to France and his music did not show any Italian influence. His first collection of pieces for the clavecin was published in 1706, and then it is supposed that he went to Paris, where he became the pupil of Marchand. Of this composer an amusing anecdote is told. He had been one of the organists of the Chapel Royal but had received only half pay, for the other half went to his wife, who lived apart from him. One Mass Marchand left the organ in the middle, when Louis himself was present, and when he excused himself saying: "Sire, if my wife gets half my income, she may play half the service," was dismissed. He went to Dresden in the service of the King of Poland where he met Bach. He returned to Paris and became a fashionable teacher. Of him his pupil Rameau says "no one could compare with Marchand in his manner of handling a fugue", but then, Rameau had never heard Bach or Handel extemporize.

Marchand used to receive a louis d'or for a lesson, perhaps the equivalent of an English guinea. Not an excessive charge for a lesson from one of the chief virtuosi of the day, but no doubt much more than Rameau could afford. Indeed, how Rameau lived we do not know, though he may have managed by deputizing for organists, many of the more fashionable of whom had pluralities. The multitudinous poor of Paris had so little money that the necessities of life could be had very cheaply. It is not possible to correlate eighteenth-century monetary values with twentieth: beer was very much cheaper then, but books more expensive. A middle-class family could live better: cheaper rent, cheaper domestic wages, cheaper bread and bacon. But a scholar would live worse: dearer books, dearer and worse artificial light in the winter evenings, dearer paper, and the expense of dressing as a gentleman. Rameau also may have received money from various theoretical treatises he wrote: some writers declare he revolutionized harmony, but surely he merely systematized the French method of teaching.

Rameau married a singer, and kept up his relationship with Dijon, visiting that city to play the cathedral organ from time to time. His teaching and his books on harmony and the somewhat austere nature of his early music for the clavecin, as compared with the lighter and perhaps, let us say, more beautiful, music of Couperin, must have made him appear as an impoverished, but rising, pedant. He is said to have been completely devoid of any personal charm. He was, it appears, a withdrawn character, a man who wished to keep his personal contacts at a minimum, even though he suffered from loneliness and awkwardness as a result. His early poverty had engrained frugal habits in him, habits which never endear and, in a successful man as Rameau became, actually offend.

But he must have had some attraction for women: apart from his wife, Madame de la Poplinière was his pupil and he had great general influence over her. Rousseau, who presumably wished to work his way into the graces of the very wealthy financier, gave out that in musical composition he was one who wished to form his style upon the works of Rameau. But Rameau put him off saying that he found it very tiring to read manuscript scores. Then Rousseau persuaded M. de la Poplinière to have his music played unedited, Rameau grumbling that the sounds produced by a man quite ignorant of the technique of composition must indeed be fine. As what sounds there were died away, Rameau said bluntly that Rousseau had no talent or skill, and what interest there was in his work entirely depended upon his thefts from others.

A very strange thing then happened, something outside the scope of this book except as it resulted in something of a change in the music of Rameau's clavecin publications of 1741. He became a great operatic success. Voltaire, whom he met at de la Poplinière's, became his supporter and wrote him a libretto. He was attacked by the followers of Lully and, when this had died down, by the followers of the new Italian school of Pergolesi. "Fame," as Dr. Johnson remarked, "is a shuttle cock," and Rameau's name was banged to and fro in controversy to such an extent that he became by far the foremost French musician of his day. His clavecin music became more elegant and charming, and ran hand in hand with his operas: sometimes Rameau would use a clavecin piece for a ballet, sometimes he would reduce a number of an opera for clavecin. This process has continued to this present day, when his clavecin music has become the basis for at least two ballets, especially the piece named "La Poule" in the 1741 collection, which everyone seems to find irresistible. This caricature of the clucking of a hen is realistic enough, but its strangeness lies in its moment of real passion towards the close.

The third great figure in French clavecin music was Mozart, a composer whose glory obscures the post-Rameauists, as they might be called. Perhaps Daquin is the one exception. His little piece "Le Coucou" is so deservedly popular that it is of interest to record that he was something of an infant prodigy, occupied an organ loft as early as the age of twelve, was a pupil of Marchand, succeeded his master as organist to a monastery of the Cordeliers and became one of the organists of the Chapel Royal.

The Mozarts, father, mother and two children, arrived in Paris in November, 1763: little Wolfgang Mozart was therefore seven, and would be eight in two months. They stayed with the Bavarian Ambassador in the Hotel Beauvais, a house which still exists and is now No. 68 in the Rue François-Miron, a street running east from St. Gervais, where a collateral descendent of the great Couperin was organist, past the Franciscan monastery where Daquin officiated, into the Rue St. Antoine. The musical centre of Paris has of course shifted. What with the *Concerts spirituels* in the Tuileries, the Opera in the Palais Royal grounds and the organ loft of St. Gervais it was in the eighteenth century decidedly spread along the north bank east of the then fairly modern Pont Royal. Now it is much further to the north, about the Boulevard des Italiens.

From the Hotel Beauvais they went to Versailles from whence the father unfortunately found no occasion to write to his Salzburg correspondents. But in later years his sister related how the Marquise de Pompadour refused to kiss Wolfgang and how he said: "Who is this who will not kiss me? The Empress did so!" He played the clavecin to the admiration of the Court, and was much petted by three of the daughters of Louis XV who were musical, having been taught, of course, by Couperin himself. His style of playing was, however, probably quite different from that which they themselves knew, for the music was in structure different. Little Mozart's earliest compositions show no trace of the contrapuntal style, "composing from the bass", and require no clavecin registration: they would have been equally effective, indeed, on a spinet. However, his improvisations may well have been in another style, but one feels that to the Court it was a social more than a musical occasion, and they were charmed and amazed by a prodigy rather than moved by a musician. Things were very different when Mozart, accompanied only by his mother, revisited Paris.

They entered the city in March, 1778, when the composer was just twenty-two, and in his first letter to his father Mozart was too taken up with the dull journey and his feelings about a Mannheim family with a member of which he was in love to explain where he and his mother were stopping. It was perhaps just in lodgings: although Mozart found he received so many invitations that he could dine out every day, these invitations were no longer from Versailles and from Ambassadors, but came from upper Paris bourgeois and the like. Madame d'Epinay wanted this musical adornment to her salon, the Baron Grimm wanted to add this Salzburgian to his collection, and the ballet-master Noverre was interested in a possible composer.

A typical instance of his life in Paris may be given, to show that he had no more position than had Rameau before he began his series of operas. And it is but to do his father left behind in Salzburg justice to say that he was constantly urging his son to write an opera suitable for French taste. But we are only interested in the clavecin and so must deal with Mozart's famous letter of the first of May, 1778, to his father.

The Baron Grimm had furnished him with a letter of introduction to the Duchesse de Bourbon, but Mozart is not clear as to why or what happened, but in effect he presented the letter to the Duchesse de Chabot, who may or may not have read it. He was ushered into what he calls a large room without any fire and as cold as ice.

> At last the Duchesse appeared, greeted me with the greatest apparent kindness, and said that unfortunately all her clavecins were out of tune, but would I not try one? I suggested that as my hands were too cold to do myself justice I would like to warm them first by a fire. "*O oui, monsieur, vous avez raison*" was all she said: she did nothing about it, but began to draw, sitting by a table in company with several gentlemen. I was quite ignored: I was left standing, numbed with cold in this great unheated room of which all the windows were open. Had it not been for M. Grimm's kindness and therefore a distaste from annoying one of his friends, I would have stalked out. However, finding that no attention was paid to me, I sat down to the clavecin and started to play my "Variations on the Minuet of M. Fischer" [which had recently been composed at Mannheim] but noticed that what I did was quite unimportant to the lady and the gentlemen occupied in sketching, so I stopped playing and got up, only to be greeted by quite a barrage of automatic compliments. So I deprecated these, and said the untuned clavecin and my cold hands rendered it impossible for me to make music worthy of my distinguished audience and that I had better return on a more propitious occasion.

To my surprise I was begged to continue playing, and really quite ordered to remain until the Duc himself arrived . . . "*O c'est un prodige, c'est inconcevable, c'est étonnant!*" leads but to the final result—"*adieu.*"

The twenty-two-year-old Mozart in fact was still regarded as a grown-up prodigy, and his grand hostesses, rather bored, were as polite as they could make themselves, which was not much. Clavecins require constantly to be tuned, all Duchesses were not either as good managers or as wealthy as might appear; surely April (Mozart's previous letter to his father suggests this visit was paid in April) would not necessarily have given Paris such a bitterly cold day which did not seem to inconvenience the fingers of people sketching, and surely this anecdote as recorded by Mozart is all very understandable. Even his Fischer variations are not such as would cause an idle dilettante to drop her sketching pencil, at least until the ninth variation when there was an opportunity of using both manuals and crossing the hands, a piece of visual drama which might have attracted.

Later on in this visit to Paris his mother died in a house on Montmartre, and the largely failing visit drew to a close. It is, by the way, rather curious that Paris, though she had once very properly named a street after Mozart, had not chosen the St. Antoine neighbourhood but a street in Auteil, whose name was afterwards changed to commemorate La Fontaine. Rameau has a short road near the old Opera site in the Palais Royal—very fitting. Couperin has not been commemorated at all. Mozart Street in London is a funny little affair lost in the wilds of the Harrow Road—so we have nothing to boast of.

To sum up: we see the clavecin composers in France were centred in Paris. To all intents and purposes, Paris was the musical centre of France even more than London was the musical centre of England. We see, however, that the clavecinists came from outside Paris, from the French provinces, from Belgium or from the Empire. The staple means of livelihood was playing the organ in church. Additional money was earned by teaching the musical daughters of the wealthy Paris bourgeois. The way to fame was either through Court appointments or through the households of the rich financiers, who were richer and more influential than the run of the aristocracy, too numerous for the size of Paris and who were about as important as subalterns in an over-officered battalion. Often the instruments the musicians had to teach on in the great shut-off houses were out of tune, and the treatment accorded to them would not be more polite than that accorded to Mozart by the Duchesse de Chabot. But the clavecinist would be content with his guinea and his art.

3. The Music

After the simple dances printed by Attaignant there is little music to be consulted until the early work of the clavecinists proper, the earliest of whom was Jacques Champion de Chambonnières who was writing a little before Purcell. He wrote little pieces whose fancy titles obscured the simple dance forms which they really were. These dance forms, especially the Allemande, Courante, Sarabande and Gigue, were served unadorned in other countries: it was in France alone that they became essentially literary in their interest. The true nature of French music has been defined with exactness and frequency, but these definitions do not seem to embrace all the facts. As far as music for the domestic keyboard is concerned, it is possible to say that on the whole the corpus consists of short or shortish descriptive pieces often with sufficient literary interest for books, reference books, travel books, *memoirs* and the like to shed interest and enlightenment upon them. This is of course not the case with most keyboard music written in other countries, it is true of neither Purcell nor Bach, true of neither Handel nor Scarlatti, though with regard to the Italian it is not quite so untrue as it is of Bach. This literary or descriptive interest of French keyboard music is an established tradition from Chambonnières to Poulenc.

The individual dance forms were probably not derived directly from lute music, but from the ballets of Cambert and Lully. Where Cambert and Lully got them from would take us too far from the subject in hand: the point to be made here is that clavecin music was often derivative. It was something that someone who had assisted at a ballet might like to hear, a dance tune played on the clavecin garnished with a pictorial impression. As for the dances, the grave, sometimes emotional Allemande, with its constant flow of quavers or semiquavers, the metrically complex Courante with its two and three beats in a bar sometimes inextricably intermixed, the slow and stately aria-like Sarabande and the quick happy English jigg, they were well known and were all written in binary form. Chambonnières starts his "La Verdinguette" in C, there is no modulation to the dominant up to the double bar, after the double bar where we might have expected a touch of subdominant we have instead the relative minor followed by the dominant, and so to a close in C. It is binary form, but not sure of itself, and indeed the binary form, except in the clavecin music of Rameau, never had the hold which it had in the Empire.

The way it broke down was the way it tended to break down in England had not Handel taken the matter firmly in hand a decade after the death of Purcell. And this was the influence of the Ground: a bass line is repeated and repeated many times, and each time there is a different tune written above it. But whereas Purcell and, when he used this form, J. S. Bach, were very strict, the French clavecinists went their own way. If the ground is repeated and the initial tune is repeated alternately with each time a different tune, then we have a Rondeau. The difference between a Rondeau and a Rondo is all the difference between contrapuntal music and sonata music, the one composed from the bass as in the Rondeau of Couperin, the other composed from the treble as in the Rondo of Mozart. In both the tune recurs periodically in the tonic key with different tunes in between, in both cases the different tunes are meant to be contrasts to the main tune, but in the one case it is the bass which is the backbone of the whole, in the other, the harmonic key structure.

From the Rondeau, which is similar when in triple time to the Passacaglia or the Chaconne, the next step among composers who were not interested in what was called the "science" of music, would be not to trouble if an engaging contrasting tune was of such a nature as not to allow the ground bass strictly to be repeated beneath it. It was the beginning of composing from the treble, though outside the sonata key system. And in time this most fruitful and popular method of composing became that of repeating a bass and its corresponding tune several times. Sandwiched between the repeats would be episodes free as to their basses and harmonies, but strict as to their length, key and rhythm.

Now this form of composition led to the greatest Rondeaux being thoughtful, rather slow pieces of music, while the sonata Rondo was usually quick, dramatic and exciting. Mozart would write a simple tune, so simple that talking duchesses could tap it out with their little feet, and this tune would later lead to episodes so dramatic, so beautiful and so interesting that the greatest musicians could be held enchanted. But in the Rondeau it was the opening bass and its tune which was the important thing, and silence was necessary before the first bar. In the Mozart Rondo we have a drama, the curtain rises and nothing in particular happens so as to give the audience time to rustle in their seats: then it becomes more and more interesting and dramatic, then at last it ends much as it began. But the Rondeau as written by Couperin at his greatest is a sort of sermon to a text, logical, exact, exhaustive and full of meaning, every word of which must be taken in.

Chambonnières, Begue, d'Anglebert and the early uncle Couperins wrote in simple dance forms, feeling their way perhaps even through a certain slackness to the slack Rondeau form. It only took a generation to perfect this sort of music: Chambonnières was at his height about 1660 and Couperin in his first publication in 1713. The primitives, then, in the clavecinist school, are duller than most primitives. The clavecin school is one of those in which only the prime products are of excellence, for the decadence is equally dull with the primitives.

Couperin, and when we write this name we mean of course the only true genius with this surname, François Couperin "Le Grand", published his pieces in Suites which he called *Ordres*. And he did not call them Suites for the excellent reason that he did not mean the individual dances to follow each other. He could not have done this because the course of an *Ordre* (for instance, the 9th) may be broken for a piece requiring two clavecins, and several Ordres are broken to allow pieces requiring a second instrument of some sort. For example, the *Musete de Taverni* in the 15th needs the chord of A major with an open fifth to be repeated as a pedal point throughout, while a *sujet* and a *contre-partie* intertwine contrapuntally above: now these two parts require not only two hands but two separate manuals. How then are you going to play the Bourdon, as the pedal point is called? By not playing the *contre-partie*, no doubt, and the piece sounds quite effective.

These interruptions in the progress of an Ordre show conclusively that an Ordre is a set of pieces like a set of Scarlatti sonatas. You may play a movement which you like in any order, and they are not huge Suites like those of J. S. Bach, even though an Ordre may take as long to play.

Having therefore, I hope, cleared the ground by saying it is unnecessary to study Ordres as such, and that the true clavecin unit is the individual piece, it would be possible to approach the music itself if the thorny subject of ornamentation did not prevent and go before.

Let us hear what can be said in favour of carrying out the full ornamentation as printed in the usual editions confronting modern pianists, ornamentation even sometimes written out in full by, as I think them to be, officious editors. First, there is Couperin's Preface to his 1713 *Pieces de Clavecin.*

> J'y ay mis tous les agrémens nécessaires. J'y ay observé perpendiculairement la juste valeur des tems, et des notes ; et a proportion du scavoir et de l'âge des personnes, on trouvera des pieces plus ou moins difficiles, à la portée des mains excelentes, des mediocres et des foibles, l'usage m' a fait connoître que les mains vigoureuses, et capables d'executer ce qu'il y a de plus rapide, et de plus leger, ne sont pas toûjours celles qui reussissent le mieux dans les pieces tendre, et de sentiment, en j'avoueray de bonne foy, que j'ayme beaucoup mieux ce qui me touche que ce qui me surprend.
>
> Le Clavecin est parfait quant a son etendue, et brillant par luy même ; mais comme on ne peut enfler, ny diminuer ses sons, je scauray toujours gré a ceux qui par un art infini soutenu par le gout, pourons arriver a rendre cet instrument susceptible d'expression : c'est à quoy mes ancêtres se sont apliqués. . . .

Couperin is quite clear. The clavecin is a beautiful but inexpressive musical instrument ; ornaments are necessary so that its music may touch the heart, which is his object in writing for it.

Landowska remarks that Couperin was strongly of the opinion that, considering all the trouble he took to mark in his ornamentation, players should exactly follow these markings, and play the ornaments exactly as set out in his *L'Art de toucher le Clavecin* ; taking away none, and adding none. Only then will his pieces make their true impression on a hearer of good taste.

Now in support of those who wish, when playing Couperin on the pianoforte, to avoid most of the ornamentation, we may bring Couperin himself once more into evidence. In the very *L'Art De toucher Le Clavecin* par Monsieur Couperin, published Chez L'Auteur, rue de Poitou au Marais 1717, which Madame Landowska quotes, we have this.

> La Douceur du Toucher dépend encore de tenir Ses doigts le plus prés des touches qu'il est possible . . . qu'une main qui tombe de hault donne un coup plus Sec, que Sy elle touchoit de prés ; et que la plume tire un Son plus dur de la corde.

In other words, the clavecin is such a sensitive instrument that its tone is influenced by the act of touch. Now the pianoforte is even more sensitive than the harpsichord, therefore all the necessary powers of phrasing are possible without having to play all the set ornamentation which even harms the melodic contour when played upon a pianoforte, because it is unnecessary.

The modern antagonist to Madame Landowska is Herr Oscar Bie, who, in a translation by Messrs. Kellett and Naylor,[1] says: ". . . his agréments are anything but pleasant. They seem to destroy our sense for the pure run of the voices, and are painful in their superabundance . . . running drills, cutting the tones deeper into the relief of the piece . . . could we hear Couperin play, we should certainly hear the pure voice more distinctly than we imagine, enfolded as it would be here and there by deeper or brighter shadows of the ornamentations . . . a technique . . . lost to us with the thorough comprehension of this music."

My own opinion is, on the whole, do as you like. No two performances need be the same, or ornaments may be varied at repeats. In practising the music, use all the ornaments, so that when playing you may be sure you are avoiding them for artistic and not for lazy reasons.

An additional piece of evidence that Couperin acknowledged the legato power of the clavecin and that therefore ornamentation was not introduced to prolong notes, as some writers too readily assume, is provided in that part of *l'Art de toucher* which deals with fingering.

Couperin sets out the following passage marked with fingering in the "maniere ancienne"

and remarks "Cette manière ancienne n'auoit" (*sic* ? misprint) "nulle Liaison. Celle qui suit est la vraye"

Having thus achieved "Liaison" he complacently remarks, "Je suis persuadé que peu de personnes dans Paris restent entêtées des vielles maximes: Paris étant le centre du bon."

<hr />

[1] *The Pianoforte and Pianoforte Players*, Dent, 1899.

Having therefore dealt as adequately as perhaps possible, in the present state of knowledge, with the difficult problem of how much ornamentation to use, we may turn to the music, and the composer himself offers invaluable information. In the Preface of his *Pieces de Clavecin*, 1713, he says:

> J'ay toûjours eu un objet en composent toutes ces pieces: des occasions differentes me l'ont fourni, ainsi les Titres répondent aux idées que j'ay ẹues; on me dispensera d'en rendre compte: cependent comme parmi ces Titres, il y en a qui semblent me flater, il est bon d'avertir que les pieces qui les portent, sont des espéces de portraits qu'on a trouvé quelques fois assés ressemblans sous mes doigts, et que la plûpart de ces Titres avantageux, sont plûtôt donnés aux aimables originaux que j'ay voulu representer, qu'aux copies que j'en ay tirées.

First we may deal with Couperin's dance pieces in binary form, that is to say in that form in which the piece is divided into two portions, each repeated, and in which the music usually modulates to the dominant and after the double bar and perhaps a rudimentary development in the subdominant, returns to the tonic for the close. This binary form is that used by both Bach and Handel in their dance numbers, their Allemandes, Courantes, Sarabandes and Gigues, and by Domenico Scarlatti in his sonatas.

Couperin's Allemandes are sad and majestic, as seen by their titles: that of the First Ordre is named "L'Auguste", that of the Second, "La Laborieuse", and that of the Third, perhaps the finest of the lot, "La Ténébreuse". As the Ordres proceed the Allemandes become less frequent and less striking, for as time went on Couperin became more and more interested in his quasi-Chaconne Rondeaux forms.

The Courantes are all of the complex 6-4 against 3-2 rhythm, usually much more complicated than the Courantes of J. S. Bach, who often introduced his cross rhythms at the cadence only. Perhaps the finest dance in this form by Couperin is the triplex "Première Courante, Dessus plus orne sans changer la Basse" and "Seconde Courante" of the 1st, an Ordre, by the way which, first and last, contains Couperin's greatest binary dance music.

The Sarabandes are similar in essential clarity to Handel's, Couperin writes out a singing ornamentation which might reasonably remind us that Handel's plain Sarabande minims should not always be left unadorned. But Couperin attempts nothing of J. S. Bach's inwardness and mysticism in this ornamentation, which, as in the greatest of the Sarabandes, "La Majestueuse" from the First Ordre, is sometimes almost lacking in originality.

Couperin seems not to have cared for the contrapuntal style of Gigue, or even for Gigues at all.   His best, "La Milordine", from the inevitable First Ordre, is a simple dance, not fugued, containing this sequence fingered by the composer himself in *L'Art de toucher.*

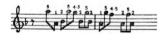

Of the little pieces introduced into the standard form of the Suite at will between the Sarabande and the Gigue Couperin makes a great deal, and is perhaps most happy in his charming Gavottes.   What could be more typical of the lighter side of our composer than "La Bourbonnoise", one of his simplest, shortest and most delicious pieces, from (of course) the First Ordre, which contains in another Gavotte in G minor with a Double "*Ornemens pour diversifier la Gavotte précédente sans changer la Basse*", a graver and tunefully sad dance measure?

A little dance called "Les Canaries" ("Espèce de gigue"—Rousseau) with a Double of singular felicity in the Second Ordre is remarkable among the galanterien, but the Minuets and Passepieds contain nothing of merit approaching those of J. S. Bach.

It is in the Rondeaux, usually pieces with titles, that we meet with amazing variety and richness.

The piece in C. minor (printed however with only two flats) named "La Favorite" in the Third Ordre at once claims the attention as one of the greatest clavecin pieces ever written by anybody.   Its direction "Gravement sans lenteur" is taken by Landowska to contradict its plain two in a bar rhythm, and she plays it as if there were four beats and the tempo "Gravement avec lenteur", but the effect is prodigious, and one feels she must be right.   Similar in style and form is the famous Passacaille in B minor in the Eighth, in response to which the historian of the fourth volume of the *Oxford History of Music* springs to life with the following:

> after each of the couplets the impressive theme is brought back without any alteration and the feeling of the whole piece may be compared to some of the Dances of Death in old German art, in which the figure of Death is shown as ready to seize representatives of every class and age of life in succession.

It is immensely difficult to play, more so than "La Favorite", because the broken chords of the theme are so difficult to roll out with the right impressiveness; and because the theme itself is rather bare, the Passacaille being very long and the theme repetitive within itself. It has little relationship with the C minor organ Passacaglia of J. S. Bach, the bass often being extremely free in the couplets, it not being fugued and, perhaps above all, there being no sense of symphonic development. Which things being so, it is perhaps surprising that both these great movements should remind one hearer at least of the gravity and weight of Beethoven; but so they do. Beethoven, a few initial difficulties apart, has always been admired among the French, and so perhaps it is not so astonishing that these early specimens of French musical art should possess the same basic emotion as that so often expressed by the great symphonic master.

The astonishing First Ordre contains in "L'Enchanteresse" a shorter Rondeau of almost equal power and gravity, in "La Bandoline" of the Fifth we are becoming a little lighter in style, and by the time we play "Soeur Monique" we have almost reached salon music, salon music of the most intellectual refinement, it is true, but not the great Couperin. It is a pity that Couperin's clavecin music nowadays is usually bought in "sheet music" and that it is his lighter pieces which are often the most studied. He was not only a composer of tinkling little fancies. He suffers from his superabundance: his most popular music bears the same value to his greatest as the "Harmonious Blacksmith" variations do to some of the other harpsichord music of his great London contemporary.

To me the most valuable because the unique piece, a piece resembling the work of no other composer whatsoever, is the long and exact chaconne in the Thirteenth Ordre called "Les Folies Francaises, ou Les Dominos". Here each time the ground bass comes again there is a different subtitle, and every sort of girl is portrayed in the way in which she meets the emotion of love. They are imagined as at a masquerade, each girl with an appropriately coloured domino. The first is the bass with a pretty tune on top "La Virginité sous le Domino couleur d'invisible", and then through "La Pudeur", "L'ardeur", "L'Esperance", "La Fidélité", "La Persévérance", "La Langueur", the neurotic "La Coquéterié" to a picture of amorous old gentlemen and then, a surprising touch of genius, "Les Coucous bénévoles sous des Dominos jaunes" which Landowska makes a *da capo* after "La Jalousie taciturne", to "La Frénésie" and so to "L'âme en peine". Like the very greatest programme music, which I suppose this is, of a psychological Proustian sort, this music is great just as music, and can be enjoyed fully just as a chaconne.   But besides this, to me it sums up much wisdom about the emotion of love, and shows Couperin very French, in that as well as a musician he had also the spirit of a great man of letters.

He wrote other pieces of programme music, that is to say, pieces in which the usually static portraits such as "Soeur Monique" move and act.   "Les Petits Ages" in the Seventh Ordre, the strange ballet-like "Les Fastes de la grande et ancienne Menestrandise" in the Eleventh Ordre with its village fair and hurdy gurdy, and the much more conventional battle piece in the Tenth, "La Triomphante".

While the clavecin music of Couperin was equally great throughout its career, though it changed from generally binary dance forms to various types of more or less strict rondeaux, we find, I think, that the greatest pieces of Rameau come from his later 1741 collection, a collection permeated by opera and ballet.   In this volume we find "L'Egyptienne", "La Livri" which is an arrangement for clavecin by Rameau himself, the charming Minuet with its companion in G major and G minor quoted in *Castor and Pollux*, "Les Sauvages", originally a dance for natives of the Caribbean islands brought to Paris for show, and then used in *Les Indes Galantes*, and other music. Of the earlier clavecin music by far the greatest is an Allemande in E minor originally published in 1724: this Allemande, grave and presenting (to the Lullyists) the terrifying spectacle of sixteen semi-quavers in the bar, is one of the greatest keyboard pieces in this dance form, and may fitly be compared with "La Ténébreuse" of Couperin or the best of Bach and Handel.

Students of form may like to examine the piece called "Les Cyclopes" from the 1724 collection.   Labelled a Rondeau, it can be exhibited as a rare specimen of sonata form for the clavecin.   The first subject, in D minor, has its exposition broken into by arpeggios requiring two manuals, but it is eventually given out in full, ending on a tonic close for bar 52.   Here we may suppose the Development section to begin: the sequential semiquaver figure and the full bar pause would lead us to imagine we were playing music fifty years in advance of the times were it not so tied to its key and its dominant. The recapitulation is exact.

Rameau was at his greatest a really great man, but the general body of his work does not sustain this reputation: Couperin, besides being much more varied, was always more of an artist in his clavecin music, and Rameau, exceptional pieces apart, must take second place to him. It is perhaps a mistake to play much Rameau, and it must be doubted how wise it is to make his clavecin music the basis for a whole ballet. But some Rameau, interspersed among other clavecin music, will always bring that feeling which one has for some composers: you say "how very fine, why do we not hear more of . . ." whoever it is. But sometimes there is a good reason for it, as in the case of Rameau.

When Mozart arrived in Paris in 1778, the only clavecinists alive were Duphly and Corrette, neither composers of any importance. Rameau had been dead rather more than ten years and Couperin much longer. Mozart made no attempt to write in their style, though he did write special music for the clavecin. He had made journeys into Italy, and had come across pianofortes. Even recently, on his journey from Salzburg, he had become acquainted with the pianofortes of Stein at Mannheim, and some of his keyboard sonatas were already pianistic.

The pieces of music for clavecin with which he particularly hoped to please the Parisians were variations: we have already read of his unhappy experience while playing his Fischer set to Mme de Chabot. The airs he chose for treatment were usually from the theatre, the sort of thing the Parisians would already know and like to hear treated. Thus an air from the *Opera comique Julie* by Desaides, a very minor composer of the school headed by Monsigny and Philidor, was the subject of nine variations. All Mozart's Parisian variations have much in common. The first variation is usually a sort of semiquaver "division"; later on there is a variation introducing trills in both hands alternately, things difficult to sound pleasing on a pianoforte, but pretty enough toys when executed on a two-manualled clavecin; Mozart also uses an Adagio variation, with a melodic line of an aria-like contour and ornament; often there will be a variation in the tonic minor; and whirling gay semiquavers will conclude.

The set to the French folk-song, used in our days for the same purpose by Dohnanyi, "Ah! vous dirai-je, maman" presents no features not to be found in the treatment of the air from *Julie*, except that Mozart must surely have been thinking of the clavichord in the tied notes of the "alto" part in the Minore variation, where the quietly intentional rub of the discords almost cries for the sensitive legato of the tangential instrument. The variations on "La Belle Françoise", a somewhat monotonous popular song, shows in the Second and

Eighth variations crossing of the hands of a type unusual in Mozart's pianoforte music but which would be effective on the clavecin, though there is the usual variation in the tonic minor which in this case is the remote key of E flat minor, a key so remote from the usual D or C as to suggest a clavecin of equal temperament, and this same key of E flat minor is also that of the Minore variant of "Je Suis Lindor". This air is of unusual interest to us. Lovers of Rossini will remember Count's Almaviva's "Io son Lindoro, che fido v'adoro", but this is not the Rossini air, that composer, indeed, was not even born. The tune was by Beaumarchais himself, and the words form the second couplet of the serenade with guitar accompaniment:

> Je suis Lindor, ma naissance est commune;
> Mes voeux sont ceux d'un simple bachelier:

Le Barbier de Seville had been performed three years before in the Theatre in the Tuileries, and these variations form the first evidence that Mozart was acquainted with Beaumarchais' work, though he had not at this time met Da Ponte who was knocking about Venice. It was of course Da Ponte who introduced Mozart to the not as yet written *Le Mariage de Figaro*. In Beaumarchais writing his own singing tunes we have another instance of French eighteenth-century literary men being musical: the pleasing simplicity of this tune shows a musical line similar to that of Rousseau. In the Mozart variations of it we have the usual features, including crossing of the hands and a highly ornamented Adagio.

Musically, the most interesting variations which Mozart wrote in Paris may not have been for the clavecin, for the set which opens the sonata in A, K.331 is so effective, and so popular, when played upon the pianoforte, that it is usually claimed as being written for this instrument. As, however, the final Rondo, the "Turkish", is clearly clavecin music, it is surely surprising that Mozart should have consorted in the one sonata music for two different instruments. These variations have all the usual Parisian features, a crossed hand variation, a Minore and an Adagio. Sing though the tune does, a clavecin can sing as well as a pianoforte, and one feels the assumption about the instrument for which the A major variations was composed is made on the premiss that the clavecin is incapable of *legato*. It is no more incapable than the early pianoforte.

Besides these sets of variations, Mozart wrote four and perhaps five sonatas. K.310 in A minor has that drumming bass so effective on the clavecin, and met with in Scarlatti and in the D major harpsichord concerto of Haydn. In the Andante there is a passage of quite special difficulty for the left hand below a trill for the right, but what is to me clearly clavecin music is the passage in C major after the double bar, with its soft low chords for the left hand while the right has a sort of cello melody to be played on the other manual: then follows the impassioned rhetoric for two manuals, one with a triplet chordal figure full of clashing suspensions, the other, the lower, with a stern *pizzicato* ending in a series of trills, music which demands the clear low tones of the clavecin, an instrument able to reproduce the pizzicato of a cello. Much of the final Presto is equally effective on either instrument.

The C major sonata, K.330, seems to me by no means so obviously clavecin music, and indeed to be one of those keyboard sonatas in which Mozart seems to have had the string quartet in his mind's ear, especially the slow movement and the little melody after the double bar in the Finale. K.331 is the A major sonata already considered. K.332 in F is surely pianoforte music, the sudden fortes and pianos being too quick for the hands to change manuals or stops in the clavecin. The final Allegro assai contains clear pianoforte writing as in the figuration introduced for the repetition of the bewitching little syncopated tune introduced after the double bar. K.333 may or may not have been written in Paris; authorities differ. The first and slow movements appear to be Mozart in his string quartet vein, see for instance the passage after the double bar and the important work the cello would have to do. The simple last movement is probably pianoforte music, as it might sound rather thin on the clavecin. Many people might think this the wrong way about: in truth clavecin music is thicker in texture than the music of the pianoforte primitives; compare, as extreme examples, J. S. Bach with Haydn.

With the departure of Mozart, alone, leaving his mother in her grave in Paris, great music for the clavecin ceased to be written. Grétry wrote some clavecin concertos, but he became too concerned with earning an operatic living during the Revolution, in which he acted as a musical Vicar of Bray, to bother much with the clavecin or indeed the new pianoforte. Such heavyweights as Berlioz were equally indifferent, and there was no equivalent to Couperin until the times of Debussy, and as for visiting foreigners, the next one to play an important part in Parisian life was the essentially pianistic Chopin.

SHORT BIBLIOGRAPHY TO CHAPTER II

Translations are given wherever known, though quotations in text are not usually taken from such translations so as not to infringe copyright.

Wanda Landowska: *Music of the Past*, Geoffrey Bles, trans. W. A. Bradley, 1926.

Jean Jacques Rousseau: *Confessions*, Everyman's Library.   (Dent 1931. 2 vols.)   *Dictionnaire de Musique* (Hachette).

François Couperin: *L'Art de Toucher Le Clavecin*, 1717.

W. A. Mozart: *The Letters of Mozart to His Family*, translated and edited Anderson.   (Macmillan 1938.   3 vols.)

Arouet de Voltaire: *The Age of Louis XIV*, Everyman's Library. (Dent 1926.)   *Précis du Siècle de Louis XV*, 1755 and 1763.

C. Bouvet: *Nouveaux Documents . . . des Couperins*, 1932.

de Saint-Lambert: *Les Principes du Clavecin*, Paris, 1697 and 1702.

de La Borde: *Essai sur la Musique Ancienne et Moderne*, 1780.

Oscar Bie: *History of the Pianoforte*, trans. E. E. Kellett and E. W. Naylor.   (Dent 1899.)

Louis Ducros: *French Society in the Eighteenth Century* (Bell 1926).

CHAPTER III

THE CEMBALO IN ITALY

———— ❧ ————

1. *The Instruments in Society*

L EAVING England and France we come to Italy, and in Italy we find,
what we will again find in the case of The Empire in the next
two chapters, a land which is geography and politics rather than one
unified nation.   England had a capital in London, and France in Paris:
both capitals strongly centrifugal, though Paris was more a vortex
than London.   But Rome was no capital of Italy, and not markedly
a capital of the Papal States, for this Papal realm had such an odd shape
that a secondary town, Bologna, was strong culturally enough to be
a northern rival to Rome.   Naples was indeed the capital of the
Kingdom of the Two Sicilies, and Venice was indeed the capital of the
great (and in our period, decadent) seafaring Republic.   But although
the traveller from Naples to Venice, if he did not go by sea, would
surely find it safer and more convenient to cause his lumbering coach
to proceed via Rome, he would have no sensation of journeying to
the capital and down again to a Province, as a land voyager from Bristol
to Norwich via London would have felt.   Naples was larger than
Rome, but Venice was the capital of a Great Power; and until she fell
suddenly on the onslaught of Napoleon, the Republic retained this
status among the nations of the world.   Thus the Court of St. James
sent to Venice an Ambassador, but a mere Minister did for Naples.
In our story in this book, the most important Ambassador was a Duke,
but the Minister at Naples was a mere Mister before he was knighted.

Besides Rome, Naples and Venice, there were other capital cities,
notably Florence, the capital of Tuscany, Genoa, the capital of the
Republic of that name, Milan, the capital of its own Duchy, Turin,

the capital of Piedmont, and the smaller ducal capitals of Parma, Mantua and Modena. The territory ruled by the Pope was as nearly divided into two as a tube of toothpaste pressed in the centre by the thumb of Tuscany. Rome herself was the cultural and social centre of the southern bulge, but though she was the administrative capital of the whole, Bologna was the intellectual capital of the northern bulge. This bulge contacted Venetian territory across the Po, a river which to this day divides the provinces of Venetia and Emilia, which latter, with the Marches, Umbria, Rome and the Abruzzi roughly makes up the eighteenth-century Papal States.

All this, however, is rough and approximate. There were constant wars and constant changes, while the history of domestic keyboard instruments runs for centuries up to 1800.

Before returning to these individual capitals, so many smaller Londons and Parises, we should turn to the society in the capitals which was the same (if different in emphasis and proportion of population) throughout Italy.

There would be the rich landowning aristocrats, usually of Italian birth, but in the north sometimes of Austrian and in the south of Spanish. In no land more than Italy did the crowned heads sleep more uneasily, whether fillets, wreaths or garlands or tiaras, whether kingly, princely or ducal, or even the imaginary laurel crown of a composer of operas. Within little Italy was played out the same comedy of balance of power which was played on the broader European stage. A Count ruling a small estate and paying homage to the Pope might suddenly find an unexpected and angry God in the shape of Louis XIV demanding that he should pay homage to him. If he does so, the Pope's troops will invade and destroy his County: if he does not do so, who can say how long is the arm of the French king?

While the pressure of France was occasional, the pressure of Spain was constant on the southern half of the Italian mainland and on the islands. The Court of Naples was often subordinate to La Granja, and even in the north the Spanish Bourbons seem to have used inoffensive duchies such as Parma as petty kingdoms for younger sons.

To the north-east the Empire, jealous even of the spiritual pretensions of the Papacy, maintained such pressure as the personal prestige of succeeding emperors permitted, ending, indeed, with battles between French and Austrian troops, for the Italian states could put no effective bar on the entry of either.

In the middle of all this, the Popes and the Doges tried to maintain their prestige by avoiding battles which they knew they would lose. They did this so successfully that Europe gasped when Napoleon executed the easy task of marching into both Rome and Venice. Both crumbled away at a touch, like floorboards afflicted with dry rot. The success of the balance of power policies of the Papal States, of Genoa and of Venice maintained these areas as purely Italian, though Genoa was selected (without being asked) as a Spanish naval base at one period.

So we have the landowning aristocrats, scheming, worried, not always Italian, congregating in the several capitals, knowing each other, not in the easy good-humoured way of the British, nor in the disciplined and King-fearing way of the French, but often hating and killing.

So much for the wealthy aristocrats. But their younger brothers, nephews and cousins, forbidden by their birth to engage in the professions or in trade, maintained a starving pride, particularly in the south, where Spanish influence predominated. In London the younger relatives of peers would engage in trade or enter the professions as a matter of course. In Paris there was always the Church and the Army at least, and the very numerous jobs about the huge and costly Court. In Italy, with its petty Courts and Armies more like bandits than disciplined troops, and its ecclesiastical appointments outside the Papal States constantly used as pawns in the everlasting game of chess played by the Papacy, the only sure method of priestly enrichment of petty nobility was offered inside the Papal States, for nephews of popes were regularly made cardinals, or, if already noble, enriched and advanced, a marquis into a prince.

All this, and one other factor, had a very great influence upon the position of women. And this position is possibly the largest single factor, from country to country and era to era, in the history of the instruments with which this book deals. The other factor not hitherto referred to, is purely geographical, and can be easily expressed by saying that Naples is half-way in a direct line from London to Alexandria. This can be expanded, by adding that the sea voyage Naples-Alexandria is shorter than the sea voyage Naples-London, because of the Iberian peninsula. Finally, what Venice was always very aware of was "an argosy bound to Tripolis" and wars with the Ottoman Empire. The Levant had great influence on Italy: the Canalettos of St. Mark's Square in Venice show untidy façades with

blown window blinds and what even may be washing; the rooms seem
bug-ridden, and no doubt were. The dress of the poorer classes was
nearer the galabieh than the coats and trousers of London. And thus
the position of women tended to be Levantine and the numbers of
poor, nobly-born, unattached young men did the rest.

Views on women were contradictory: they were angels; on the
other hand, they were so lascivious that if they looked out of a window
on to the street it must necessarily induce in them an unworthy emotion. They were wise, and could inspire poets; on the other hand,
they were so stupid as to have all professions closed to them. These
contradictions are part of the male view of the female throughout the
world, but nowhere in Italy was the juxtaposition more poignant for
the women. In the Levant proper all women were kept under sub-
jection, but Italy had sufficient commerce with Vienna and Paris and
London for some women to achieve the same independence of life as
a man. Queens of Sweden and of Poland came to live in Italy and
exerted great cultural influence, rich English ladies toured the land:
one imagines Mrs. Thrale, when Signora Piozzi, very much wore the
trousers. Emma Hamilton caused amazement and something like
adoration in the streets of Naples. And all the time the women were
trained into habits of intrigue by the convention of the *cavaliere
servente*.

"Surely the ladies of England have *cavalieri serventi*?" asked a
young widow, travelling alone in a coach from Bologna into Tuscany,
of a certain Abbate. The priest said no, they did not, and the girl said
she was sorry for them, adding that a *cavaliere servente* was the pleasan-
test sort of man there was. "As a matter of fact," she continued,
"at the moment I am without one. Will you be my *servente* till we
reach Florence?" But the secular priest, who was Mozart's librettist
Da Ponte, was saved further embarrassment by the ingress into the
coach of two much younger men, both much more admirably suited
to the young widow's purpose. It was not, by the way, morals that
caused Da Ponte embarrassment, for he had done much of that sort of
thing in his day, and he was only in secular orders with no Church
appointment. It was merely that he did not like her.

Perhaps the shortest way to explain this convention is a bald historical one. The warrior would go away to fight and would appoint
a gentleman, often a relation, to look after his wife in all faith and
honour. During the seventeenth century the ground floor of his
house would always be full of male retainers, partly a bodyguard,

partly a riffraff of dependants, and the lady must be protected even from these. When life became more civilized, as it did during the eighteenth century, and there was no longer any real need for the servant cavalier, the tradition was maintained. It was the done thing. The girl, married without love to a man she might not have met before her wedding day, would expect to have a *servente*, and if she liked him better than her husband, she would become his mistress. Her husband committed a solecism if he pretended to notice. In the Goldoni comedy set to music by Wolf Ferrari and known in England as *The School for Fathers* we have such a situation, but the translation and the London setting makes the London audience quite miss the point. The uneasy husband in the corner is scorned by the Londoner because he does not throw the *servente* out, but the Venetian eighteenth-century audience enjoyed Goldoni's portrait of a husband so rustic as to be unable to manage the minimum necessary politeness of being easily civil to his wife's *servente*, and unable to find, apparently, some-one else's wife to whom he could act the same part.

So we have throughout Italy a worried and often impoverished nobility with its women usually uneducated and spending time in endless intrigue. Who had time and patience to make music in the home? Very few, as music, except in Rome, was not an affair of state rooms in palaces and of salons in private houses. It was an affair of the public opera and of the Abbate.

There is perhaps no more picturesque class of ecclesiastic than that to which Da Ponte and Liszt equally belonged. With the French title of Abbé or the Italian of Abbate, they went about the world enjoying respect combined with freedom. In the Papal States every third man was an ecclesiastic of some sort, in Venice (rather anti-Church) there were many fewer, though about ten times as many as in modern London in proportion to the population. Naples was full of priests, secular, monastic, or beneficed. The Abbates received no income and were under no discipline, and had usually attained their rank by passing examinations in the only universities open to them, that is to say, those completely under the ruling of the Church. The Abbates travelled about, attended the opera, taught in the universities, enjoyed young ladies as both pupils and mistresses, or formed one of the retinue of a cardinal or a duke.

In England we may imagine any lady or gentleman, adventurer like Drake, a queen like Elizabeth or a wool merchant like Sir Thomas Kytson playing the virginals. In France the clavecinist would alight

G

from his black polished coach with its gilt facings to teach a king's mistress. We will see in due course that in Germany a typical figure would be a small town schoolmaster quietly playing fugues to himself in his study on his clavichord. In later England the typical harpsichordist would be a foreign gentleman, florid, his portrait painted by Gainsborough, a protégé of a duke, with an extensive and remunerative teaching practice around the new suburbs north of the town, perhaps around Soho Square. In Italy I imagine an Abbate playing an out-of-tune harpsichord, or cembalo as he would call it, in his lodgings, whiling away the time before conducting his landlady's daughter to the opera, a service which, courteously rendered, allowed his rent to rest in arrears.

It follows of course that the music in these times and countries was very different. However courtly or bourgeois or religiously introvert it may have been elsewhere, in Italy it was nothing if not operatic. And it was to the opera that all musical Italy looked, the Church itself copying opera, and nowhere more than in Rome where opera as such was usually forbidden. Much is usually made in biographies of Mozart of his boyish ability when in Rome to write down after one hearing a *Miserere* of Allegri. But this piece of music had been copied officially at the request of the Emperor, only to prove quite ineffective when performed at St. Stephen's in Vienna. The Emperor accused the Pope, who in turn accused the organist of St. Peter's, of not being frank and honest, and copying inferior music so as to retain the true Allegri. But this was not what had happened, the truth being that the music itself was of no superb merit. It was the combination of the manner in which it was played, sinking slowly to a whisper, working loudly to an impassioned climax, together with the chanting, the incense and in fact the whole stage management of the High Altar of St. Peter's, backcloth, wings and all (i.e. reredos, choir stalls and all) which resulted in an operatic masterpiece.

The academies where the budding musicians were taught have often been described, and we will come across them later as we make our Italian tour in a page or so. Most of the boys were sent there free, for if they were orphans or bastards or poor legitimates, there was often some kindly wealthy man to adopt them. The poet known today as Metastasio was the son of a poor macaroni seller, and was adopted. Da Ponte was not born with this surname, but it is that of the diocese of the bishop who befriended him and paid for his education. The Cardinal Bishop of Palestrina befriended the son of the wine grower Pierluigi, thus making the name of this diocese famous throughout the church music-loving world. Even as late as Puccini this Italian tradition remains, the son of the poor organist of Lucca being much helped by Queen Margherita.

In these academies the boys studied as we shall shortly see, and those with good voices were castrated besides. One presumes this was usually done to the bastards and the orphans. These castrated boys, *castrati*, sometimes grew up to extreme affluence and power, millionaires and the advisers of kings like Farinelli, Prime Minister of Spain. But more often they were turned out into the world of Italy with a spoilt voice and a spoilt personality, to add to the crime and poverty of the land.

Naples was the chief city with schools such as has been described. Boys from the age of eight upwards were admitted, and those unlikely to make a living at music were from time to time discharged and given a sum of money. The harpsichord (called in Italy and hereafter in this chapter except in quotations, cembalo) instructors were named Maestro Secolari, and were often old pupils retained. Each of the three chief schools had its own dress: one had a blue uniform, a second a white one with a black sash, but the one penetrated by Dr. Charles Burney in 1770 had pure white as its dress. Burney alluded to:

> a *Dutch concert*, consisting of seven or eight harpsichords . . . all performing different things and in different keys. . . . The jumbling of them all together in this manner may be convenient for the house, and may teach the boys to attend to their own parts with firmness, whatever else may be going forward at the same time: it may likewise give them force, by obliging them to play loud in order to hear themselves; but in the midst of such jargon [there were singers and fiddlers in the same room] and continued dissonance, it is wholly impossible to give any kind of polish or finishing to their performance: hence the slovenly coarseness so remarkable in their public exhibitions; and the total want of taste, neatness, and expression. . . . The beds, which are in the same room, serve for seats to the harpsichords. . . . Out of thirty or forty boys who were practising, I could discover but two who were playing the same piece . . . during the winter, the boys rise two hours before it is light, from which time they continue their exercise, an hour and a half at dinner excepted, till eight o'clock at night.

Dr. Burney, who was very pro-Italian in music, adds that this regime must in the course of a number of years produce great musicians.

Yet he can also remark on their "slovenly coarseness". Budding cembalo composers were penning away in the same room, so that production of music was immense in volume, but much of it marred by habits which it is extreme, but not untrue, to call "slovenly coarseness" in composition when, in the third section of this chapter, we discuss the music of men like Rutini.

In this Neapolitan din and confusion of this school dressed in white was an English boy of Italian descent, Stephen Storace, pronounced in London with an English accent, but in Italy as an Italian name. His sister was Ann Storace, the singer, later known in England as Nancy Storace, and to be the "creator" of the role of Sussanah in the first performance of *Figaro* in Vienna in 1786, Mozart having met brother and sister a little before.

Meanwhile, outside these schools of boyish and of eunuch genius, the streets were as turbulent and as noisy. Only, indeed, for general indiscipline, to be compared with London. "If I compare the impudence of the townsfolk of London and Naples," wrote the boy Wolfgang Mozart to his sister in Salzburg a few months before Burney paid his visit to the music school quoted above, "I really think Naples is even worse than London, for the *lazzaroni* here have a sort of brigand chief whom the King pays to keep the rest of his fraternity in order." At the Opera there cannot have been much royal attention to the composer at the cembalo for Mozart tells us that, to appear taller than his Queen, the vain little King stood upon a stool, not a very comfortable way of attending to the music of Jomelli. In this lack of attention, however, the King was merely following royal precedence, for his predecessor who had actually taken sufficient pride in his capital to build the second largest theatre in all Italy—and that is saying a good deal—would talk for the first half of the opera and sleep during the second.

One more view of Naples before we leave for the north. There is the English Minister, lately knighted, in a house full of bric-à-brac, but with a fine cembalo on which his first wife played so well that she played to the boy Mozart, though not without preceding trepidations. She was not the only performer in that household, and Mozart by no means the only visitor. We have the invaluable Dr. Burney again. "Having the honour, this day, of dining at our Minister's, I was very much entertained in the afternoon by the performance of a fat friar of the order of St. Dominic, who came there to sing *buffa* songs; he accompanied himself on the harpsichord." In 1782 Lady

Hamilton died, and four years later the English Minister, the respected antiquarian scholar of European reputation and listener to Neapolitan cembalo music, took as his second wife the discarded mistress of a nephew. He married Emma Lyon, and the new Lady Hamilton made a sensation at the Neapolitan Court. As she wrote to her former lover, "We had a small diplomatic party, and we was sailing in our boat, the K[ing] directly came up, put his boat of music next us, and made all the French horns and the wholl band play . . . I have him in my train every night at the Oppera." And, later, "the King and me sang duetts 3 hours. It was but bad, as he sings like a King. I am singing a duetto now of Paisiellos, that makes every person cry."

If we now take, in imagination, the rutted coach road to Rome, rutted by the wheels of the coaches of Handel, Mozart and Domenico Scarlatti, we will find in the Papal territories a different society, but one just as stimulating. The landed aristocracy was here largely replaced by Cardinals, who were not all holy men, or even learned men. Cardinal Ottoboni, for instance, quite young, gay, music-loving, had the merit of having a Pope as an uncle. Operas were performed, not in a public theatre, for that was forbidden, but in the private palaces of the Monsignors. In that of Ottavio Corsini on one occasion no less than nine Cardinals were present, as well as many ladies of fashion. Cardinal Ottoboni gave weekly concerts, and himself composed, and was the firm friend of Corelli. Between Corsini and Ottoboni there is a great gap of decades, but none in social activities. Rome remained the same until Napoleon entered and behaved with such ill-breeding. But at this point we must describe the Arcadians.

Vestiges of Arcady were still to be found in the suburbs of the northern manufacturing towns of England before the 1914 war. I remember one in which each member of a sort of local culture club invented a maxim or apothegm, and these were all collected together and printed in a little book cased in red leatherette. At another session of this circle a young man, fired by Wagner, astounded the members to such a degree by his attack on Mendelssohn's *Songs Without Words*, that the female president of that assembly, the lecture terminating rather sooner than was timed, could think of nothing better than to suggest that the young man play some of the pieces he had spent an hour in denigrating. This conception of people meeting to exchange artistic and philosophical ideas started in Italy and reached its maximum degeneracy in the island to the north in a space of about three hundred years. But with it was originally mixed another idea. And this notion was to the effect that wealthy noblemen and noble ladies, their lives tangled by intrigue and soured by debts and gambling losses, their livers ruined by drink and their morals by promiscuity, thought how charming it would be, to become shepherds and shepherdesses, walk out in the sweet fields, call themselves by pastoral names and, for an afternoon at least, live simply and talk purely of the soul. The first great society of this sort was the Arcadians of Italy, and the last, the Souls of late nineteenth-century London, though to say that about the last is perhaps unkind and perhaps an exaggeration: the Souls' morals, in any case, were impeccable.

The Queen of Sweden and Cardinal Ottoboni were Arcadians, and at the Cardinal's weekly concerts Arcimelo would greet Terpandro and Protico, or, in other words, the musician of the palace, Corelli, would welcome his colleagues Alessandro Scarlatti and Bernardo Pasquini. On some other day of the week an Abbate, decorated with the name of a shepherd, would welcome the musical Arcadians, and, with Terpandro at the cembalo, cantatas of Protico would be sung.

If we leave Rome, with its official no-opera, but plenty of chamber music, plenty of operatically-written oratorios, and plenty of opera during High Mass, and with the Pope and the Cardinals banqueting in the Vatican on the eve of some feast, say on Christmas Eve, to most secular music set to most sacred words, with the maestro banging on the cembalo the figured bass to keep the musicians and singers together, if we leave, reluctantly, this decadent Rome, we should surely journey to Bologna, through the Papal Territories, and taking the same route as the Mozarts, father and son, in 1770. So we lumber in our unsprung coach through Civita Castelonia and reach the Adriatic coast at Loreto. Then through Sinigaglia and at last inland to Bologna, sleepy with the mountain and sea air, aching with the jolting, and, one fears, bitten by the bed-bugs of the Italian inns.

Bologna, because of Padre Martini, was the centre of "science", a word invariably used from about 1640 to 1840 to denote great contrapuntal skill and the ability to impart polish. The word now means nothing, for contrapuntal problems are solved like he who solves a chess problem by altering the rules governing the moves of the pieces. In the rhythmically and harmonically simple systems of the two centuries mentioned, complexity, including rhythmic and harmonic complexity, could best be introduced by fugal devices. But Padre

Martini, renowned though he was throughout Europe as a contra-puntist, wrote his cembalo sonatas in a smooth operatic tune with simple accompaniment, and was far from reaching a Cimarosian standard, let alone a Scarlattian.

Outside the town lived the retired Farinelli, an old man with his cembalos, to which he gave names, so much did he value their company, so quiet unless played upon, so graceful, so immobile. A cembalo given him by the Queen of Spain (he was private singing *castrato* to the King and Queen for very many years) he named Coreggio, and other instruments were named after Titian and Guido. He received both the Mozarts and Dr. Burney in his princely cembalistic retirement. One of the instruments described by the Englishman was a cedar wood cembalo made to Farinelli's own directions, the naturals were black and the sharps whited with mother of pearl, "but the most curious property of this instrument is, that by drawing out the keys the hammers are transferred to different strings, by which means a composition may be transposed half a note, a whole note, or a flat third lower at pleasure, without the embarrassment of different notes or clefs, real or imaginary."

And so we leave Bologna, where we have seen the priestly hands of Martini and the unsexed elderly hands of Farinelli upon the black naturals and the mother-of-pearl sharps, and the question is, shall we turn south-west into Tuscany to reach Florence, or continue north, round the Adriatic curve, to Venice? This latter imaginary journey, because of the pull of the great names of Mozart, Handel and the Scarlattis, seems to have fixed itself in the eighteenth century, and Florence is of earlier interest. A note may suffice. In this city a group of amateurs desired to perform Greek drama, and one or two of their number essayed the task of writing music they thought might be similar to the music of the ancients. It is most doubtful whether Euripides or Sophocles would have recognized, or even taken any pleasure in, the result, which was a sort of modal measured song to an accompaniment of many instruments, sometimes mildly contrapuntal in character and written out, but often harmonic and very simply harmonic, and arranged from a figured bass. This figured bass was similar to that which developed later, except that intervals more than an octave were pointed out. In cases in which Padre Martini would have written 4/3, an early Florentine would write 11/10. But the composer at the cembalo would know all about that, and there would be no difficulty. Besides the two cembali, which from the earliest times seem to have been the foundation of operatic music, the one to direct the orchestra from and the other to play accompaniments, there was a whole mass of heterogeneous instruments; all the instruments that there happened to be in the palace at the time, one imagines. Violins of all sizes, from *piccoli* (small ones playing very high) to double basses playing very low. As well there were harp-like instruments, regals, brass and wind instruments, the latter often out of tune. The noise would have been rustling and dim, except where the trumpets rang out in a song on the subject of *Vittoria*, and throughout would be heard the measured musical clang of the conductor's cembalo, keeping the whole in time.

With this paragraph on Florence, we can proceed along the usual route for Mozart or for Handel, through Parma, Mantua, Verona and Vicenza, to Venice herself: Venice, the great Adriatic capital, which, as a metropolis should do, absorbed most of the cultural life of the provincial cities into itself.

The northern land boundary of the Republic abutted on the Empire, though it was French and not Austrian troops which brought about the sudden downfall of this hitherto Great Power. Yet the proximity of Vienna was always felt, just as Levantine art was always felt, and Venice would be a city where a Viennese cembalo might be played by a priest sitting to it near a carved coffee table recently imported from Jaffa. It was one of these German cembali that Dr. Burney inspected in the residence of an Imperial emissary, "a very curious keyed instrument which was made at Berlin, under the direction of his Prussian Majesty". It had an abnormal number of stops, and could sound like a harp, a harpsichord, a lute or a pianoforte: this last is surprising, and one wishes Dr. Burney had given a diagram of its hammer action. Like Farinelli's cembalo outside Bologna, it was capable of mechanical transposition.

But though this instrument at least came from the north, musical influences came largely from the south, from Naples, and from Alessandro Scarlatti. And this Neapolitan had begun to make a change in his use of the cembalo, which influenced—and this to us is important—the practice of his renowned son Domenico.

Previously he had used the cembalo alone in *recitativo secco*, the strings entering for the (often very short) *ritornello*; the contrast between the two tone values must have been very great. Even his arias were mainly accompanied by the bare figured bass, a viola da gamba player supporting the cembalist, who would make what he could of the music in the way of imitation. But now Alessandro Scarlatti used the strings much more and *recitativo secco* much less. What is even more startling, he would not only cease to figure his basses, trusting to the resource of the experienced cembalist, but would omit the cembalo altogether, having string tone unsupported by the constant percussive tang or the harp-like arpeggii. This pure string tone must have sounded strangely bewitching, while the re-entry of the cembalo would have added drama to the scene. Alessandro composed little for the cembalo alone, but there is a set of variations on a theme of Corelli: it is said to have influenced the early music of his son, who was still in Venice studying under Gasparini. In Venice also was the Duke of Manchester, the English Ambassador, and also in the city was the younger brother of the Elector of Hanover, one Prince Ernest. To this Adriatic city Handel made his way from the west, and then we have the famous masked ball.

At this masked ball in Venice an unknown man played upon the cembalo, and Scarlatti, among the dancers, listened and said: "That must either be the famous Saxon or the Devil himself." It was indeed Handel: this was the turning point of his life, not because he met Scarlatti, but because he met the Duke of Manchester and the brother of George of Hanover.

We imagine a Venetian palace, and brilliant toccatas and involved improvised fugues and gusty variations: we readily imagine Handel and Scarlatti technically faultless and, in the glow of genius, producing impromptu music which the world is the poorer for losing. In modern times such a scene could hardly be reproduced. Whoever we may think to be two of the foremost composers of the age, they are not the same people as two of the foremost pianists. The pianoforte, with all its merits, introduced a specialization foreign to the cembalo and the clavichord. But that is not the only comment to be made on this famous meeting. There is another. Handel and Scarlatti may have used only the three middle fingers of each hand. Of course, in the flush of ideas convenience may have suggested the use of the thumb and little finger, just as consecutive fifths or octaves, or passages in fugues in which voices disappear and completely new voices enter (with a sort of layer upon layer effect), were suggested. The ideas ebbed and flowed, and musical form and the fingering followed. But to use ten digits was not what was taught, and might even have been disavowed by the players.

To be taught the cembalo introduced the neophyte into a mystery, and perhaps it was not good for him to know too much too quickly: there were tricks of the trade which had to be paid for in *scudi*, though no doubt the Irishman Roseingrave might have preferred guineas. This London harpsichordist, whom we will meet later in the last chapter of this book, became a firm friend of Domenico Scarlatti, and this is how he himself, by way of the pen of that able itinerant journalist, Dr. Burney, describes their first meeting. It has sufficient similarity to the Handel–Scarlatti one to make one wonder if it was not the Italian equivalent of the northern "clavichord in the garret" legend of Handel in Halle, Arne in London and to some extent J. S. Bach in Ohrdruf. But to return to Roseingrave in Venice where he was invited to a party at the palace of one whose name was inscribed in the Golden Book (a stud book of thoroughbred human Venetians), and asked to play the cembalo for the company. He complied, and:

> finding myself in rather better courage and finger than usual, I exerted myself, and fancied by the applause I received, that my performance had made some impression on the company. After a cantata had been sung by a scholar of Gasparini, who was there to accompany her, a grave young man dressed in black with a black wig, who had stood in one corner of the room, very quiet and attentive while I played, being asked to sit down to the harpsichord, when he began to play, I thought ten hundred devils had been at the instrument. I had never heard such passages of execution and effect before. The performance so far surpassed my own, and every degree of perfection to which I thought I would ever arrive, that, if I had been in sight of any instrument with which to have done the deed, I would have cut off my own fingers. I declare that I did not touch an instrument myself, for a month.

Domenico Scarlatti, like the lady who sang the cantata, was a pupil at the time of Gasparini for vocal composition.

A cembalo player perhaps nearly as expert as Domenico Scarlatti was already a professor at one of the Venetian equivalents to the forcing school of vigorous coarse genius we have inspected with Dr. Burney at Naples. This man was Hasse; with a handsome figure and effectively baroque manners, a rising opera composer, "il caro Sassone" seemed to have the world at his feet. But the cembalo music to which he put his name, including the sonata in D which is to be found in one of Pauer's collections, was to be quite put into the shade by the popular beauties of his operas. He shone in eighteenth-century Europe with great glory, but is now one of the dead volcanoes of music, like his senior, Alessandro Scarlatti.

Gasparini had in Marcello another pupil of fame in his day; Marcello's instrumental music is still very occasionally to be heard. He was of a family to be found in the Golden Book and became one of the Council of Forty. His cembalo music has been described as brilliant but empty, and there may indeed be an amateur finish to his work. But there was in this epoch so little professional polish anyhow, as we will see in the third section of this chapter, in the plane of genius rather lower than that of Domenico Scarlatti, that I do not really feel Marcello suffered as an artist by being born into the ruling oligarchy of the Republic.

Galuppi was a fellow pupil of Marcello under Lotti, who was at one time organist of St. Mark's and later in life to write the music sung from the Doge's barge while afloat to celebrate the annual Venetian marriage with the sea. Galuppi was born on one of the islands, Burano, and called, therefore, in a land which nicknamed almost every composer, "Il Buranello". Later on he went to London, but it was Galuppi as a young man that Browning addressed in his poem of the men and women of eighteenth-century Venice.

Well, (and it was graceful of them) they'd break talk off and afford
—She, to bite her mask's black velvet, he, to finger on his sword,
While you sat and played Toccatas, stately at the clavichord?

It was most unlikely to have been a clavichord, an instrument which will be dealt with in a later chapter. It was not popular in Italy; it was unsuitable for Toccatas, which always contained, and sometimes entirely consisted of, a quick rush of notes; and it could not have been heard at all, were the audience never so quiet, in the halls and rooms of a palace in carnival time with their flung-open double doors. But then cembalo does not rhyme with sword, has two syllables and a feminine cadence.

He goes on, however, to the famous and apt mention of the dominant pedal:

Hark! the dominant's persistence, till it must be answered to!

and then comes:

> Brave Galuppi! that was music! good alike at grave and gay!
> I can always leave off talking, when I hear a master play.

But it is to be doubted if they could leave off gambling, an even more favourite amusement of the dying export and import centre of the Mediterranean. The great merchant houses inherited by disappointed men finding their initiative stifled, were further ruined by gambling. Even at best, the inheritor himself would take an estate in the interior and busy himself farming. It was not to farming, however, that the impoverished gambling brother took himself, but to a quarter of Venice named San Barnaba, whence the adjective Barnabotic. Da Ponte, the Abbate, had been doing very well at the Ridotto, where the gaming took place. He returned home to his lodgings, owned by a poor nobleman whose sister was the Abbate's mistress.

> When her brother saw all the money I had unthinkingly piled on the table out of my pockets [recounts Da Ponte] he gave a shriek of joy and his Barnabotic claws soon raked the golden pile into two handkerchiefs. While he feverishly did this, the following conversation took place:
> "Been gambling?"
> "Yes, Your Excellency."
> "Do you know how much you won?"
> "No, Your Excellency."
> "Would you like to double it?"
> "Yes, Your Excellency."
> "I'll go and open a bank at the Ridotto. Don't worry, the money is as good as won."
> "No, Your Excellency."
> He did not appear to know quite how to take this last "No", he ground his long teeth and mocked "Yes, Your Excellency! No, Your Excellency! Are you willing or not?"
> "Yes, yes, Your Excellency," for I felt it useless to say "No".
> "Good: bring my sister with you and follow."
> "Yes, Your Excellency."
> "And don't keep me waiting."
> "No, Your Excellency."
> Then he ran down stairs and I went along with his sister, scratching my head and cursing "His Excellency" and the Golden Book and the whole of San Barnaba.

This anecdote of the seamier side of Venetian life must bring to an end our imaginary tour which started at Naples, halted at Rome, visited Farinelli and Padre Martini at Bologna and ended at Venice.

The similarity of the structure of Italy with that of the Empire either is already clear, or will be clear when the succeeding chapters have been perused. What is different is the whole tone of society, lighter, gayer, I think no wickeder, but certainly more amusing. Musicians were continually being exported: the visiting Duke of Manchester persuaded Handel away from Venice, a Beckford captured the boy Clementi. Musicians were also imported, as Handel and Mozart, only to be exported again later, and usually with an Italian musical soul they would never lose. To us in this book, the greatest home-produced and home-educated export was Domenico Scarlatti to Iberia.

Italy, quarrelling, usually poor, full of petty wars, cruelty, intriguing, almost laughable in hypocrisy, and sleepiness, was not a great instrument-making country in point of numbers, but we have only to think of the violin-makers of Cremona to be aware of the danger of stressing cembalo-making poverty too much. But the cembalo never ranked very high: the human voice, artificially produced or feminine, came first, and the violin second. Very many more *castrati* were manufactured than cembali. Where would we be without Dr. Burney?

To persons accustomed to English harpsichords, all the keyed instruments on the Continent appear to great disadvantage. Throughout Italy they have generally little octave spinets to accompany singing, in private houses, sometimes in a triangular form, but more frequently in the shape of our old virginals; of which the keys are so noisy, and the tone so feeble, that more wood is heard than wire ... I found three English harpsichords in the three principal cities of Italy, which are regarded by the Italians as so many phenomena.

Before we make a brief survey of some early instrument manufacturers and their surviving instruments, there must be a word on nomenclature. An early Italian word, towards the end of the fifteenth century, was *clavicymbal*, from which clavicembalo, and thence cembalo is clearly derived. An instrument made with the strings in an upright position, so that it looks like an escritoire, or a harp fitted with a keyboard, was called a clavicytherium. An instrument stringed like an English virginal in a box and equally an instrument with the keyboard at an angle to the strings, was called a spinet. The word gravicembalo was sometimes used for clavicembalo: it is merely a different spelling and possibly originated in a dialect in a different part of the peninsula.

Almost all the instrument makers were in north Italy, none seem to have been in Naples, and in Papal territories northern Bologna was just as important as meridian Rome. This is what we might expect from general principles; the inventive and manufacturing parts of Italy have ever been the north.

Of the north, the Republic of Venice was the chief manufacturing state. In 1500 we find spinets manufactured in the capital and James (see Bibliography: he will be extensively drawn upon for what follows) gives Giovanni Spinetti as the inventor and the namer of the oblong spinet, and therefore Mr. James is a challenger of the epinette theory, and is possibly a loser owing to the modernity of his first date, drawn from an instrument inscribed *Johannes Spinetus Venetus Fecit*, A.D. 1503.

The virginals now in the Victoria and Albert Museum and said to be Queen Elizabeth's, may have been made in Venice, by Benedetto Floriani, in 1571.

A spinet in the Donaldson Museum of the Royal College of Music bears the inscription: *Johannis Celestini Veneti MDXCIII*, and is a charming portable instrument, though of short compass, with only four octaves.

A true cembalo, though of only one manual, made in Venice in 1574, is now part of the property of the Victoria and Albert Museum, though not at the time of writing in its due place there. It has a singularly rococo case, garlands of flowers occupy the panels, while the whole of the inside of the wing flap is richly decorated with goddesses, satyrs, angels and allegorical figures. The presence of a grinning satyr shows the worldly, or, as that word has hard and shallow connotations, humanistic approach to cembalo music.

In the interior of the Republic, Verona and Padua were most active. Verona was the seat of a small family keyboard instrument manufacturing industry: there was a spinet in existence in the Museum of the Conservatoire of Paris dated 1523 with the inscription *Francisci de Portalupis Veronen*. The compass of this little instrument is four and a half octaves, with black naturals and white sharps. Padua, though not more important than Verona for our limited purpose, is in the total history of keyboard music of great interest, for Cristofori, a cembalo maker, came from Padua, and later moved to Florence, where he started to make the new pianofortes as well. He made a cembalo for a son of the Grand Duke of Tuscany, whose territories are less important to us than those of his almost surrounding neighbour, the Pope. In Rome one Geronimo from Bologna made a cembalo in 1521, and here again we have only one manual and, by the way, no stops. The Italians at this date seem not to have experimented very much in construction, having once achieved the couched harp with the keyboard endwise to the strings. The case here shows a complex abstract design, while the under wing has no paintings as far as can be ascertained, for here again the instrument is not back in the Victoria and Albert Museum. Yet learned Bologna and the capital of the Church are disappointing in their output and are far from rivalling Venice. We nowhere in Italy find a great House like Ruckers in the Low Countries, Taskin in Paris, Kirkman or Shudi in London.

Milan, famous in musical history for its Scala, and frequently the first city come upon by the traveller, is rather off the Naples, Rome, Bologna, Venice line which seems to have been the cembalo making, playing and composing axis. It was so absorbed in opera, was much smaller at this time than Naples, and the Spanish Crown, which thought it owned the Duchy, had a repressive rather than, in the Neapolitan case, a fertilizing effect. When the Industrial Revolution came to Italy at length, and much after cembalos had given place to pianofortes, Milan became larger and richer than Naples. However, in Rosso the city even in earlier days had one famous manufacturer of cembalos to whom the wealthy Lombard families would give commissions to manufacture. A spinet in a particularly lavishly decorated case, dated 1577, should be in the Victoria and Albert Museum. A sixteenth-century writer says of Rosso (I use Engel's translation) "This brilliant craftsman made among his other works a spinet of rare beauty and quality with keys entirely of precious stones, and with the most choice ornaments . . ." The comment may be made, I think, that it is not the golden case of the watch that makes it useful, and we may deduce from Burney that that part of the Italian instruments which actually made music was the subject of far less loving care than the mother-of-pearl sharps and the St. Cecilias and Apollos of the wing flap.

2. *The Composers*

In England, France and Germany there were, as far as concerns our book, two or three composers of outstanding eminence who lived all their lives, like Couperin, in the land of their birth, or who at least lived most of their working lives in a land of their adoption, like Handel.

In Italy there is only one great cembalo figure, Domenico Scarlatti, and he, like his lesser brethren, found it financially useful to export himself for a term. In the case of Scarlatti this term was a long one, of no less than twenty-five years. As there is no chapter devoted to the Iberian Peninsula, an isthmus of narrative connecting the life of this Scarlatti will be found in Appendix I.

The other great names are those of visitors, Handel and Mozart. Neither wrote cembalo music of importance which has come down to us, but both were so very much influenced by their Italian visit, that a paragraph or so must be given to each.

Searching among the lesser Italian cembalists for a second to Domenico Scarlatti is like searching for a second to J. S. Bach among the organ composers of Germany. There is no second. His father, in the history of opera a great and neglected figure, has left us little cembalo music, though there is some chamber music in which a cembalo fills out the figured bass. But among the crowd of Italian composers of the fourth rank there is one man of the third, called by Stendhal (no less) "the Molière of Italy", and, in another sentence, he is compared with Haydn. "There are two routes which lead to communicating pleasure, the style of Haydn, and the style of Cimarosa; the latter can never be imitated by fools."

Cimarosa was a Neapolitan, born when Domenico Scarlatti was ageing in Spain. Cimarosa's life is exactly typical of that of the average Italian composer, the type of life we have already depicted. That is to say, he was of poor parentage, in his case his mother is said to have been a washerwoman. He was adopted by a priest. He was in due course sent into one of those deafening academies in Naples, with eunuchs resting under the roof, cembalos going incessantly like public-house electric pianos in the "cantena", and trumpeters blowing away on the stairs. He was also like the typical Italian composer in that he left the country for a while, going to the Court of Catherine of Russia to compose operas. After four years he found the Russian winters far too cold, and he translated himself to the Imperial Court at Vienna, all this time writing opera after opera, among them *Il Matrimonio Segreto*, the overture of which at least is still played and enjoyed. The Emperor so liked *Il Matrimonio* that it is said that he caused the whole opera to be repeated the same night, though he did allow them all to have supper first. Another anecdote is told of Cimarosa, how a painter tried to flatter him by denigrating Mozart, and Cimarosa replied by asking the artist how he would like to be praised at the expense of Raphael.

True to type to the very end, Cimarosa returned to Naples to die, but there met tragedy. He backed the wrong horse, the French horse, during the Napoleonic wars, and when the Bourbons came back, largely owing to the activities of the lover of the English Minister's wife in his own town, he was imprisoned. When let out, he thought Venice safer, and there he died. Stendhal, writing seventeen years later, a year after the Congress of Vienna when the new music of the Romantics and the new instrument, the pianoforte, had begun to flood Europe, described how he came upon a bust of Cimarosa. "He was a large man: the muscles of the face, all strong and prominent, would conceal the great genius from those who have not studied well the science of Lavater; the expression of the countenance is open and gay; the principal intelligence resides in the parts round the eye."

How far we can go with Stendhal in praising Cimarosa will be discussed in the third section of this chapter.

To return to the great names, and the Scarlattis in particular. Alessandro Scarlatti, born in Naples, spent much of his life in ecclesiastical appointments in Rome, not from choice, but because his numerous and successful operas did not bring him in enough money to live on, there being no copyright, and provincial cities would mount his works and pay him nothing. His son Domenico was born in Naples and educated by his father and by Gasparini of Venice. Domenico returned to Rome, but his father wrote to Duke Ferdinand, son of the Grand Duke of Tuscany, saying that Rome offered "no roof to shelter Music, which lives here in beggary" and that Domenico appeared to show even greater promise as a cembalist than as an opera composer. We have already had a picture by Roseingrave of this black-wigged, quiet and brilliant young man. Tuscany offered him something inadequate, and he was surely glad to become *maestro di càpella* of St. Peter's and later to voyage to Lisbon, where he made Court connexions which resulted in his stay of twenty-five years in Madrid. It was a long way away, but not so far as to prevent his paying visits to his native land, and we know something about one of them at least.

Domenico Scarlatti, from his place in the Lisbon Court, was called to Naples to his father, whose last illness was upon him. When he arrived he found that Hasse was staying with his father: the two great composers of opera, one representing the older generation, the other the new: one the great favourite of yesterday, the other of to-day, present an unusual picture of mutual kindness. To the ordinary music-loving Venetian or Florentine or Viennese of the previous generation, the greatest living composer would not have been Purcell, but Alessandro Scarlatti. And now that the master was dying, the citizen's sons and daughters would have been equally sure that the greatest living composer was not Bach (of whom they would not have heard), nor Handel, nor the son Domenico, but Hasse the Saxon. Alessandro had had a full life indeed: towards the end he had restricted his movements between Naples and Rome, and his duties in both cities. He had also turned to expounding the foundations of his art, publishing *Regole per Principianti* in which he said: "To my thinking there is no other rule in music worthy of a man of genius than to please that sense the delight of which is the sole object of music." The sentence is as translated in Grove, and like almost all the *obiter dicta* of the foreign Great seems as stilted as meaningless.

Domenico Scarlatti found opportunity of playing before Hasse, and the latter, according to Burney, "allowed him to have been possessed of a wonderful hand, as well as fecundity of invention".

To these three in the house at Naples came Quantz the flautist. On hearing of his arrival Alessandro said something neither stilted nor meaningless, but much to the point: "You know that I cannot endure players of wind instruments, for they all blow out of tune." However, this prejudice must have been overborne by Hasse and Domenico, for Alessandro played the cembalo to Quantz on the flute. And here we have another wooden, or in this case ambiguous, statement, this time by Quantz on Alessandro's cembalo playing. The translator makes him say that Alessandro "played in a learned manner". These phrases need translating, not only from Italian or Latin into English, but also into equivalent English, bearing in mind changes in idiom during the last two hundred years. One supposes that Quantz meant that old Scarlatti's filling up of the figured bass in his (Quantz's) flute sonata was skilfully contrapuntal, even astonishingly so, but perhaps not quite what the composer intended.

The old master lingered on a few months, and when he died his epitaph was written by Cardinal Ottoboni.

At length the time came when Domenico himself, aged nearly seventy, in turn came back to Naples to die. His old La Granja colleague Farinelli (see Appendix I) came back to Italy a few years later, and settled, as we have seen, with his cembalos with their picturesque names outside Bologna. When Burney was in Vienna he met a man named L'Augier, who said he knew Scarlatti in Madrid, but there is something wrong with the chronology. In general, L'Augier testified that Scarlatti, in his later years, "was too fat to cross his hands as he used to do, so that these [his later sonatas] are not so difficult as his more juvenile works which were made for his scholar and patroness the late Queen of Spain, when Princess of Asturias." . . . Scarlatti used to admit that he broke the rules of composition and that his music imitated the melody of tunes sung by carriers, muleteers and common people. The music of Alberti and several other modern composers did not in the execution want a harpsichord, as it might equally well, or perhaps better, be expressed by any other instrument, "but as Nature had given him ten fingers, and as his instrument had employment for them all, he saw no reason why he should not use them." This message, so to speak, from Madrid was uttered in ignorance of the harpsichord music of J. S. Bach written a thousand miles to the east in Leipzig. Bach's harpsichord music is just as essential to the instrument as is Scarlatti's, just as difficult and, in the famous Gigue of the B flat Partita, required crossing the hands, and in the Fantasia in C minor shows a Scarlatti texture, wit and fire, not to speak of binary form. Bach may possibly have known of Scarlatti's sonatas, for he kept up a large correspondence and his continual hospitality to all who passed through or near Leipzig would have kept him in touch with all European musical activities. Scarlatti's sonatas, or at least some of them, were published both on the Continent and in London, and it is quite possible that a volume of them lay upon one of J. S. Bach's flugels.

So much for the Scarlattis, whose great prominence in their own day and copious output has in our day been reduced to a few facts, a pen portrait or so, and the occasional twang of an harpsichord over the Third Programme of the B.B.C.

Let us turn to a much better-known figure, Handel, who left Hamburg for Italy with no prospects and only his savings. However, he had designs on the same Ferdinand that Domenico had, and perhaps the two arrived in Tuscany together, both young men, both indeed of the same age, the one the son of a great composer residing in the neighbouring Papal States, the other the son of a bourgeois in far-off Halle. But, whether they met there or later, they struck up a friendship as rapidly as Handel had done with Mathieson, or Scarlatti had done with Roseingrave. Handel in the princely and magnificent palace, the Pratolino, in the Tuscan hills near Florence, wrote cantatas and re-wrote part of his opera *Almira*. Then he went on to Rome, and Sir Newman Flower[1] has discovered a record dated 14 January, 1707, which reads: "There has arrived in this city a Saxon, an excellent player on the cembalo and a composer of music, who has to-day displayed his ability in playing the organ in the church of St. John to the amazement of everyone." Cardinal Ottoboni became his patron, and so he must have met many Arcadians, including of course Corelli and Pasquini and the father of his friend Domenico Scarlatti. The Cardinal himself was only a little over forty, and was able to move among the young equally easily as among the middle-aged. But another patron also appeared, another "nephew" of another Pope, not this time a cardinal, but a marquis promoted to prince, Prince Ruspoli, and the prince appears to have seduced Handel from the cardinal, for Sir Newman Flower quotes an entry in the Ruspolian archives which reads: "Paid for the carriage of the bed and other things for Monsu Endel." But it appears that the bed and furniture did not come from the Ottoboni household, but from the Roman equivalent of a furniture hire service.

While his headquarters were at Rome, Handel had nevertheless found time to pay a flying visit to Venice. He met the Duke of Manchester, who was the British Ambassador, and the duke was the first of the English who was captivated by the music of Handel. He also paid a visit to Naples, where his cembalo playing captivated the Cardinal Viceroy. In Rome once more he seems to have become restive, even though a third cardinal had recently written libretti for him to set, and he returned to Hamburg, stopping at Venice on the way for performances of *Agrippina*, enchanting a prince of the House of Hanover.

Thus Handel's Italian visit was essentially a prolonged stay in Rome under the patronage of a Pope's nephew and of a former's Pope nephew, the one a prince and the other a cardinal. One may imagine

---

[1] *George Frederic Handel*, Cassell, 1923.

him an unimportant being in these villas and palazzos, unimportant
except when His Eminence wished for music to entertain his friends.
Unimportant also because young and poor. Important guests do
not have their beds hired in from neighbouring warehouses. We
may also imagine Handel playing the cembalo, one-manualled instruments to whose tuning he himself might often see, delighting if not
astounding his audience of prelates and ladies, playing, too, the operatic
cembalo, directing his music at performances of cantatas and oratorios
in Rome, and the full theatrical opera in Venice. We may imagine
him fired by the beauty of Italian singing, especially the sopranos,
both woman and castrated, for later in London he used Italian singers
whenever he could. At last, having taught the Italians nothing of his
Protestant solidity, but learned much of their grace and poise, he
lumbers out of Venetian territory into the Empire on his way back to
his own country and to England.

How different was the visit of Mozart about sixty years later, though
Italy had not appreciably changed, except that Imperial influence instead of Spanish now extended in the north. Various wars and political
goings and comings had altered the political administration of the
south, but Spanish influence, though waning, was still present. In
Rome Clement XIV was Pontiff. He is famous for his suppression
of the Jesuits, an Order chiefly known to Protestant opera-goers by the
funny hat worn by Don Basilio (in the words of his creator "chapeau
noir rabattu").

Milan, now under Austrian influence, was the first destination of
the Mozarts : they passed down the Po Valley where the boy of fourteen
received much admiration, and found themselves at last in the entourage
of the Austrian Governor of Milan, Count von Firmian. Here the
boy played before a distinguished gathering, including the Cardinal
Archbishop. The rest of his tour we already know : how at Bologna
he met Padre Martini, how, passing through Florence on the way to
Rome for Holy Week he struck up a friendship with the English boy
Thomas Linley, how in Rome he wrote out the *Miserere* from memory, how in Naples he and the first Lady Hamilton played to each
other. One may safely add, that if the boy Mozart is ever the subject
of a film, it will be Nelson's Emma and not the first Lady Hamilton
who will be seated at the cembalo. And no doubt a year or two will
be added to Wolfgang's age.

Mozart, like Handel, would have played the cembalo at the opera,
and extemporized in private houses : like Handel he carried out of

Italy all the musical virtues which the country had to offer, and none of their musical vices.

Before closing this section we must make a rapid tour, from Naples to Venice, to be sure we have met all the numerous composers at work.

In Naples Leonardo Leo, who wrote a little cembalo music including a delightful Arietta still sometimes played, died of apoplexy while seated at his cembalo. Domenico Paradies was born in Naples, and had gone to London to teach the harpsichord, returning to Naples at the end of the eighteenth century in his old age, though he died (like Cimarosa) in Venice. He wrote a great many cembalo sonatas, but only twelve *Sonate di gravicembalo* were printed in his lifetime.

In Rome there is much we have missed, and especially Frescobaldi, the great and influential organist of St. Peter's. He belongs to the earliest epoch of music for the cembalo, and was a contemporary of Orlando Gibbons. We have already met his pupil Froberger, when the latter was a refugee into England. Frescobaldi's style is severe, contrapuntal, and organistic. Froberger wrote music more cembalistic and achieved some Sarabandes of great, if short, beauty. Another pupil of Frescobaldi's was Michael Angelo Rossi, who published a collection of *Toccate e Correnti* for organ or cembalo, and this collection became popular and was soon reprinted. Frescobaldi is to some extent reflected in these pieces by his pupil, though Rossi has passages of true cembalo brilliance. The "Toccata in A" usually printed in Purcell editions as by the English master is attributed on one manuscript to Rossi; though the bold use of syncopation is much in Purcell's manner, the style is Italianate, and the piece may well be seventeenth-century Roman.

Bernardo Pasquini was a Tuscan who came to Rome to play the organ in one of the churches, and therefore (for he wrote many operas, too) did the same sort of work and presumably lived the same sort of life as his contemporary Alessandro Scarlatti. His cembalo music is important and will be dealt with in the next section: he may be regarded as a sort of link between Frescobaldi and Domenico Scarlatti—perhaps rather a frail link. A pupil both of Alessandro Scarlatti and of Pasquini was Durante, who wrote some quite unimportant cembalo music. Alberti, after whom is named the arpeggaic bass figure, died near Rome, and part of the next section will be devoted to a measured defence of this usual figure of scorn.

In Florence was born Marco Rutini, a slightly younger contemporary of Cimarosa. His admirers claim that his cembalo sonatas belong to the best literature of the instrument. Hardly. They are inferior to Cimarosa, who is himself third rate.

Lastly, there was Giovanni Gabrieli, who was born and died in Venice, organist of St. Mark's, and who lived before Frescobaldi, being a contemporary of Byrd and Palestrina. Palestrina wrote nothing for cembalo, and Gabrieli has nothing for the organ or spinet to make him equal in originality to the Englishman, Byrd. Nevertheless, his music is the best that the whole of Italy produced in the sixteenth century for the instruments dealt with in this book.

This ends the section of Italian cembalo composers, a hard-working lot, crowded together, depending all their lives on patrons, over producing, and writing with more power than polish, using time and time again the same clichés. Among them periodically came composers from other lands, astonishing them, and harpsichords from England, whose workmanship astonished them still more. Then they too would travel, to England to teach, to Spain to delight monarchs, and to Russia to astound. Italy has always been the land of song: were it not for the genius of Domenico Scarlatti and the visits of Handel and of Mozart and the great influence Italy had on these northerners, were it not, lastly, for the genius of her instrument makers, notably Cristoferi, one of the creators of the pianoforte, Italy might reasonably have been omitted from this book, like Spain or like America. But once we look beneath the surface, what bustling life in what sunshine, what pathetic love of native city, what enterprise, and what highly-coloured patrons!

And so we leave the land where the secular cleric amuses himself with the sonatas of Domenico Scarlatti, playing with fat hands on the mother-of-pearl keys, and awaiting his mistress to take her to the opera.

3. The Music

The texture of the music we are about to survey is usually extremely simple: tune and accompaniment. Not even so much tune, just a series of clichés arranged in sequence over an Alberti bass. The defence of the cliché is that the art of composition is the art of arranging masses, like architecture.   The detail of the masses may be unoriginal, nevertheless a Handel can produce as massive an effect as a Nash, even though the detail of both is so much conventional stucco ornament.   Of course, Handel's detail is often highly intricate and original, as is Domenico Scarlatti's, but I am anxious to show why the lesser Italian cembalo music is worth inspection at all, and I must defend both treble and bass.   So much, then, for the treble.

Now for the accompaniment and a defence of the Alberti bass, and this will take us much longer.   Alberti, the "inventor" of the Alberti bass, or at least one of the chief manipulators of this device, was presented to the British public by Walsh in the guise of eight harpsichord sonatas, which are said to be meagre and dull owing to over-dependence on the Alberti bass.   Paradies, Galuppi, Handel in his "Italian" vein, Rutini and others certainly depend very much on this type of bass, which, in its simpler forms and when the harmonic progressions are commonplace, inevitably tends to degenerate into cliché. A certain passage of Handel, from a portion of his Fantasia in C major is, key apart, almost exactly note for note Paradies, but it is quite possible that neither copied the other, but that the restricted texture of the Alberti bass does limit the number of possible permutations and combinations of melody and accompaniment when writing in the "classical" style.

Nevertheless, the constant odium in which the Alberti bass seems to lie is almost as monotonous as the bass itself.   There is a good deal to be said on the other side.

In the first place, about 1740, there was approaching a time of great change in keyboard music, and, indeed, in all music.   A change as great in its way as that inevitably inaugurated by publications like *Parthenia*, when great vocal composers like Byrd and Gibbons found themselves writing for an instrument which did not take kindly to a vocal texture.

The Alberti bass, by freeing a composer from contrapuntal problems was, perhaps, of great assistance to him in the problems of form. The Alberti bass, with a tune on the top, of 1740, would become the scorn of the future.   Scarlatti used it, however, extremely little, and Handel used it (or Waltz his cook used it) perhaps as a quick means of getting the paper filled up.   But the Alberti bass, like most other things, can be good or bad of its sort.   And a good example, with a top which is melodic and a bass which is interesting, forms almost two free parts, and, with the melody, three parts in all. Such Alberti bass is as difficult to play as a fugued passage. Enemies of the Alberti, which is to say almost all musicologists, say that it gives the impression of bustle without the strain of working out real parts or of playing them. But the right accents and right degree of prominence of a good specimen of Alberti presents problems all its own. Lastly it is the true type of accompaniment when a composer wishes to treat the keyboard instrument as a homophonic singing instrument. The harmonies of a good Alberti merge into the melody and seem to sustain it, and the whole is essentially pianistic in its effect. It presents a characteristic tone and contour. Because an Alberti bass would be ridiculous (intentionally or not) on the bassoon or cello, it does not follow that it is out of place on a percussive instrument which, like the clavichord or pianoforte, can be coaxed into song. And, by the way, the Alberti bass sounds best on a clavichord, as the notes of the tenor register are so sweet and true.

So much for the texture of much of the music. Now for the form. This was usually, indeed almost invariably, binary, with a double bar half-way through, each section repeated. There was a growth, if it is a growth, towards a definite second subject, usually in the dominant, and after the double bar there was a growing, though never very prolonged or, indeed, interesting, development section. Pieces called sonatas were often in just the one movement, and by far the greatest composer in this form was, of course, Domenico Scarlatti.

His music might be divided into three periods. The first would be his Italian years before his Iberian journeys. Young, brilliant, a composer of many operas, one would expect the sonatas of these years to be full of technical difficulties. The second period would be his Iberian adventure, with his short sojourn in Lisbon, his much longer one in Spain, usually at the Royal Palace of La Granja, outside Madrid. The Iberian sonatas would be those like No. 338 in G minor in Longo's edition, in which you hear the strumming of guitars, or a snatch of passionate evanescent song, as in No. 461 in D. Lastly would come his simpler pieces. But there is no scholarly way of dividing his five hundred and fifty printed sonatas, and guess-work is worse than the present disorder.

Scarlatti's sonatas are nowadays often played on harpsichords and usually very quickly, except of course when the music is obviously slow in tempo. The effect is brilliant and solid—solid because of the constant doubling of parts through the use of stops, brilliant because of the great skill of the modern performers and the contrasting use of two manuals.   Yet to me the effect of several Scarlatti sonatas played in this way is one of slight boredom.

In another part of this book I suggest the experiment of playing Beethoven, even last period Beethoven, on a harpsichord, and if I now suggest the playing of Scarlatti on a clavichord I do not wish to be misunderstood.   Beethoven certainly did not write Op. 101 for a harpsichord, just as Scarlatti did not write any of his sonatas for a clavichord.   But playing such a work as the sonata in F minor, Longo 383, quietly on a clavichord, brings out a meditative aspect of Scarlatti usually ignored by our modern harpsichord players, and which is one of the reasons why a prolonged Scarlatti harpsichord recital is trying to the attention.   It is a mystery of our art how it is possible to play a work in quite different manners and, provided the interpretation is intelligent and coheres its parts, give an equally beautiful result.   It is as though a piece of music was like a solid body, any solid body, from a gem to a large building.   See it from this angle on a sunny morning, or see it from another on a misty winter's evening, and the building, though the same, is completely different in its emotional effect.   One wishes to avoid aesthetic theory, and quite frequently Scarlatti's insistent guitar rhythms give the obvious tempo, yet there is great pleasure to be drawn from this composer by playing quietly and easily those sonatas which answer to such treatment.   As for instance, that in C minor, L.352, whose marking, *allegretto*, is usually interpreted at a pretty brisk pace.

There is another thought in the interpretation of Scarlatti which might be dwelt upon for a moment.   We have seen that the cembalos of Italy were often of one manual only, and the seventeenth-century ones were usually without stops of any kind.   It is therefore arguable whether the wooden banging and shoving (this is being very rude) of some harpsichordists as they change register and put on or take off octave couplers are in keeping with the music.   They certainly are in keeping with works like Bach's Italian Concerto, and harpsichordists so often play Scarlatti's music as though Bach had written it.

Scarlatti very rarely used the Alberti bass and uses little ornament. His trills should not, I think, invariably be taken brilliantly.   For instance, in the D minor L. 413, if this pastoral piece is taken at 70 dotted crotchets to the minute, a trill played thus is enchanting:

It is a great pity that Scarlatti is rather locked up in the eleven or so volumes published by Ricordi and edited by Longo. It is true that "slim volumes" of selections may be bought, but these so often print and reprint the same sonatas, as Mr. Dunhill's Augener edition and the Peters edited by Sauer. The second volume of the edition Sauer did for Augener contains fairly fresh material. But it is not as though Scarlatti wrote about a score of good sonatas and over five hundred bad ones. Often, it is true, Scarlatti will use the same basic idea much more than once, but even this is surely of considerable interest. What is wanted is an edition containing about sixty sonatas not already printed by Augener.

But we must leave the one great man of the Italian cembalo school, and get on to Cimarosa. His sonatas are like Scarlatti's in that they consist of one movement only. Cimarosa, though lacking a Longo, is in a way better off than his greater predecessor, for the Paris firm of Max Eschig have put out an edition of thirty-two sonatas of his, arranged in three volumes. His texture is much simpler, for in the second half of the eighteenth century cembalo music concentrated on expressive melody of an operatic kind, to the detriment (if simplicity is a detriment) of rhythm and harmony. While this sort of thing

reminds us of Scarlatti  it must be admitted

this sort of hand crossing is very barren Scarlatti, and the modulations that follow are of a most obvious description. It is a degeneration of the Neapolitan school, and uses formulae which must have been equally known in Vienna. Take this of Haydn (or is it Cimarosa?):

and compare it with this of Cimarosa (or is it Haydn?):

As a matter of fact the latter is Haydn, from his 27th Sonata, dated 1776, when Cimarosa was twenty-seven and Haydn forty-three.

There is no point, perhaps, in wondering who copies whom: it was a common formulae in a development section, from which section both uses of the same cliché come: Alberti bass, arpeggio figure, and sudden tonic minor.

What is endearing about Cimarosa is his spirit of comedy, it is music to be played to such scenes as depicted in Longhi's *Blind-Man's Buff*. The sort of little tunes which Rossini or Donizetti were later to invent for their comedy situations while the characters sang a patter recitative, constantly occur as second subjects or as intruders into development sections in the cembalo music of Cimarosa. And not only is Cimarosa delightful in himself therefore to any lover of *Don Pasquale* or of *Il Barbiere di Siviglia* but he sheds a new light on Haydn. Haydn was something besides the successor to Handel in his polyphonic oratorio choruses, something besides the predecessor of Beethoven in innumerable symphonic passages, mysterious or dramatic; something more than the perfecter of the string quartet. He, like his friend Mozart, had the spirit of Italian comedy, which neither Handel nor Beethoven had. Haydn, by bad fortune or lack of ability, is the composer of no comedy now presented: but those who turn back again and again to Haydn for something they do not find in Beethoven, and do not know what this something is; those who, by living in the country or an overdose of the spirit of C. H. H. Parry have avoided Italian comic opera, yet turn again and again to Haydn, will find what they look for in Rossini and Donizetti. And in the cembalo music of Cimarosa, slight though it is compared with the vigorous and ranging keyboard music of Haydn, they will also discover what they want.

Cimarosa is sometimes compared with Mozart, but I never have followed these constant Mozartian comparisons. J. C. Bach is said to sound like the supreme master. The fact is, that all composers of this epoch used figures of speech in common; what Mozart did incomparably was to change these completely by his genius. It is not helpful to compare Cimarosa with Mozart: so far from Mozart being typical of his century he is *sui generis*. But a Haydn comparison is permissible, and after playing Cimarosa for a week or so, we return to Haydn with clearer eyes, as a writer of sunlit pianoforte comedies (besides, goodness knows, much else). But Scarlatti? No, Cimarosa had only vestigial remains of his great predecessor, and Scarlatti persists, unchallenged by Cimarosa, as the one solitary first-rate cembalo composer which Italy has produced.

A large number of cembalo sonatas were produced by the fourth-raters: how numerous they are, and so often how dull!—Browning's Galuppi, for instance, with an almost constant Alberti bass moving, as often as not, from position to position by consecutive fifths.   Even more unblushing than these Alberti consecutives are those passages in which the triads are just pluncked down, without "Alberti-ing" them, and here the consecutives glare from the page.   This is done so often by Galuppi and other minor composers that it must be deliberate, and there is no doubt that in the background of eighteenth-century harmony these consecutives are most piquant, once or twice.   But not constantly.   It became in fact, I believe, just a bad and lazy habit. Any modern amateur pianist wishing to improvise a typical Italian sonata need not worry about his left hand, triads in root position can just follow his bass line, even if this is stepwise.   What, however, the modern amateur may fail in, is the sudden surprising comic little tune, arch, singing, which suddenly occurs to cheer, as particularly in the case of the Florentine, G. M. Rutini.

But it is dreary work talking of the lesser Italian cembalo composers, who are just as tedious as the lesser French clavecinists.   The two schools are indeed somewhat symmetrical, with a Couperin equal in interest to a Scarlatti (both of them members of musical families), with a whole army of privates under these two generals; though the two seconds-in-command are not of equivalent rank, for Rameau is very near indeed in stature to Couperin, while Cimarosa is not much more than a private.

When we turn to the Fantasias and Toccatas we turn to an earlier and, as far as minor composers go, more interesting and fresher epoch. Both Gabrieli and Pasquini were organists, and their work is often for organ or cembalo, and Gabrieli's in particular is usually taken as part of the musical ancestry of J. S. Bach.   Gabrieli's texture is polyphonic and makes play with little figures and points of imitation against a *cantus firmus*: often very effective if played at a reasonably quick pace:

but between the tenor and the bass *cantus* are ugly consecutives, so out of keeping, one would have thought, with the style of the period. Turning up Byrd to see how fussy he was over consecutive fifths, and spotting a possible one (the interweaving of the parts obscures it), I am struck by Byrd's superiority in every way to Gabrieli: firmer, richer, more mature. Byrd was fourteen years older than his contemporary. It is a change to turn to the later Pasquini, and his best work, or at least most amusing and arresting, "Toccata con lo Scherzo del Cucco", which perhaps is the best keyboard cuckoo piece in existence; it is certainly longer and more varied than Daquin's clockwork bird. Pasquini's cuckoo even changes to its summer repetitive note.

Gabrieli is the composer of the best Italian Canzone's, though this polyphonic form tends to be dull until the advent of the greatest Canzone writer, J. S. Bach. Gabrieli is, however, very varied and so keeps up the interest: many of his sections have to be played briskly in spite of the long notes; the following is really a springy 6/8 rhythm:

It is Gabrieli's Ricercari which make most appeal to me, and which place him in the very forefront of sixteenth-century instrumental composers. These fugal movements, usually strongly modal, are more interesting and vigorous than the equivalent Fantasias of Orlando Gibbons, who came a little later, and whose works would surely have been called Ricercari in Italy. There is in particular a Ricercare in the Dorian Mode of Gabrieli which is as strong and firm as Bach himself, but although playable upon a cembalo is surely organ music —organ music without pedals, that is to say.

This is the place for a short note on Michelangelo Rossi's ten Toccatas for (specifically) cembalo, published in 1657. The music is syncopated to obtain the maximum feeling of quaver motion in 4/2 time, but none of these Toccatas have the same breadth and feeling of largeness of the one in A usually included among the works of Purcell but sometimes attributed to Rossi. Nor in these 1657 *Dieci Toccate* are there any with the dramatic and moving recitative of the Purcell piece. But Rossi has many touches of purely instrumental brilliance, such as passages of sixths well laid out for the two hands.

Before we leave this polyphonic music and return to the homophonic style in such Suites and Variations as we may find, we will discover in the Fugue a link between the austere school of the Venetian
Gabrieli and the Neapolitans.

We can start with Gabrieli writing a fugue on an unusual, and
beautiful subject

which, in the tonal answer, is transformed into

and which has for counter-subject the gay

But the actual progress of this most promising material is disappointing.
Some of Pasquini's fugues have equally appealing expositions, but
equally prove disappointing in the modulating sections. Alessandro
Scarlatti wrote some cembalo fugues: there is a 6/8 fugue in F minor
on an interesting syncopated theme, worked out in four voices,
though only three are usually sounding at the same time. "The
dominant's persistence" leads to a worthy end. A fine piece of music,
but not obviously cembalo music.

If now we turn to his son, we are on familiar ground. Every
schoolgirl knows this eighteenth-century version of the Kitten on
the Keys

though (if the cat's fugue tradition has any authenticity at all) I
always feel it was a mature and very firm-footed cat, the quavers
merely being her supple tail.

"Non aspettarti in questi Componimente il profondo intendi-
mento, ma bensì lo scherzo ingegnoso," wrote Scarlatti in the volume
of thirty of his sonatas dedicated to the King of Portugal with the
flattering letter invariable in those times. "To the Reader," he added,
"dilettante or professor, whichever you may be, do not try to find in

these compositions the profundities of great art, but rather expect a
certain wayward gaiety, which will teach you to be at your ease with
the cembalo." Not a good translation, mine, I fear, but quite sufficient to provide an answer to those who castigate Scarlatti for his fugues
which, by means of using passages of sixths and other devices, diminish
to two parts towards the end.

Another fugue which it would be impossible to score out into four
parts without "overlapping" and getting into six or even eight parts
of which only two or three would be in use, starts off with two
engaging subjects,

with the phrase I have marked almost constantly in use. This gives
a Handelian effect—though it is more correct to say Handel's fugues
have often a Scarlattian effect.

The Suite form, untouched by Scarlatti, was never much used by
his fellow countrymen. But although Frescobaldi's style is usually
severe, contrapuntal and organistic, some of his keyboard music,
though advertised as "di cembalo et organo" seems essentially for
the domestic instrument, especially in consideration of "Partite de
diversa arie e corrente, balletti . . ." as the edition "Stampato l'anno
MDCXXXVII per Nicolo Borbone in Roma" says.

In the first of these Partitas there are no less than four Correntes
end on, the first in D minor with no flat in the signature, the second in
A minor, the third in F with a flat in the signature and the fourth in
G minor with only one flat in the signature. All are in binary form
and each is short, about 32 bars. They are "tuney", essentially
homophonic, and with too many thirds in the right hand part to be
particularly interesting except historically.

The second Partita consists mostly of Ballettos, pieces with four
minims to a bar leading to Correntes with 6/4 time signatures. All
these several movements are related in some way, by the movement of
the bass, or harmonically or even sometimes melodically, making a
whole series of interlinked short movements of considerable historical
interest. Pasquini wrote some short suites, with each movement
short, and few movements. A Partita, so called, in B flat, for
instance, starts off with a 15 (!) bar Allemanda, follows with a 33 bar

Corrente and finishes with a 36 bar Giga; 114 bars for the whole Suite. My exclamation mark is not for the shortness, but for the complex rhythm 15 bars suggests; though examining it, it seems so rambling as to have no bar rhythm at all, Pasquini adding extra beats in the same harmony to give an opportunity for his parts to bustle meaninglessly about. The truth is, I think, that Pasquini is always at his best when he is engaged in setting down a definite tune, which in this Allemanda he was not doing, with the result that his little arias are often most charming and finished. The Italian Gigues are usually very short and of the obvious 6/8 pattern to be found in Handel's Suites.

Domenico Zipoli published sonatas using the term correctly enough, *sonate de chiesa*, but they were really suites, and the succession of toccatas, with (Purcell-like) versos, and so forth, contain movements which are really only suitable for the organ, in spite of the title-page's "per Organo e Cimbalo". Other movements are arpeggaic in general texture, and have an interest and modernity similar, but in my view inferior, to Croft. Zipoli often reminds one of Handel, though in fact it is only that Handel wrote in the same tradition, a tradition known to most Englishmen only through Handel. A Pastorale in 12/8, a Largo in C major, and a Piva (compare the Pifa of the Pastoral Symphony) and brisk Gavottes all help the Handelian illusion: but a so much weaker Handel!

Sets of variations are uncommon in Italian cembalo music, Pasquini being more guilty than most in this form. His variations on broken-backed popular tunes are dull, and in a sort of mixed style, being in neither the severity and harmonic experiment of the earlier Byrd nor in the later homophonic and operatic style. By broken-backed, I mean the sort of melody which starts off well, very beautifully indeed, in its first section, only to disappoint in its second by giving what is only a prolonged and barren cadence.

Much more interesting for the mind to dwell upon, though certainly rather peculiar, are Pasquini's sonatas for two cembali. One eagerly follows the clue that leads to the (as one hopes) precursors of the Mozart for two pianos in D, Italian comedy music of the most superb sort, only to find that disappointing Pasquini supplies us only with two sets of figured basses. It is clear that two skilled musicians, who had learned plenty of what was in those days called science, would make harmonious music out of them. Their present-day aesthetic value is so slight as not to be there: however, all those pianists

I

who take pleasure in music for two pianos and who wish to polish
their rough ability to extend a figured bass may surely be cordially
recommended to try Pasquini's sonatas *a due cimbali*. It is almost,
indeed, as though Pasquini wrote them for that very purpose, as
exercises for his pupils and for pupils of his times in the ages to come.
Some movements are very simple: what, for instance, could be easier
and more decorous in a truly Anglican manner than:

or what gives opportunity to rivals growing in ease and brilliance
on the two keyboards than:

The British Museum has a MS. copy of these figured bass sonatas;
the press mark is Add MSS. 31, 501. Those with no access to the
British Museum will find the figured basses of one complete sonata
on pages v and vi of the late Mr. J. S. Shedlock's *Selection of Pieces
composed for the Harpsichord by Bernardo Pasquini*,[1] and on p. 42 and
following a completely written out sonata by Shedlock. Someone
coming into the room and with the ordinary, what one might call
Promenade Concert, ear on hearing the opening Allegro, is sure to
say, "Isn't that Bach?" If a more musical person came into the room
and said, "Is that possibly Pergolesi?" then I feel you would have
hit the mark, and produced that *intermezzi* music which Pasquini
may have had in mind. The *due cembali* were composed in 1704 and
La Serva Padrona twenty-seven years later. Except for Gabrieli and
Domenico Scarlatti, the cembalo composers wrote music for worldly
Abbates to play before going to the opera.

SHORT BIBLIOGRAPHY TO CHAPTER III

Article entitled *Cembalo* in the *Encyclopaedia Italiana*.
C. Burney: *The Present State of Music in France and Italy*, 1773.

[1] Novello, 1895

P. James: *Early Keyboard Instruments* (Peter Davies, 1930).

The Letters of Mozart to His Family, Anderson (Macmillan, vol. 1, 1928).

da Ponte: *Memoires* (Routledge 1927).

Newman Flower: *George Frideric Handel* (Cassell 1923 and 1947).

Vernon Lee: *Studies in Eighteenth Century Italy* (Fisher Unwin).

Sismondi: *History of the Italian Republics* (Routledge).

Ranke: *History of the Popes*, vol. 2.

L. Torchi: *La Musica Instrumentale in Italia*, Turin, 1901.

G. Pannain: *Le Origini e Lo Sviluppo Dell Arte Pianistica in Italia*, Naples, 1919.

L. Ronga: *Gerolamo Frescobaldi*, Turin, 1930.

CHAPTER IV

THE FLUGEL IN GERMANY

1. The Instruments and the Society

WHY the flugel? This word means a wing, and has always been given by the Germans to keyboard instruments whose flap, when opened to expose the sounding-board and the strings over it, formed a wing. Thus a harpsichord as well as a grand pianoforte are both flugel. There is no word for harpsichord alone. Clavier is usually taken to mean the quite different clavichord, though it obviously, as in Bach's *Clavierubung*, sometimes does mean the harpsichord, though never that instrument exclusively.

The Germans never seemed to have been in the forefront of quilled instrument manufacture, the clavichord being the first object of their care, and then, with Silbermann, the beginning of that great pianoforte manufacturing industry which has continued to this century, if not to this day.

Perhaps the Netherlands was the main source of flugel, for this country exported to many lands, including both England and Germany, and its great Ruckers family is perhaps the greatest harpsichord building family in history. The actual number of flugel in the Holy Roman Empire, which we take in this chapter as synonymous with Germany, was probably far less than the number of clavichords, a much cheaper and indigenous instrument. France and England were both much wealthier countries, and in spite of the Empire's swollen aristocracy, there were probably more harpsichords and clavecins in the world than flugel, it being explained that these are merely English, French and German words for the same instrument.

The aristocracy of the Empire was a ruling one, and varied from the great Electors and their noble courts to Baron Thundertentronckh, whose flugel, presumably played by Pangloss, was surely invariably out of tune, and as invariably declared to be a perfect instrument in a perfect imitation of Versailles. Then there were the Courts of which the Female was musical and the Male not, like the Berlin Princess of "what the French call *l'embonpoint charmant* (who) . . . plays the harpsichord well herself, as I was assured, and was very curious and conversible about music: even while at cards. . . ." Dr. Burney, it is hardly necessary to state in view of the characteristic phrase "curious and conversible" is our informant.

Sometimes the Female was quite in the background and the Male Musical in the ascendant, like the quite terrifying Monarch at Potsdam who "always stands behind the *maestro di capella* [i.e. the man at the flugel] in sight of the score, which he frequently looks at, and indeed performs the part of *director-general* here, as much as of *generalissimo* in the field".

From Frederick the Great down in scale of revenues and of power is a long fall to the Duke of Wurtemberg, who however retained in his employment a man Dr. Burney considered to be the greatest harpsichord player in Germany: Schubart, the possessor of a perfect double shake. The duke's chief passion was for opera, for which entertainment he employed a large number of singers and instrumental musicians, including "fifteen *Castrati*, the court having in its service two Bologna surgeons, expert in this vocal manufacture. . . . His passion for music and shows, seems as strong as that of the Emperor Nero was formerly. It is, perhaps, upon such occasions as these, that music becomes a vice, and hurtful to society. . . ."

More balanced was the Elector of Saxony, whose grandfather had been also King of Poland, in his capital at Dresden. To Burney he said:

"You love music?" "Yes, Sir." "Have you been in Italy?" and upon my answering in the affirmative, his Electoral highness appeared to be pleased, and desirous of entering into a more particular conversation; but, throwing his eyes around, and seeing the foreign ministers, officers of state, and a number of strangers and people of condition eager for notice, and expecting their share of attention, he turned about, and spoke two or three words to prince Beloselsky, the Russian minister. . . .

This question "Have you been in Italy?" was obviously the

conversational gambit in the Empire and was constantly addressed to Mozart, the answer never being heard and being invariably followed by the grave advice that that is where he should go to polish up his art!

Sometimes marriage tamed the Musical Male, as in the case of Prince Leopold of Anhalt-Cöthen, who when a bachelor was the enthusiastic patron of that noted flugel player, J. S. Bach, and when married could bear to part with him to the religious and mercantile bourgeois of Leipzig.

In the capital itself, in Vienna, was to be found the best musical aristocracy of all, with a Gluck to teach the archduchesses. Gluck in his old age settled down with his wife and adopted niece singing to his own flugel accompaniment. And in Vienna was also Countess Thun, of eighteenth-century musical women surely the most charming. She played the flugel to Dr. Burney. "Her taste is admirable, and her execution light, neat and feminine; however, she told me she *had* played much better than at present, and humorously added that she had had six children, and that 'every one of them had taken something from her'. She is a cheerful, lively and beneficent being, whom everyone here seems to love as a favourite sister."

Even Mozart, most difficult to please, was delighted. Some nine years later after the Burney meeting, Mozart wrote from Vienna to his father in Salzburg: "The Countess is the most loveable and delightful woman I have ever met," but later shows that she had deserted the flugel for a "beautiful Stein *pianoforte*" on which Mozart played, and so she must leave this chapter.

Other society, both aristocratic and musical, was immense. "Vienna is so rich in composers, and encloses within its walls such a number of musicians of superior merit, that it is but just to allow it to be, among German cities, the imperial seat of music, as well as of power."

The flugel, in other words, was not a middle-class instrument. The middle-class boy, the young Handel, for instance, or the starving Haydn, would practise on the clavichord. Only as he rose in the world would he come across the flugel, and this instrument might be anything, from a tuneless old box, crazy on its legs, to some magnificent reconstituted Ruckers model or some newly imported Shudi and Broadwood from England. This instrument would be in the palace of the local sovereign, or in the first floor of the large house in Vienna. For Vienna was quite unlike Paris with its shut-in *hôtels*, and quite unlike London with its fine family town mansions. It even then consisted largely of flats. An imperial edict gave over the ground floors of all houses to the army: then the aristocrats, such as the Esterhazys, the Thuns or the Lobkovitzs, lived on the first floor: the successful poets and singers and composers, such as Metastasio or Porpora, lived higher up, how high accorded to income, while the starving artist, such as young Josef Haydn, lived in the very top, his clavichord not being heard at all, in no possible way inconveniencing even the Porpora below. While the count on the first floor, listening to his flugel played by the musician he patronized, might, if he chose, be socially unaware that anyone else resided in the whole building.

It was in such a setting that the young Haydn, serenading in the street for a fee, was drawn in by the comedian Kunz up not more, one gathers, than two flights, to play a storm on his flugel for him. But it was only up one flight he had to mount when he was presented (as all musicians sooner or later were presented) to the Countess von Thun, and she was so horrified at his poverty that at first she thought there had been some mistake: but not after he had sat at her flugel and started to improvise. . . .

In some parts of the Empire an Ecclesiastic held sway, like the mild Sigismund and the far less mild Hieronymus of Salzburg.

These Lords Spiritual, like their Temporal brothers, liked to rule their dominions and liked also to mix in the great world of the big cities, whether Berlin or Dresden, but particularly in Vienna, whither both Mozart and Haydn were brought in the train of their, shall we say, "owners"? An Irishman named Kelly, by no means castrated, though the pupil of the singing eunuch Aprile, wrote in his reminiscences that "all ranks of society are doatingly fond of music" and describes the opera at Vienna, with Salieri at the flugel, "a little man with an expressive countenance . . . extremely like Garrick".

This opera in Vienna was part of the Royal Palace, as was usually the case, for instance in Paris. London, with the city aloof from and sometimes suspicious of the Court, had its theatres in the intervening land between London and Westminster. But on the Continent, and especially in the Empire, whether in the great capital or the country seat like that of the Esterhazy's, the theatre was part of the personal environment of the reigning prince.

The arrangement of the opera orchestra at Dresden is given by Rousseau in his Dictionary, and is reproduced here, because two flugel

appeared similarly at Berlin and Stuttgart at least, and perhaps elsewhere, even in Italy, whence perhaps the practice derived.

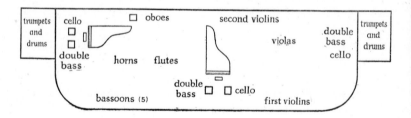

The composer or the director of the performance sat at the flugel
facing the stage, the side flugel being used for accompanying. From
the first instrument what we would now call the conducting took
place, the giving of the tempo, giving cues to the instruments, keeping
the singers and the orchestra together, and so forth. During the
recitatives, when the orchestra could rest, the conductor could rest
also, and his colleague at the second flugel would accompany the
recitative from the figured bass.

The really extraordinary thing about the disposition of this
orchestra at Dresden and at other opera houses is not so much the
presence of two flugel, but the way the three double basses and the
three cellos are situated. Each flugel has a pair of such instruments,
the players obviously reading the bass part over the flugel player's
shoulder, and this proves that the recitative was not accompanied by
solo flugel, but by double bass and cello as well. This is a point that
modern producers of *Figaro* should bear in mind, for the more modern
of these do introduce a harpsichord for the *recitativo secco*, but usually
it plays alone.

But even this pairing off of the cellos and basses might have been
deduced from other practices of the time, but how can the lower
string pair at the right hand of the orchestral pit be explained? On
each far side we have the trumpets and drums disposed, after the
fashion of the century, for these martial instruments were added to the
score rather than ever became part of it. The fiddles and violas were
on the right of the conductor and the wood wind and brass (i.e. the
horns) on the left, the bass strings sharing the score with the flugel
players; and all alone, a solitary cello and a solitary double bass, with
no flugel part to share, and sitting under a powerful military battery.
I suspect J. J. Rousseau's accuracy, in spite (or even because) of the

fact that this Dresden plan has been copied by several historians, in toto, and without analysis but with, in fact, most obedient acceptance. Yet there are some obvious errors in Rousseau's table of reference, and I think he was in a particularly careless mood that morning at Motiers when he drew his diagram; perhaps he was being plagued by "clergymen, relatives and bigots of all sorts" coming in from Geneva.

Those who attended performances of Mr. Benjamin Britten's *The Rape of Lucretia* will have seen just a little something of this old method when Mr. Britten himself happened to be conducting. His score rested on the top of a pianoforte, which was in the same general position as that of the central flugel in the Dresden orchestra, and from this keyboard he accompanied his recitatives, recitatives which from time to time drifted sufficiently near the eighteenth-century formalism as to include full closes. When the orchestra was to play, then Mr. Britten rose from his keyboard and conducted with his hands in the usual manner, without employing, of course, any figured bass. So his pianoforte fulfilled the function therefore, not of the central flugel, but of the side flugel, being moved, so to speak, to the centre for purposes of convenience only.

These two flugels and the players on them were the occasion of the brawl between Handel and Mattheson in the opera at Hamburg. During the run of a Mattheson opera *Cleopatra*, Handel sat at one or the other of the flugel, and when Antony, sung by the composer, had made his final exit with the opera not quite finished, Mattheson would descend from the stage to take over Handel's instrument. But on one occasion Handel refused to leave it, and he and the composer had a heated argument, stated by some to have lasted half an hour, inside the theatre holding up the performance, and that Mattheson tried to knock Handel away. It must be remembered that in our late-maturing eyes both composers were mere boys at the time: undergraduates, so to speak. The two angry boys, followed by an amused crowd, eventually left the theatre to an open space outside, and drew their swords, a thrust by Mattheson being deflected by one of Handel's enormous buttons, and his sword being in consequence broken. It cannot have been a very good sword.

I am inclined to think it must have been the side flugel which was quarrelled over, for even in rowdy eighteenth-century opera the giving over of the main direction during the run of an act would have caused too much break, were it done ever so amicably. Likewise, in the anecdote of Handel challenging a difficult singer to make good his threat to jump from the stage on to the harpsichord, "Well, jump then, and we will see if you can jump better than you can sing", it was the side instrument which was in question.

J. S. Bach's public flugels were those in the churches, whither they had been introduced for figured basses during *ritornelli* where the organ was unsuitable and for solo recitative accompanying, and those in the university concerts inaugurated by Kuhnau, the *Collegium musicum*. There would be two flugel here, as in an opera house, one for the figured bass and the other a solo instrument in flugel concertos. In Bach's concertos for two flugel or more, possibly there was no figured bass instrument present, for the keyboard parts are so interwoven and so continuously playing as to leave no filling in to be done. A third, fourth, or even fifth, as in the case of the A minor concerto, keyboard instrument, playing a part different in essence from its companions, would, one thinks, have been clearly redundant.

But the single flugel for concert use, in concerti grossi, and the like, was decidedly not considered unwanted. C. P. E. Bach was as fierce for the figured bass in concerted music as he was for ornaments in solo music. He pointed out however large the body of strings, a flugel can always be heard, especially if you listen from above.

The answer, however, to this, surely is, "Well, don't listen from above", a thing in any case not usual except from boxes in the opera. In the case of his father, J. S. Bach, his general tendency towards chamber music—that is to say music in which every part is fully articulated both with itself and the whole, a tendency clearly seen in his violin and flugel sonatas—may have helped to keep out the extra accompanying flugel from multiple keyboard concertos.

When Bach got home from his *Collegium musicum* concerts he would find there a peculiar brand of flugel, being a two-manualled instrument fitted with a set of pedals, like an organ, enabling it to play music written on three staves and requiring octave couplers. It was for such a flugel that the Trio Sonatas so often nowadays classified as organ music, were written.

He also had two *lautenclaviere*, one of which may have come down to him from his great uncle, Johann Nikolaus Bach, organist at Jena. This was an instrument with an ordinary keyboard but wired with lute strings, and plucked like an ordinary flugel. The other one had recently been built under his own direct orders, and not only was furnished with metal lute strings but gut strings as well, the lute strings sounding an octave above the latter. When the lute stop was drawn the instrument sounded like a real lute provided the sound was immediately damped by falling jacks felted with cloth. When the lute stop was silent, the gut strings, two to each note, sounded like the gloomy large bass lute, usually called a theorbo. These theorbo strings, undamped, gave a greater possibility of legato playing, while the four-foot metal strings gave the necessary brilliancy.

Bach also had an ordinary two-manualled flugel and several smaller plucked instruments which, if they were spinets and had a wing-shaped cover, would come under the heading of flugel.

It was presumably on the two-manualled instruments that the famous duel between Marchand and Bach took place. The Parisian clavecinist, in disgrace at Versailles, and travelling very much for his health, met J. S. Bach by an arrangement made by another Frenchman, who was concert master at the Court of the King of Poland in Dresden. The King himself was not to be present, but there was a sort of musical jury, and the contest, as amusing to eighteenth-century aristocrats as cock-fighting, was to take place in the house of the Prime Minister. Bach was there and we suppose tuned his flugel in the, for him, usual quarter of an hour: I always think of Bach tuning his flugel as a sort of Sir Henry Wood, very matter of fact, very exact and very single-minded. Marchand, however, did not turn up, a circumstance which allows all patriotic German biographers of the master to let go with a whoop of triumph. The King did not feel like this: he had already awarded Marchand a couple of medals, but did not bother to give Bach anything.

The practice of carrying smaller flugels from house to house was obviously not confined to Mozart. We find for instance that the Abbé Vogler, a figure at once romantic and sinister, sent to his house from a bourgeois party in Mannheim for his two small flugels with which to play "his tedious engraved sonatas" with Mozart. And if we like to picture the Empire in a bird's-eye view, we may think of flugel in the palaces near the large cities, of the flugel in the apartments of the first and second story, of flugel in coaches moving from house to house within the cities; while in the attics and in the country places, were the much more modest clavichords. We may also picture flugel in carts being drawn in from the Low Countries.

These towns of interest to us would be in three groups, firstly, those strung along the Rhine from Strasbourg, visited by Mozart, to Dusseldorf, visited by Handel, but of chief interest Bonn, visited by both these composers and the birthplace of Beethoven.

The second group is formed of the towns strung along the Danube, from Ulm and Augsburg to Pressburg, below Vienna. Thirdly we have a central and northern area, from Prague, visited by Mozart and Beethoven, to Lubeck, visited by Bach and Handel and for the same purpose; and from Cassel in the west, visited by Bach, to Berlin in the east, where Handel, Bach, Haydn, Mozart and Beethoven at various times played the flugel. But Berlin was never Vienna in spite of these constellation of names, for the composers did not stop in the Prussian capital, as three of them were glad to do in the Austrian.

This dispersion of flugel among so many towns over so large an area forms a strong contrast to the disposition of clavecin in France and harpsichords in England. In both these countries the instruments and their manufacture were concentrated in the capitals. Visiting composers had little temptation to journey far into the provinces, and intellectual and musical society was all to be found within a twenty-mile radius of the main seat of the Court. The only similarity in dispersion to Germany was Italy, whose political constitution was a similar jig-saw in pattern and in effect, though a jig-saw formed by quite different causes.

2. The Composers

Germany was very much a country of organists at the time of development of the plucked string keyboard instrument, and as this instrument, called in Germany flugel, often had two manuals, power of registration by means of stops, and answered very well to organ touch, it followed that organ composers touched the flugel as though it was an organ. The first composer to make any difference at all in his writing for the two quite dissimilar instruments was perhaps Froberger. He had studied much in Italy under the great organist Frescobaldi, and became Court organist in Vienna. But he escaped to England's shores to avoid the dismal scenes on the Continent of the seventeenth century. He seems to have left the Continent with suffic-ient money, but was robbed on the way, and arrived destitute. In his extremity, he looked for any work, and applied to Westminster Abbey, then recently reverted to Anglican worship under the Restoration. All the Abbey could offer Froberger was the job of blowing the organ, which duty he undertook. Froberger, though fifty years behind England in his appreciation of how to write for domestic keyboard instruments of the plucked string kind, was yet one of the most noted organists of Europe, and in pumping the Abbey organ was in the position of a general unable to slope arms. On one occasion, when the King was present with his Court in the back choir stalls (one assumes), Christopher Gibbons, the Abbey organist, was duly playing, but Froberger let the pressure drop and the organ began to fade and weeze. Christopher Gibbons in a fury appears even to have left the console to upbraid him—perhaps he went so far as to sweep out of the Abbey. But while Gibbons was doing this, Froberger managed to make his way to the keyboard, and, presumably, got someone to replace himself. He began to improvise, and his style was recognized by one of the ladies present, and Froberger was presented to the King, with the result that he later played the harpsichord before Charles in Whitehall. What Christopher Gibbons thought about all this is not really very hard to guess—it is all part of the perpetual refugee problem.

This little anecdote may very well do for a composer whose work for the flugel was small in quantity and usually dull in quality.

As for Kuhnau, an altogether more interesting and important figure, he has been dealt with at least in part in the second section of the chapter devoted to the clavichord in Germany. It is enough to say here that he became organist of St. Thomas's church in Leipzig the year before the birth of J. S. Bach, and in 1700, sixteen years later, became Cantor of the School of St. Thomas, and held that position until he died, his successor being, of course, J. S. Bach himself. Here again you get the organ influence.

This influence, however, quite disappeared in the genius of Bach, though he was probably helped by having a job at one period of his life which mainly consisted of playing on and writing for the harpsichord, to the equal exclusion of two things he is usually connected with, the human voice, and the organ.

This period was the six years he held musical office in the court of the Prince of Anhalt, a smallish principality to the north of Halle and south-west of Potsdam. Not much is known of his daily life at this place, in the white three-storied gabled seventeenth-century country mansion, or in the small town alongside it.

At the time Bach became the music director he was still, by modern standards, a young man, and his prince, by the same standards,

not much more than a well-educated, musical and travelled boy.   He
appears to have been generous, too, and Bach received 400 thalers a
year.   If we can at all take a flugel as a commercial average, and equate
the large double-manualled instrument which Bach left at his death
and which was valued at 80 thalers with the £160 which a similar
new instrument would cost to-day, we might suppose Bach's Cöthen
salary was equal to about £800 to-day.   On this he had to bring up a
growing family of children, but basic living expenses, bread, bacon,
beer and rent, were cheap in the smaller towns of the Empire.   Bach
himself was by no means always at home: he seems to have fretted for
a church and an organ, and was more than once absent trying for
another job.   Then, too, he went with his prince and miniature
court to Carlsbad, where he may have met the youngest son of the
Elector of Brandenburg just about the time when that title was to be
augmented to that of King of Prussia.   This young man's courtesy
title was that of the old rulers of the territory, the Margrave of Brandenburg, and is famous in the annals of music as the commissioner of
the six varied *concerti grossi* first performed at Cöthen before the
Margrave.   The handwritten full score and parts were eventually
sent to Berlin, but allowed to let fall on the library table without
comment, and eventually to be stacked in a corner uncatalogued.
They were rescued after the Margrave's death.   But Bach had a
second copy of the score and parts for use at Cöthen, and we may have
no doubt of the brilliant thing he made of the fifth of the set, which
is that one with the important flugel solo part, making indeed almost
a flugel concerto.

Such flugel solo music as the English Suites and the Chromatic
Fantasia and Fugue, and chamber music for which there were fully
written out flugel parts like the sonatas for flugel and violin, were
written at Cöthen.   While almost all chamber music of this period
has a flugel accompaniment consisting of a figured bass supported by
a cello, Bach made real trios of a two-instrument work sometimes,
with the violin, flute or gamba playing one part and the flugel two
parts, making perfect three-part writing.

The worries of life for a musician in those days were as intense as
they are to-day, but no doubt quite different.   In order to obtain this
Cöthen appointment Bach had to endure a few weeks' imprisonment,
his previous ducal employer being a relative on very bad terms with
Anhalt-Cöthen.

His first wife died suddenly when left at home during one of the

Carlsbad journeys, and Bach for affection and his family's sake re-
married, a soprano singer from across the Elbe being the young woman
in question.

His young prince's marriage with a woman with no music in her
heart made Bach look for other work.   To be the musical bear-leader
of a young prince must in any case have been, however gilded, a somewhat undignified existence.   And to have his musical life so completely woven round the flugel could have suited Bach no better.   He
was not a one-instrument or a one-form composer, but surely happiest
when exerting his art in all directions except the one thing he never
touched, opera.   Nevertheless, unimportant to the master though
they possibly were, to us his flugel compositions are among the greatest
written for the instrument.

Bach had of course played upon and written for the flugel before
the Cöthen period, and did so after it at Leipzig, a period of his life
more dwelt upon in the chapter devoted to the clavichord, an instrument with which Bach unlocked his heart.

Of Handel we have much less to say, and what there has already
been said in connexion with the flugel belongs more to the social
and picturesque background of the subject.   He left Germany for
Italy at the age of twenty-one, and none of his flugel music was written
in the Empire.

Gottlieb Muffat, however, spent his whole working life in Germany, the main part of it in Vienna where he was organist to the
Court and teacher of flugel to the children of the imperial household.
Three generations of eighteenth-century archduchesses have in fact
been taught by the most eminent of European composers—a subject
for a book for anyone to pick up.   Gottlieb's father had studied in
Paris, where he was more impressed by the music of the opera and
ballet than of the clavecin: leaving Paris he became organist of Salzburg
Cathedral, presiding over the instrument for which Mozart was to
write so many concerted sonatas *da chiesa*.   He retired later on to a
town on the Danube above Vienna, where his son Gottlieb was born.
Gottlieb, as we have seen, made the short journey to the capital and a
prosperous career.   Gottlieb inherited much of his father's outlook,
but instead of writing pieces of a ballet-like character for strings and
flugel figured bass, he wrote similar pieces for solo flugel.   Both
father and son made their works great affairs, many movements,
divisions and sub-divisions, almost like an opera with its acts and
scenes, and with playful or literary titles.   Gottlieb Muffat, to us the

more important of the two, called his works by the euphonious if not informative title *Componimenti musicali*, and they make music of a surprisingly modern sound for a contemporary of Bach and Handel, owing to this operatic influence. The place to deal with them again will be in the next section of this chapter.

Haydn must make a fleeting appearance. Although I have already given my opinion that his keyboard music was for clavichord in his Vienna days and for pianoforte as he became a great man in the little world of Eisenstadt, his Concerto in D for keyboard instrument and orchestra is obviously harpsichord music: the repeated notes of the accompaniment in the first movement being meaningless on a pianoforte, but rhythmical and amusing in the Scarlatti manner if played with suitable registration and on a different manual from the tune.

Wagenseil could be the subject of a much longer paragraph if his music were more interesting. He was also a teacher of archduchesses and it was to him that the five-year-old Mozart, seated at one of the imperial flugel said: "I am going to play a concerto of yours, will you please turn over for me?" Wagenseil's harpsichord music is simple in texture and tuneful in the Muffat manner in effect, though without Muffat's power of fancy.

As to Mozart himself, he was not quite born seated at a flugel, for if this image is persisted in, it would be truer to say he was born with a violin bow in his hand, placed there by his father. But both the infant Wolfgang and the child Nannerl were very much brought up on the flugel, and Wolfgang's childish music is written for it. It was a flugel concerto which Leopold found his infant son, covered with ink for in his zeal he had continually thrust the quill deep in the inkpot and wiped the superfluity off with his hands, engaged upon when he returned one day to the Salzburg home. Leopold wept with joy and pride at the musicianship displayed in the score, but said the flugel part was too difficult. And so it proved, at least for the infant composer, who then defended himself: "It is a concerto, and must be practised before it can be performed."

Presumably Wolfgang quickly overtook his older sister who studied the manuscript book written for her by the father and called in French in that cosmopolitan household *Pour le clavecin Celivre appartient a Mademoiselle Marianne Mozart 1759.*

The children soon set out on their journeyings, their father showing them to the wondering princelings of the Empire in 1762, as well as to the Emperor himself. Next year began their grand tour, and the clavecins of France and the harpsichords of England knew the prodigious touch.

On the outward journey, confining ourselves in this chapter to Germany, they passed from Salzburg through that central section of towns delineated a few pages back, and so to the western or Rhineland series, beginning with Heidelburg where the Elector of Mayence was ill and no higher dignitary than the dean of the cathedral was caught to be impressed. He, however, caused Wolfgang's name to be placed on a memorial by the organ as a remembrance as perpetual as might be: the organ and memorial lasted about fifty years. Working their way down the river, the Rhineland was left at Cologne and Germany not regained until three years had passed, and Wolfgang had very nearly died. Poor Leopold and his wife were quite worn out with travel and anxiety, while the indications are that the money saved from the expenses was by no means equal to the praise received. They re-entered the Empire from Switzerland, passing through Ulm to the Danubian cities and to Salzburg.

Before Wolfgang was properly in his teens, fatal age for the exploitation of a true infant prodigy, another journey to the east was undertaken, wholly within the boundaries of the Empire, through Vienna to Brun and Olmutz, where Wolfgang again nearly died, this time of smallpox. He was amused by the archbishop's chaplain who came to teach him cards, and we may well imagine how Wolfgang, that mathematical genius, speedily became a consummate player. He was also taught fencing, though this certainly a little mysterious; surely an odd way to speed convalescence. Nannerl also succumbed and also recovered. She lived to old age, so perhaps it is unfair to consider Leopold the murderer of his son; but what a childhood! Worn out with travel and sickness; buoyed up by genius and music; playing the flugal dizzy with fever while admiring dukes and duchesses shower compliments and snuff-boxes, Leopold standing in the background hoping rather for a few thalers.

The three Italian tours, more important musically than the Imperial, French, English and Netherlandish, are part of the Italian chapter of this book.

Until Mozart left for the important, disappointing and indeed tragic Paris visit he made soon after his twenty-second birthday, those domestic keyboard compositions he wrote were all for the flugel. However, keyboard writing was at least as much for the organ as for the flugel, and writing in general as much for the violin as either,

K

for it was Leopold's instrument. Mozart had also to write numerous ecclesiastical compositions to please the Archbishop of Salzburg, while symphonies were never far from his mind. His heart was with opera, and he had composed several while in his teens. Thus his pre-Paris flugel output is not large, just variations, some sonatas and one or two concertos. After his Paris visit he wrote very little flugel music, for the new pianofortes, especially those of Stein, more and more attracted him. Mozart's life is the watershed between old and new. Like J. S. Bach he was divided: Bach's heart was with the clavichord, his mind was with the flugel. Mozart's heart was with the pianoforte. The pure flugel compositions of Bach and Mozart show these composers in the brilliance and mental power of their genius, but it is the clavichord and pianoforte compositions which show them as poets. Thus these two composers, towering and universal geniuses though they were, do not tower over the rest of the harpsichord repertory: Couperin, Domenico Scarlatti, Purcell, not to mention Handel, have equally valuable contributions to make.

The central position of Haydn, therefore, is not germane to our subject. The friend and admirer of Mozart, who both influenced him and was influenced by him, equally had his flugel days past. And the teacher of surly young Beethoven, too, was equally far from the flugel. This musical epoch of Haydn's influence, separated by so few years, is a different one from that with which we are dealing.

Yet the name of Beethoven cannot properly be ignored. It was surely on a one-manual flugel, perhaps the equivalent of the English spinet, that his displeasing father taught him to be an infant prodigy, failed, and saw to it that Beethoven for the rest of his life suffered under strain, sometimes strain of an intense description. Only true and glowing genius could have driven Beethoven on under treatment which would have turned a mere talent away from a, to him, hateful art. However Leopold may have worn out his son on the flugel, his genuine kindness and affection allowed Mozart's mind and heart to blossom naturally. But the flugel for the young Ludwig and his loutish father must have been the time when his soul was warped, so that for the rest of his life his desires and achievements were at variance: desiring to be pure, he contracted syphilis; desiring to marry, he died a bachelor; desiring to write opera, he wrote one imperfect though essentially great specimen.

To take the taste of this out of the mouth and to end this section more genially, we may turn to:

But here is the finger of God, a flash of the will that can,
Existent behind all laws, that made them and, lo, they are!
And I know not if, save in this, such gifts be allowed to man,
That out of three sounds he frame, not a fourth sound, but a star.

In other words, Robert Browning's *Abt Vogler*, a very noted flugel player in Germany. All his life, and indeed to this day, he has been detested by some, among whom was Mozart, and loved by others, among whom was his pupil the great Weber. He was detested, in what might be called his first period, by the Padre Martini of Bologna, who had refused to teach him as lacking in talent and powers of concentration. But in Rome he secured lessons from Mysliweczek, a Bohemian composer of some popularity settled in Italy. Vogler, desiring to attach to himself the essential legend, would boast how as a boy in Wurzburg he would practise the flugel all night long. But he pleased the Pope who made him Apostolic Protonotary and Chamberlain: neither post as high sounding as might appear, there being many holders of both offices and most with nominal duties and equally nominal salaries. But to an adventurer of personality the outside of the cup is of great importance, and this ape-like man, with his short trunk and long arms, was now dressed in a black mantle with purple stockings and gold shoe buckles, and began a habit of ostentatious prayer.

He went to Mannheim to become Court Chaplain, and at a party he met Mozart, who disliked him even more than he had done Clementi. However, he was very popular with the ladies of the Court: he became a Kappelmeister and started to teach the flugel, keeping pupils waiting in an ante-room while he addressed very long and presumably silent prayers to his Maker, to the edification of his pupils who would after be in no mood to discern any technical faults in his mere musicianship. His teaching seems to me to have been on the lines of those modern professors who advertise their capacity to teach the piano by post and without the drudgery of scales.

After a time he wandered away from Mannheim, stayed for a while in Darmstadt and there and in Vienna was kind to Weber, for which his sins, if he had any but a ruthless determination not to die of poverty, be forgiven him.

On the occasion of the Mannheim party referred to, he played, with the unhappy composer present and suffering, a concerto of Mozart's, possibly that in E flat, K.271, recently composed in Salzburg.

"He played too fast . . . and usually just guessed the bass, and made up both melody and harmony as he went along if he got into a fix. His rapidity is simply extraordinary, you can follow him neither on the score nor by looking at the keyboard. . . . All we can say is, not that we have heard flugel playing, but that we have *seen* it," and then Mozart, more gravely, asks: "In what does the art of playing music at sight consist?" and answers the question himself most excellently: "it consists in playing music in the right tempo, and in giving all the phrases and passage work appropriate expression, so that the listener might imagine the composer himself was playing."

3. *The Music*

Flugel music falls easily into various sub-divisions, so that this chapter can end with the uniformity wished for, and need not be split among the various composers as had to be done in the clavichord chapter. Perhaps this is because the clavichord is so personal an instrument that the composer himself is the sole creator of its music, but since the flugel was a more public and formal instrument, the composer owed something (sometimes, indeed much) to other music and to tradition.

But before embarking upon the ten sub-divisions which seem to me to be necessary, it will be as well to get the subject of ornamentation out of the way.

Perhaps flugel ornamentation is more difficult than any other. In the case of the virginals and the harpsichord there is ground for dispute as to the amount of ornamentation desirable on a pianoforte, and also ground for dispute as to whether the unornamented melodic lines of Handel should, nevertheless, be ornamented. The ornaments of the clavecin are, though plentiful, quite clear, and it is then merely a matter of personal taste as to how many should be included for modern performance. The clavichord was not much used for ornamentation by J. S. Bach, and C. P. E. Bach has himself left us details of how to ornament his sonatas, details which are hardly necessary for most pianists to absorb, for his music is rarely studied; in my view not unjustly, seeing that Haydn, who used few ornaments, did the same sort of thing so very much better.

But in the flugel we have a large territory to consider composed of many musical centres, unlike the clavecin and harpsichord, where all the important composing and playing went on in Paris and London, each with its central and well-understood tradition. And then, in the flugel, we have a highly sophisticated public art, not the intimate personal art of the clavichord. Lastly, unlike the music for the clavecin, though admittedly like that for the clavichord, the music covers two quite different styles, which might very shortly be classified into that of composing from the bass (i.e. the "Goldberg Variations" of J. S. Bach) and composing from the treble (i.e. any of the variations of Mozart).

In the case of the flugel there is extra fog, owing to the lateness of the rediscovery of the music of one of its two great exponents, J. S. Bach, and the changing phases of this rediscovery. At first, and in some centres still, it was and is supposed that the right way to play Bach, the Bach style in fact, was each note clear and round, no expression, pretty fast, and rather mechanically, especially in fugues when the subject, be it never so conventional, had to be prominent. Then there was the romantic reaction, when Bach was to be played as though it was Schumann. Then the scholar-poets like Busoni came to the fore. This great composer, player, editor and Bach-lover goes so far as to repeat the theme at the close of the "Goldberg Variations" almost unornamented, the basses in octaves and the whole an octave lower, with a most impressive effect. And why not? That sort of doubling and registration is perfectly possible on the flugel, and ornaments which might sound well with one registration might sound poorly on another. In modern times we have flugel (or to be pedantically precise, clavecin) recitals giving this music on the instrument for which it was composed. But there are only a few harpsichordists, and the tendency is to rustle, dignity and brilliance. We have not heard performances by artists with other temperaments, and we should not too hastily assume that Lucille Wallace or Wanda Landowska have uttered the last music on the subject.

In the front of most modern editions of flugel music, be it by J. S. Bach, or Mozart or Gottlieb Muffat, there is usually an editorial note as to how to play the ornaments. But different editions give conflicting advice. Similarly with books on the subject. The late J. A. Fuller-Maitland in 1925 did not hesitate to contradict Schweitzer's 1905 opinion as to how to play the Sarabande in the G major Partita; while the authoritarian Dolmetsch, taking his information largely from Frederick the Great's flute instructor, lays down laws which, if followed always and followed exactly, would dehydrate most music.

To try to clear away the fog, and with the support of general precepts of two great men, C. P. E. Bach and Schweitzer, and the actual performances of Busoni, I will dare to tackle the very vexed question by asking why composers wrote ornaments at all? Beethoven used very few, Chopin's ornaments are of quite different origin and simple to follow, Debussy used none. Why should the seventeenth and eighteenth centuries have forborne to have written in their ornaments with the same clarity as Chopin?

It is possible to think of three answers. First, musical shorthand. The flugel composers wrote a very great deal of music, and to help themselves, they used in the figured bass a harmonic shorthand, and it seemed natural to them to use a similar melodic shorthand as well. Thus quite a long movement in two parts, equally suited for an aria or a violin or cello solo with figured bass accompaniment, could quickly be written, especially if the parts were repeated if in binary form, or if it was *da capo* in aria form. The composer had some pupil rule him paper, and then quickly wrote down the treble and bass: ornaments on the treble and figures under the bass, and there was an aria for a *castrato* for the next opera, or something to amuse a flute-playing duke. The composer himself would play the flugel part, and superintend the performance, and would surely alter and amplify within the scaffolding of his general idea during the actual playing of the music. There is no evidence whatever that either J. S. Bach or Mozart concerned themselves with the difficulties of players in the distant future on a different instrument and in cities that were then swamps, vast forests or a collection of a few wooden huts.

A second reason for ornaments was that the composer did not much mind how a performer other than himself managed. He was free to ornament, and quite expected to use initiative. If he was not an artist at all, then the performance would in any case be ugly. But if he was a true musician, then the ornamentation would be truly musical, and there would be no need to examine the actual performance against the written signs. Nowadays the score is the thing: deviation from the score is an error on the part of the artist. Then the performance was the thing, deviation from the score mattered only when the performance was poor. The romantic conception of inspiration, taken from the theologians' idea of the Bible and its writers, has remained long after the origin of the idea is disbelieved in by many. An agnostic is quite ready to believe J. S. Bach was inspired. But there is no evidence that any classical composer thought himself inspired, except Handel during the composition of *Messiah*. Do not let us cease to use this noble and poetic concept of the origin of artistic greatness: but we are talking now of a great pile of flugel music written at different times by different men, and all we need say is, if some of it is inspired, then its performance requires also an inspired artist, for there was never any actual inspiration in the notes and symbols themselves, but only in the spirit behind them.

A third reason is possibly harmonic. The figured bass method of writing is suitable to a simple harmonic system, but breaks down at intricacy and subtlety. Beethoven wrote out his ornamentation in long notes, and in his C major piano concerto he also supplies a figured bass, with a congested result. The two lines of figures needed by Bach and Mozart swell to four, and we have this sort of thing:

It is not really to be supposed that there was a second pianist present filling in a figured bass with the first cellist reading the repeated A flats over his shoulder. I take it that this was just a habit, a habit which was discontinued when it became altogether too laborious and obviously pointless. This passage just quoted is harmonic in interest: what gives point to it is the viola line, with its A natural against the A flat of the bass. The only composer before Beethoven who wrote like this, that is to say, who wrote passages of mainly harmonic interest as part of a grand scheme, was Haydn, and that composer did not usually, I think, figure his symphonies.

Bach and Mozart would have been less likely to need to write in this manner, Bach being essentially contrapuntal and Mozart always being rather too athletic. When Bach has recondite harmonic effects they arise from the interplay of parts or from the grind of the melodic flow against a smoothly marching bass.

When this sort of thing turns up

from the *recitative stromente* of Cantata No. 51 (and I must apologize for my clumsy filling in of the figured bass), it is so much simpler to write grace notes and simple figures, which is what Bach did do.

The voice has the treble line, the cello the bottom line, and the flugel player, resting his harmony on the bottom line and not knowing the treble line, will put into his flugel the B of the Ninth and both the D and C of the 6/5, and the A of the second Ninth.   That is to say, these discords are essential to Bach's harmonic scheme.

Now flugel music was not figured when it was to be played solo, but the flugel composers were usually busied on concerted music of various forms, and many of their concerted habits were still on them when they wrote for solo flugel: thus the harmonic continuance of grace notes.

To recapitulate.   When faced with an ornament, I think that the modern player should first ask himself if it has any particular harmonic significance, and if it has, to be sure to bring out that note which gives it such significance, as in this passage from the Sarabande of the G minor English Suite of Bach,

where the grace notes marked with an asterisk are of great harmonic power, and should be accentuated and dwelt upon, the subsequent resolution on E and C sharp being unaccented.   This sort of harmonic ornamentation, if not quite confined to the flugel in Germany, was much more common there than in France or England, where clavecin and harpsichord ornamentation was mainly melodic.

If the player, however, decides that the flugel ornament has no particular harmonic significance, he may decide that the interest is purely rhythmic, and gives a sort of orchestral or tam-tam colour to the music as in the constant little three or four note skirls in the Alla Turca of Mozart's A major sonata, K.331.

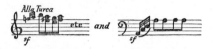

If, however, the player decides that the ornament is neither harmonic nor rhythmic, I feel he may arrange the notes very much to please his own ear. This advice (I hope not foolish advice) of mine applies to all music discussed in this volume, and not just to the flugel in Germany. An example of this melodic freedom, as I believe it to be, has been given in the chapter devoted to the cembalo in Italy, and concerns one of Scarlatti's best known sonatas.

If we decide, as I hope we may, that this question of ornamentation, one of the most vexed questions of seventeenth- and eighteenth-century music, has been dealt with as fully as my limited abilities allow, we may turn, freed and fresh, to the music itself.

PRELUDES, FANTASIAS, ETC. The most important examples of this sort of flugel writing come from J. S. Bach's initiatory movements from his Partitas and English Suites. The English Suites, which are perhaps the crown and glory of the Suite form in all its centuries of history, owe their flattering title to the accident that the Prelude of No. 1, in A major, is based on a theme from the gigue of a Suite in the same key by one Dieupart, whose *Six Suittes de clavessin* were published in London and parts of them copied out by Bach himself.

The English Suites' preliminary movements are all called Preludes, but they differ among themselves considerably, and range to long movements of an orchestral type. The first movements of the Partitas likewise are usually on a large scale, but have different titles, Prelude, Sinfonia, Fantasia, Overture, Preamble, and Toccata. We can find out how to play these and other large scale movements by examining Bach's orchestral music. We will then surely discover that Bach coloured quite differently from Mozart: we have long stretches of one colour succeeded by long stretches of a contrasting colour. It therefore seems unreasonable to indulge in long *crescendi* or *diminuendi*. Where it is thought that, were the music orchestrated, Bach would employ only his handful of *concertanti* players, then the music should be as chamber music, with each part beautifully clear. But when it is felt that Bach calls in the *ripieno* strings and perhaps his trumpets and drums as well, then not necessarily more loudness, but more fullness should be employed, doubling octaves and transposing up or down an octave as the ear of the player dictates. Playing the flugel, this is surely what would have happened, and it must be always remembered that if this music is played on the pianoforte it is necessarily a transcription. If respect for the written notes and the idea of literal inspiration has very much taken hold of a player, then perhaps he might restrict himself to the quite different clavichord music, and leave the flugel music alone.

J. S. Bach's Fantasia in C minor, a separate work, is full of interest and brings to mind the cembalo music of Scarlatti. This music appears to be pure flugel and to have no orchestral connotations. The Chromatic Fantasia is also pure flugel, and is an astonishing example of Bach's range of expression, being completely different from the Fantasia in C minor in structure and in texture. All editors of the Chromatic Fantasia, however much they disagree on points of interpretation, agree at least on the degree of latitude to be allowed a modern pianist. The quasi-recitative passages may obtain a world of meaning, the arpeggios may be doubled and other means of a similar nature used to give maximum rhetorical effect to this piece of impassioned music.

It is certain that one or two of the Preludes from the *Well Tempered Clavier* are for harpsichord, just as it is most highly probable that the majority are for clavichord. One of the A major fugues is usually quoted as being obviously flugel music, but it does not follow that the accompanying Prelude is, for Bach often mated two pieces of music from different sources. The D major of the second book seems to me obviously orchestral and therefore flugel. I say obviously, because Bach's orchestral way of writing would be quite ineffective on the clavichord, which is a sort of miniature string quartet.

After Bach, a very long way after, the most interesting Preludes for flugel are possibly those by Muffat in *Componimenti Musicali*, there being a Fantasia in G minor which is pure flugel and very tuneful. In fact, Bach was the only composer I can think of to write orchestrally

for the flugel in Preludes, Fantasia and the like. Other flugel composers graduated from the organ to the flugel or came to it quite fresh.
I am of course speaking only of these Prelude and Fantasia-like movements, not of sonatas or variations or fugues.

Kuhnau in his *Clavierubung* wrote some fairly interesting flugel
Preludes, but more to my mind are the efforts of J. L. Krebs to write
in the manner of his old master, J. S. Bach, while giving this manner a
later smoothness. In Kreb's *Clavierubung* there is a series of Chorales
divided into three movements, first, a free Preamble, then a Chorale
Prelude, and then the Chorale fitted with a figured bass. It is only
the Preambles which are of interest, and their interest is sometimes
considerable, so charming is the mixture of Bach-appearance in the
text of the music and euphonious sweetness in the playing. This
euphony plus the correct appearance is obtained by omitting those
ornaments which are the result of inner-ear harmonic clashes. Kreb's
inner-ear obviously had no harmony outside the most polite usages
of the mid-century.

FUGUES. These are always associated with Bach: as W. F. Bach
wrote his fugues for clavichord, and as Mozart was using a pianoforte
at the time he came under the influence of Handel via Baron von
Swieten, it is true to say that the only fugues there are of any musical
value for the flugel were written by J. S. Bach. As only one or two
flugel fugues are to be found in *The Well Tempered Clavier*, the chief
collection of fugues is in the musically secondary group of Toccatas.
Most of these are long and go with a great swing. There are two
fugues in A minor of similar type: one indeed is claimed to be the
longest fugue of musical value in existence! There is the great fugue,
certainly the greatest flugel fugue ever written, which comes after
the Chromatic Fantasia. Then, very nearly flugel, anyhow to be
placed nowhere else, is the E flat music for the Lautenclavier. Of
Bach's fugues this is one of the freest, and is consequently easy and
delightful to play, with plenty of "air" in the parts.

VARIATIONS. Here, more than ever, we are on high ground, very
near the top of Parnassus, and it is out of the question, if the proportions of this volume are to be kept at all, to deal adequately with
the great interest not only of the "Goldberg Variations" in themselves
but of their salient contrast to the several variations written by Bach's
only flugel peer, Mozart. This discussion would involve repeating
the views of Parry and other writers with a similar outlook, attempting
to negate their view of Mozart's variations as comparatively shallow

music, showing the quite different ends of Bach and Mozart and consequently their quite different means, and then dwelling section by section on the variations themselves.

The blunt, few and brutal facts about the "Goldberg Variations" are, that a Count Kayserling suffered from insomnia: he had a flugel player in his employment as a matter of course, and thought that when he woke up, say at three in the morning and was unable to sleep, it would be pleasant to listen to music. So his unfortunate *maestro* had to sleep in the next room and be ready to get up at all hours and to perform. No good *maestro*, one imagines, would have put up with this. But if Goldberg, the man's name, was able to play the music which Bach wrote for him on the Count's instructions, he must have been one of the greatest flugel players of the Empire.

The scheme of this vast musical edifice is harmonic, and is founded on a bass. Every other variation is a canon: between the canons Bach's imagination roved and produced the most varied of forms, including passionate and profound adagios. Just, however, when the good Count was dropping off to sleep, as he may well have done if his musical taste was merely shallow, Bach produces real fireworks in the shape of a quodlibet on popular songs. As insomnia music surely the "Goldberg Variations" are the worst ever: as a set of variations for flugel they are the greatest ever: as a set of variations for any instrument they are one of the very few greatest ever. Of all flugel music this music is the most characteristic for the instrument.

Only two of Mozart's variations need or should be mentioned here, because he wrote many of his sets while in Paris, and they come in the chapter devoted to the clavecin in France, while his greatest examples, the set on a theme from an unimportant opera of Gluck and the set transcribed from his own clarinet quintet, are probably for pianoforte. First of these two actually for flugel is a set on an air from an opera by that small, brown, vivid-faced conductor of the Vienna Opera in the Imperial Palace, Salieri, the man nearly twenty years later thought by some to have poisoned Mozart out of jealousy. Here, in the first variations of Mozart's maturity, composed in 1773, perhaps, and in Vienna, when he was sixteen or seventeen (he was born at the beginning of the year 1756, so any Mozart age calculation must allow for this) we have only six variations; later he was to write double that number. The third variation on Salieri's pleasant tune transforms it entirely, both melody and bass, keeping merely the cadences and general feel, and Mozart makes a silk purse out of this pretty, pink

and well-bred sow's ear, giving a melodic line which one would love
to hear sung by a colaratura soprano.   The fifth variation is the Adagio,
a feature constant in Mozart's scheme, and the rippling demisemi-
quavers of accompaniment demand the flugel with its separate manuals,
and power of delicate registration. It is difficult on many and impossible on some pianofortes to prevent such an accompaniment from
sounding muddy.

The other set was on a minuet by an oboeist attached for a time
to the Mannheim Court, where Mozart met him and wrote these
variations.   The oboeist, Fischer by name, later went to London and
married a daughter of the painter Gainsborough, moving in the J. C.
Bach and Abel circle in Carlisle Street for a time, until these elderly
gentlemen (for they were a generation older than Mozart and Fischer)
died.

Mozart, who wrote the "Fischer Variations" five years after the
Salieri set, must have thought highly of them, for he carried them to
Paris, and on one occasion, travelling in Germany, he sent home to
Salzburg for his sister to send them on to him. Fischer's tune is,
however, dull, mannered in a dowdy way, and it is difficult to receive
much pleasure from any of Mozart's twelve variations; even the Adagio
is uninteresting.   But as flugel music they are brilliant, with demisemi-
quaver runs, octave appoggiaturas, crossed hands on different manuals,
and the whole tenth variation can be played with every octave coupling
stop drawn.

It is perhaps just as well to mention that Haydn's variations, some
of which are very beautiful, are certainly pianoforte music.

DANCES.   J. S. Bach's Partitas and English Suites are chiefly composed of dance movements; of these the Sarabandes are usually the
most intimate and emotional, and some of them are replete with
harmonic ornaments.   An alternative set of ornaments, or perhaps
more correctly, an optional way of playing the melodic line, is given
in some cases, and this working out by the composer himself of the
ornaments is of deep interest.   Although J. S. Bach was more sparing
in his ornamentation than many other composers, he was by far (this
is bold, but I think justified) the most artistic in their manipulation.
Even such a great artist as Couperin sometimes seems guilty of adding
ornamentation because the look of the page was otherwise bare, and
there are runs merely to fill up gaps.   Bach's ornamentation is so very
poignant in his slow movements and so witty in his fast.   There is, in
short, always a temptation present to concentrate on J. S. Bach to the

exclusion of all else in a volume of the sort I am attempting to write, though in colder blood one would realize that there are several other composers just as fine, though in different ways. But there is such power and vigour behind his genius that it sometimes sweeps you right off your feet. It is surely a critic's duty to pick himself up again.

The Gigue of the first Partita is quite different from most Bach and indeed from all other Gigues by any composer whatever. It is one of those pieces of music which can equally be played slowly on a pianoforte with use of a sustaining pedal and quickly and with fire on a flugel: in this respect it has the same quality which I seem to discern in the first movement of the "Moonlight Sonata", which will make a fleeting and possibly surprising appearance later in the chapter.

It is hoped that students of flugel music will not overlook Bach's Lautenclavier Suites, particularly that in A minor.[1] People with access to an organ but not to a harpsichord may agree with me as to the excellent effect produced by using octave couplers, especially on the upward runs of the Prelude and the bass of the Sarabande. The Minuet is one of Bach's most graceful essays in this dance rhythm. Then there is also the E minor Suite,[2] in the Prelude of which all sorts of experiments in registration most usefully can be made, and also with a Sarabande of unusually low *tessitura* and most expressive and thoughtful melody which again requires octave couplers. It is this sort of experiment which makes one realize that the harpsichord family is nearer to the organ (even allowing for difference in attainable legato) than either is to the pianoforte. Few pianofortes could produce, even under the touch of a Solomon, sufficient clarity matched with sufficient depth for this noble Saraband.

To go down from these Sarabandes to those of Muffat is indeed a descent. He is much more at home in his gracious Minuets and brisk and breezy Bourrées, where he often can stand the comparison with Bach. He was a lively and entertaining composer who during his lifetime must have been thought the only German peer of Handel in Suite writing.

Dolmetsch, quoting Quantz, Frederick's tame flautist, lays down that Bourrées should be merry and short. Well, Muffat gets full marks. He says Sarabandes should have majesty: here J. S. Bach would fail

---

[1] Peters edition, No. 214, page 18 *et seq.*
[2] Peters edition, No. 214, p. 32.

as against Couperin, Bach having much more than majesty. Courantes, surprisingly, are also to have this majestic quality, but here one feels Potsdam must have been rather cut off from what was happening elsewhere. Personally, I distrust these quotations from Quantz's *Versuch einer Anweisung die Flote* . . . published in 1752. He was too much of a king's canary not to have been narrow and doctrinaire.

SONATAS. Kuhnau's sonatas, whether "programme music" from the Bible or the *da chiesa* form adopted for domestic use, have been dealt with on the assumption they were clavichord music. It may, therefore, be useful to deal with J. S. Bach's works in this form, for they appear to be flugel music. They were not written as *da chiesa* sonatas for the flugel in the first place, but transcribed as such from other sources. Some of the music, I am sorry to say, seems to me too dull to be mentioned, but the D minor sonata, a more mature work and taken from Bach's own sonata in the same key for solo violin, is of great beauty. To prevent the reader turning over the pages or to the index, it is fair to remind him that the *sonata da camera* was chamber music in the form of a dance suite; while a *sonata da chiesa* was chamber music to be played in church and consisted of slow—fast—slow—fast movements, all in the same key, for a solo instrument or instruments and figured bass, one or both of the fast movements being usually a fugued allegro. It is the second slow movement of this sonata which must detain us. In *tessitura* and general effect it is not dissimilar from the Sarabande of the Lautenclavier suite mentioned above, and, if no harpsichord is available, demands an organ. The marking Andante is to me questionable: its gravity and the low pitch of its opening melody seem to me to require something near Largo, which is its type, rather than the more intimate connotations of Adagio.

After Bach we have Mozart, with no sonatas of importance intervening. Mozart, of course, wrote in the new style, that of C. P. E. Bach and Haydn, only with the compactness and brilliance needed for the flugel. There are five mature sonatas preceding his Paris visit, K.279–283 inclusive: K.284 with its octaves and thirds and left-hand passages is usually taken to be pianoforte music.

These five sonatas (together with the pianoforte sixth just mentioned) were all composed on the instructions of a nobleman who appears to have avoided payment. They were written in Salzburg, though the sixth may have been written later in Mannheim, just at that juncture in Mozart's life when he began to become acquainted with the pianofortes of Stein. I feel a little uncomfortable in writing

about the five sonatas for the flugel.   They seem to me rather inferior
to the Paris set, in which his mind was necessarily set on the clavecin,
the pianofortes originating in Italy, Germany and England being late
in introduction to the French capital.

But these five Salzburg sonatas are neither (so it seems to me) pure
flugel nor pure Stein, using this word instead of pianoforte to denote
that early version of our modern instrument for which good writing
tends to be like a quartet rather than an orchestra.   The Salzburg
sonatas are orchestral, but not so in the flugel manner, which is that
of the orchestra of the concerto grosso and of the old classical opera,
now dying out.   The long sections of *forte* followed by long sections
of *piano*, with *ripieno* and *concertante* sections, are quite absent from these
sonatas, which are orchestral in the modern manner and of Mozart's
own early symphonies.   Even with pedal stops it is difficult to see
how he managed his immediate tone transitions, with their occasional
sforzandos.

Yet if we assume they were intended for the pianoforte, they are
not in the string quartet style, but too thin to be orchestral.   It is as
though Mozart was already discontented with the flugel and was
reaching out for something different, that "something" not being the
clavichord.

What I consider to be by far the most effective flugel music of the
set is in the 6/8 Adagio from the F major K.280 where this sort of thing
is excellently well laid out, with just time enough for the right hand to
move from manual to manual as the *pianos* and the *fortes* denote:

But what does puzzle me is such a passage as this,

from K.279, lovely though it is, with the cellos churning in the bass.   It
seems to require a body of strings, and I quite fail to see how the flugel
player could obtain the requisite contrasts of tone.   There is no time at

all to change the registration, a mechanical procedure taking here at least a crotchet or the manual, and the immediate finger action of the clavichord or pianoforte is required. There is not much evidence either way, but sometimes I feel these Salzburg pre-Paris sonatas are easier to consider as his earliest pianoforte ventures written at a time (for even Mozart was human) before he had grasped the deficiencies of the instruments at his disposal. When he had grasped their lack of orchestral colour, he then wrote for them as he would for a string quartet. As the pianofortes became more powerful he once again essayed the orchestral manner; with what difference can be seen by comparing these Salzburg sonatas with the Fantasia and Sonata in C minor.

We are straying a little from our strict subject. To conclude this argument, it follows that, if the Salzburg sonatas are all pianoforte music, not just the last one in D, K.284, Mozart returned to the clavecin while in Paris. But this should occasion no surprise; besides being the greatest of artists, Mozart, like all his fellows, was a craftsman, able to turn out the music required for the instruments available. Lastly, it also follows that very few flugel sonatas exist of any merit. Indeed, the clavecin produces no sonatas except those of Mozart; neither does the cembalo inspire sonatas, in the modern sense of three movement works; while the best the harpsichord could rise to were the works of Arne. We can make, therefore, a generalization true, but startling: there are no sonatas of real importance for the harpsichord family, whether this means the harpsichord in any country or its smaller relations, spinet and virginal, at all. Also, all the great sonatas were written for the clavichord which were not written for the pianoforte. Sonata form and sonata style were born with the clavichord and graduated to the pianoforte. There are exceptions to this generalization as individual taste prompts one or another to say "What about Rutini, what about J. C. Bach," and so forth; but as a generalization I feel it may stand. The Suite was the great harpsichord form: the Sonata the great clavichord form.

Now to the "Moonlight Sonata" and Op. 101: a startling transition after a startling generalization. Now I do not for one moment wish to combat accepted history and tradition that Beethoven wrote for the pianoforte, preferring indeed not the Vienna instruments loved by Mozart but the stronger and harder machines of Broadwood of London. Nor do I wish to make argumentative capital out of Beethoven's title-pages, "for harpsichord or pianoforte". Indeed, the

L

word "flugel" covered both instruments, and it is obvious what Beethoven was writing for.

Nevertheless, he was born into the Haydn and Mozart era, and just as he figured the bass of his C major pianoforte concerto without for one moment expecting a harpsichord among the orchestra to fill up the harmonies, so in my opinion he followed a certain amount of tradition in his mode of writing for the pianoforte. If anyone will take the trouble to play the first movement of the "Moonlight Sonata" on a harpsichord or even on an early pianoforte, marking the rhythm of the dotted quavers not as trochees but as curt iambs before the ensuing minims, and with the bass most clear and prominent, he will find the music raising itself away from the schoolgirl's dream of the lovers on the lake to something more classical, more reserved and a great deal more grim and, to my mind, impressive. It is only the modern pianoforte with its muddy tone which obscures the tread of the bass. In other words, if this movement is played as if it were written by Handel, there will be a real gain in its emotional qualities.

Even more Handelian and harpsichordistic is the Adagio of Op. 101, especially the downward chromatic tread of the grace notes which form the real bass, and are like the plucked strings of double basses, falling at last to the tonic pedal ready for the return of the first subject of all. There is no need to apologize for dragging in Handel: his spiritual affinity with Beethoven is obvious. What I must apologize for is dragging Beethoven into this book. And I do so not to attempt to persuade people to play Beethoven on the harpsichord as a matter of habit, but to do so occasionally, so as to see music rather more through his eyes, and to feel the strength and clarity of his basses and his Handelian majesty, rather than his mere storm and stress, romantic passions and the like. It is, indeed, a plea to view Beethoven as if descended from the composers who form the subject of this book, who were the composers Beethoven chiefly knew, rather than to view Beethoven backwards through the music of Brahms and Wagner.

DUET SONATAS. There is one example of one flugel four hands by Mozart in B flat, K.358. It was composed in 1774—that is to say, much earlier than its Köchel number would suggest. There are two others as well, but they are not listed by Köchel or Wyzewa and Saint-Foix as belonging to this pre-Paris period at Salzburg and are presumably *juvenalia*; with which music I do not propose to deal, as belonging more to the study of Mozart than to the study of the flugel.

This B flat sonata is a pleasant work whose *molto presto* is full of whimsical, even sly high spirits, but it cannot compare with Mozart's later music for pianoforte duet. The keyboard of a one-manual flugel and of a pianoforte would be equally narrow, and it is hard to see how two adult females could possibly fit themselves in. We know less about the circumstances attending the music written at Salzburg because, of course, Wolfgang had much less occasion to write letters when he was at home. Nevertheless, however it was managed, duet sonatas for the narrow domestic keyboard of the eighteenth century were coming into favour across Europe, there being pianoforte examples by Clementi.

FLUGEL CONCERTOS. This is a very important field of operation, and includes such a work as the Italian concerto of J. S. Bach, music for solo flugel written in the strict concerto style with *concertante* and *ripieno* sections. The slow movement, like those of his first two Brandenburg concertos, diminishes from orchestral to chamber music texture, and we have an involved and prolonged melody of great emotional power floating over a bass as rhythmically strict as a ground bass, though harmonically freer. The opening of the first movement is one of those passages where all the octave couplers of the flugel may be drawn, and this registration should continue until the piano indication for the left hand, and a new tune, *forte*, in the right signalizes the entry of the solo instrument, registered plain without octaves and played on a different manual from the accompaniment. In playing this music on the modern pianoforte it is surely permissible to employ the damper pedal for the orchestral introduction, and to use the soft pedal if of the sliding type for the solo instrument. It is sometimes possible, by half depressing the soft pedal, to strike the two strings (the third being out of range owing to the pedal depression) on the unworn parts of the hammer felts, producing a quite different timbre, most suited to the contrast here desired.

Besides this great original work, Bach also arranged sixteen concertos by various composers, Vivaldi among them, for flugel. Here we see the same difference between the *concertante* and *ripieno* sections. Perhaps the best of the Vivaldi transcriptions is No. 4 in G minor, where the player is helped by having an ornamented version of the melody on his entry and only two part harmony, though of course Bach's own concerto is better in that the player has a quite different melody and accompaniment to help him mark the contrast. Other effective concertos in this set of sixteen worthy of study for the light shed on flugel practice and performance is No. 14, also in G minor, but from an original by Telemann.   Here in the Adagio we find the chamber music style intervening between two orchestral movements, the melody being violinistic against a bass line to which, in imagination and possibly in fact, figured harmonies would be added.   No. 16 is also of interest, for its original may have been written by a nephew of Bach's Weimar patron, the Duke of Sax-Weimar: on the other hand, it may have been written by Vivaldi; only vulgar eyes pry into aristocratic mysteries.   In the third movement of this concerto we see again the *ripieno* opening and the solo intervention with a different theme, and helped by its *tessitura* height to make the necessary contrast.

To a pianist accustomed to romantic music, possibly the best introduction to the harpsichord is the Italian concerto and this set of sixteen transcriptions by Bach, for they are so very different from anything in the nineteenth-century pianistic repertoire that the player would be bound completely to adjust his approach.   It would, indeed, be like learning to swim by jumping into the deep end.

There are two very well-known flugel concertos by J. S. Bach for solo instrument and strings, in D minor and in F minor, and both are supposed by some scholars to be derivations from an unknown source, though other scholars inquire sarcastically who this unknown genius capable of writing such powerful music was.   As to its power, vigour and expressiveness there can be no two opinions, and these concertos retain their power and dignity, even when played in the same series of modern symphony concerts as the most booming and flashing of romantic concertos; even when played on pianofortes by exquisite romantics and with strings enough to have furnished all the orchestras of the Holy Roman Empire; even when played under a stick conductor drenched with applause; even when played without a figured bass or with an organ performing that function with romantic little snatches of tune sticking themselves forward like Victorian plaster angels in a severe building.

He wrote others, too, but these manifestly derive from his own violin concertos.   One fact is therefore obvious, that the solo flugel concerto, to Bach, was something of a makeshift.   The violin concerto he knew and wrote originally for, but the flugel concerto solo was something to play when for some reason a fiddler of the requisite technique was not handy.   As to the D minor and F minor, they may be genuine Bach, their violin originals being lost.   Bach introduces into episodes of the D minor the most lovely keyboard effects, lovely

even on a pianoforte, and doubly lovely with the two manuals and
two or three different timbres of the flugel at disposal.

Mozart's keyboard concertos rank among the more important
of his instrumental music, much more important, for instance, than
his violin concertos. They were a genre which attracted him from
babyhood, and as soon as he came across the pianoforte he adopted it
with enthusiasm, and displayed a style of writing quite different from
the styles shown in his solo sonatas. The flugel concertos proper were
experimental studies of his childhood and boyhood and were transcriptions not, as in the manner of Bach, from violin concertos, but
from flugel sonatas by minor German composers, Mozart adding an
orchestral accompaniment and some symphonic *ritornelli*. Thus the
first original concerto is perhaps also the last flugel one (that in D
major, K.175, written in Salzburg in 1773). It is not a characteristic
or even a very interesting work. To Mozart the concerto was something you used a pianoforte for.

CONCERTOS FOR TWO OR MORE FLUGEL. The only important
specimens of this sort of writing are the two by J. S. Bach originally
written for two flugel, and the two for three and Mozart's one for
three. Bach wrote other works in this genre, but they are transcriptions from violin concertos, while Mozart's E flat concerto for two
solo instruments is almost certainly pianoforte music. The distinction
of the Bach works is that they can be played perfectly agreeably without their accompanying strings, just as music for two pianos. The
keyboards rattle along throughout: sometimes, as in the opening of
the D minor for three flugel, in unison with the strings; sometimes
tossing the fabric from keyboard to keyboard, or with the strings
plucking a simple accompaniment; sometimes with the strings wholly
silent, as in the slow movement of the C major for two flugel; and
occasionally they reinforce a syncopation, as in the last movement of
this work. Mozart's writing for three flugel is very different, not
only because his symphonic habits, already growing upon him, made
it so, but because it was music to the order of an important Viennese
lady for her to play with her two daughters, one of whom was only
a beginner, so the work has one weak part. It may in fact justly be
regarded as an amplified work for two keyboards, for Mozart added
an arrangement for such a diminished combination in the score itself.
The music is of no great interest, and cannot compare even in sparkle
with such a movement as the C major fugue for two flugel from the
Bach concertos. In the last movement, however, a varied Rondo,

the middle episode has a truly early Mozartian melody of equal grace
and simplicity. This concerto is what may be called the watershed
work: works after it were pianoforte, works before it, usually flugel.
Though written for the three flugel-playing ladies of Vienna, it was
afterwards repeated during a visit to Mannheim. He wrote home to
Salzburg, "And what came next after the symphony? Why the
concerto for three claviers. M. Demler played one, I played another
and M. Stein the third. Then I played alone the last sonata, the one
in D, for Durnitz, then my concerto in B flat, and then I improvised:
a strict fugue in C minor, a sonata in C with a rondo at the end, all
quite out of my head. There was a considerable hubbub at the end.
Stein kept making faces and showing astonishment: Demler was always
laughing: that is the way this curious man shows pleasure."

Now Stein was the celebrated manufacturer of the new pianofortes, the D major sonata referred to, K.284, is pianoforte music as is
the concerto in B flat, K.238. I think we may be certain that this
concert was given on flugel using the word to mean grand pianofortes.
It is not really a pity that Mozart used the word clavier, which could
not possibly in this context have meant clavichord, for the word
flugel is equally vague, being attachable to any keyboard instrument
with a wing cover, though used in this book to denote the harpsichord
family as the only German word available. It was, by the way, this
great pleasure that Wolfgang's music gave and gives which made the
composer a little suspect in some quarters in late Victorian and
Edwardian circles. He was possibly a little too sensuous to be spiritu-
ally in earnest. A German writer, of some influence in these circles,
even going so far as to call Mozart's works "mere music", as opposed,
for instance, to the deep philosophical utterances of Strauss on the
subject of Zarathrustra. So much for Demler who couldn't help
laughing with pleasure.

CHAMBER MUSIC. At the risk of being tedious it is necessary to remind ourselves once more that all Bach's chamber music required the
presence in the room of a flugel. Sometimes the flugel would play
the harmonies from a figured bass, a cellist or gamba player doubling
the bass line and reading over his shoulder to do this. Sometimes
Bach, however, treated the flugel with its two manuals as a two-part
instrument, writing in two parts for it and so making three or four
real parts with one or two solo instruments, wind or strings as the case
may be. The most notable of this sort of writing occurs in the fifth
Brandenburg Concerto and in the concerto for Flute, Violin and

Flugel in A minor. The Allegro is also to be found in a solo flugel version. In both these works figuring occurs for the flugel player to execute at such times as he has no two-part writing: the figures stop immediately the second part, usually the treble, enters. As we have seen in the case of the solo flugel concertos, either original or arranged, the slow movements in the Brandenburg No. 5 and in the A minor concertos are for solo instruments only, the string being excluded.

Now with Mozart the case is quite different. In his chamber music the flugel would not be present much after his eighteenth or nineteenth year, and even before that it would do no filling-in of basses. After that time, the pianoforte would be present or not in quite the modern manner; that is to say, usually shoved on one side, and present, somewhat to the chagrin of the string players, for occasions when the composer was ill advised enough to write a pianoforte trio or quartet or quintet.

The flugel comes into this chamber music mostly in his sonatas for that instrument and violin. They were essentially flugel sonatas with a violin almost *ad libitum*. As time went on the violin became more and more important, and by the time Mozart changed to the pianoforte the relationship was that of equality.

Now we have come to the end of our survey of the chief music written for the flugel, and we note great richness and variety of forms, but dominated by only two masters, J. S. Bach and Mozart, owing to the fact (as I think) that the concurrently growing sonata was a thing for the clavichord and not the flugel, so only a portion of the works written were for flugel, while in England and in France all domestic keyboard music written by the great men of those countries was for the harpsichord family right until the introduction of the pianoforte towards the end of the eighteenth century. I have also tried to show that the flugel was the bewigged instrument while the clavichord was the instrument of the soul. The new romantic movement strongly apparent in literature had its effect in clavichord and pianoforte writing, but did not effect the flugel at all. It could not, it could only kill, not bend it. The flugel is not and cannot be a romantic instrument, though as there is a classic tradition behind almost all the early romantics, and especially behind Beethoven, it can be very instructive to play some romantic music on the flugel from time to time. Lastly it may be said that, while the tradition of the harpsichord family never completely died from the domestic keyboard music of other countries, and the influence of the clavecinists (I mean the spiritual not the technical influence) especially is apparent in Debussy and Ravel, in Germany the flugel influence died out completely, but the clavichord influence remained even (if I dare say so) in Brahms.

SHORT BIBLIOGRAPHY TO CHAPTER IV

D. F. Tovey: *Essays in Musical Analysis: Chamber Music "Goldberg Variations"* (Oxford University Press 1944).
Newman Flower: *George Frideric Handel* (Cassell 1929).
Eric Blom: *Mozart* (Dent 1935); *The Letters of Mozart to His Family* (Macmillan 1938, 3 vols.).
C. S. Terry: *Bach's Orchestra* (Oxford University Press 1932).
Charles Burney: *Continental Travels* (Blackie 1927).
Einstein: *Mozart* (Cassell 1947).

[This edition of Burney is listed here as an inexpensive one volume, very much edited and abridged, but not inadequate. Real Burneys, so to speak, are expensive, as his travels rank among antiquarian books. His *History*, however (but not of much use in this chapter), was reprinted this century by Foulis and is cheaper to buy. All "Burneys" are out of print and must be sought for in second-hand bookshops.]

CHAPTER V

THE CLAVICHORD IN GERMANY

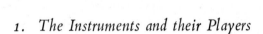

1. The Instruments and their Players

IN the mind's visual eye we must retrace our steps from the long, lean, two-manualled, handsome and aristocratic harpsichord to deal with many thousands of little black boxes, little boxes not unlike the virginals to be found in England in the sixteenth century, but usually far less ornamented and, as musical instruments, far different in quality, but certainly not inferior.

It will be remembered that the virginals were instruments whose strings were vibrated by a pluck: the keyboard, not at the end of (as in the harpsichord) but by the side of the strings, caused the jack to rise, and a thorn plucked at the string, while a roofed bridge bounced the jack back with sufficient escapement to prevent the string being plucked twice.

Looking down on an opened clavichord, there is no immediate visual difference from a virginals. The strings, about as many and about as long, range from one side of the box to the other, and on one side is a set of tuning pins. The keyboard is arranged along the long side of the box, as in a virginals. Then perhaps two differences will appear: firstly, there is no straight bridge over the strings, and secondly, part of each string is damped with a piece of felt. Plainly, if this was a virginals, the instrument would not play. The jack, on being knocked up, would not descend, and would have to be pushed back with the finger. And secondly, the string would not sound, because the end of it was damped.

This is something of a teasing or schoolmasterly way to approach the secret of the clavichord, but it is probably necessary to combat

what may be a general impression, that a clavichord and a virginals
are much the same sort of thing.   Several widely-read books, which,
as dog does not eat dog, will not be nominally eaten at least on this
page, read as though the clavichord, virginals and spinet evolved into
the larger and more resonant harpsichord; while this instrument in
turn evolved into the pianoforte.   In fact, the only resemblance between a clavichord and a pianoforte on the one hand and a virginals
and harpsichord on the other is a visual one.   Coming into a room
containing all four instruments with their cases lowered, an obvious
division would be into the two little ones and the two big ones.
While a harpsichord is an evolved virginals, to stress my point I would
rather agree that the pianoforte was an evolved clavichord rather
than there should be thought to be any relationship between clavichord
and virginals, for they are as apart as a cor anglais and a French horn.

The keyboard of a clavichord is, in the usual way, composed of as
many individual keys as there are notes to be produced.   Each key
can be thought of as a dinner knife.   The ivory handle when pressed
down elevates the steel.   Suppose the end of the steel to be turned up
half an inch, then we have the principle of the clavichord.   Press the
ivory, the steel blade rises and impinges upon a stretched string, which
wishes to vibrate.   Only part of it may do so, for the other part has
been damped.   But one part does vibrate and can be made to continue
to do so by increased and relaxed pressure on the ivory handle.

The difference in sound between a plucked string and a pressed one
is tremendous.   In the old square or modern grand pianoforte the
hammer comes up from below and strikes the string, and then falls
back.   In a clavichord the blade (called a tangent) comes up from
below, and immediate release of the key causes it to fall at once.
Damper action in the pianoforte (I am not alluding to the perpetual dampers on the unused portion of the clavichord strings) stops
the sound on removal of the finger.   So the action in the pianoforte
and in the clavichord is the same when they are played *staccato*.

I have not pictured the complicated mechanism actuating the felted
pianoforte hammer as it does not concern this book.   But this simple
diagram will show, I hope, that there is no essential difference between
staccato strokes in both instruments.   And that for clarity of mind it

is not useless to say that the one instrument is the ancestor of the other, and that neither have anything whatever to do with their accidentally similar neighbours, the virginals and harpsichord.

It is in *legato* playing that one of the great differences between the clavichord and pianoforte occur. When the pianoforte key has been depressed, the finger loses all control. What perpetuates the note is not the hammer head, which has fallen, but the absence of a damper, which absence is due to the retention of the finger on the key. Here again misunderstandings occur because of the clouded minds of some pianoforte teachers. Various touch exercises do not, cannot, alter the quality of a note when struck: no amount of pretty wrist rotating round a stationery finger has the least effect on the pianoforte. Exercises help the fingers and, one fears, have an effect on the imagination of the player, but have no such effect on the ears of the hearer. Anyone who will watch his own playing on a square or grand instrument will realize that all he can possibly do is to strike the wires (actuated primarily by his fingers) at various speeds. As the hammer head is impelled upwards, like a stone from a catapult, there is not even a question of various forces, it is only a question of speed. Great speed produces a loud note; slowness does not even reach the string owing to the counter pull of gravity. Touch on the pianoforte cannot have any meaning as applied to a note in isolation. It can and does have great meaning when applied to a series of notes in a musical phrase. Exercises help to give the individual fingers the necessary muscular powers, and the hearing mind gives them the necessary musical sensitiveness. But the individual tone of each note is a purely mechanical matter, and that is why some people say that the pianoforte is a percussion and not a singing instrument at all: not, in its strict sense, a musical instrument at all.

But no one can say the same thing about the clavichord, which is a singing instrument though, when played staccato, it can be a percussion instrument. The tone of a note taken in isolation owes everything to the finger, which can control it throughout, and nothing to mechanism.

The reason for this is, that the tangent does not automatically fall back immediately after it has touched its string, but remains in contact with this string as long as the finger is on the key. Consequently relaxed and increased pressure will produce a legato touch not too dissimilar from that of a bow on a violin for the comparison to be altogether absurd. Common faults of singing, wind playing or string playing, such as scooping or bulging, are possible to commit on the clavichord; and with the avoidance of faults we have corresponding beauties.

Another characteristic of singing instruments is their power to heighten the pitch of notes at the climax of phrases, a thing which is usually done instinctively, but which the pianoforte cannot do. But the clavichord can do it. It is to be explained this way.

The greater the tension on a string, the more numerous per second are the vibrations and the higher the pitch. A key firmly depressed means a tangent strongly holding up its vibrating string, which tends to become stretched beyond its normal length, and so gives this slight singing heightening of pitch.

At this point it seems necessary to admit what was not mentioned before so as to keep the issue clear, that the virginals and harpsichord share with the pianoforte the percussive faults mentioned: inability of the finger to control quality of tone as apart from quantity, and to heighten pitch. The clavichord stands apart, then, from all keyboard instruments, including the organ and harmonium, in the directness with which the finger plays upon the strings.

There is, therefore, no keyed instrument whatever better calculated to awaken musical abilities (as apart from muscular power), the more so that the pressure on the strings to be exercised by the finger tends to make the instrument out of tune, while its small size and easy access to the tuning pins allows the player to tune it himself. Only, therefore, a real musician can tune and play a clavichord. The ear can be the only arbiter of taste, and brilliant scales and *arpeggii*, anyhow unsuitable to the instrument, cannot cover deficient musical sensibility, and some people think they can do on the pianoforte.

At a large musical party in Vienna given in honour of Dr. Burney in 1772 a child of eight or nine played Scarlatti on a square pianoforte: i.e. a pianoforte which is to the grand as a virginals is to the harpsichord, an instrument in which the keyboard lies parallel to the strings and not at their ends. "The neatness of this child's execution," says Dr. Burney, "did not so much surprise me . . . as her expression. All the pianos and fortes were so judiciously attended to: and there was such a shading of some passages, and force given to others, as nothing but the best teaching, or greatest natural feeling and sensibility could produce. I inquired upon what instrument she usually practised at home, and was answered, 'the clavichord'. This accounts for her expression, and convinces me that children should learn upon that . . .

and be obliged to give an expression . . . to whatever is their first tune."

The origin of these subtle and delicate instruments was possibly earlier than the beginnings of the virginals. While the virginals required a certain degree of evolution in the mere mechanism, a monochord may have required almost none at all, if we imagine a monochord to be an instrument with a single string, damped at one end, and played upon by a series of tangents each with its own key. Those tangents further removed from their keys would bring into play a greater length of vibrating string and thus attain a deeper pitch. So quite a series of notes could be struck, perhaps a whole, no doubt modal, scale. But chords could not be struck, and such use was perhaps outside the idea of the original inventor, this being, according to the late learned Francis Galpin, Pythagoras himself, who used the instrument for scientific reasons. But by the Middle Ages the idea of having more than one string gained favour until at length there were almost as many strings as there were keys, but not quite as many. In the treble the distance along a string required for a semitone is small, and so the strings in the treble were used for more than one tangent, and the clavichord was *gebunden*. Some writers claim that this showed that such instruments could not have been tuned in equal temperament, but I do not myself see why.

In a monochord there is great ease in tuning. If the keys and tangents have all been correctly spaced and adjusted in the first place, the string can be tuned by any convenient note, and all the other notes will then sound true. The same principle applies surely to *gebunden* clavichords: the tangents at the treble end would have to be initially made for equal temperament, and the tuning of each string to one of its several notes would bring the others into line. But a *gebunden* clavichord built on perfect temperament could not then be retuned for equal temperament, it is true, but it is a somewhat theoretical truth. Intervals in the treble impress themselves less on the ear than in the middle registers, and it is doubtful if a clavichord tuned to equal temperament almost throughout its range except for its treble would be unplayable. Chords could be struck, for their constituent notes usually affect the middle registers. A series of thirds might indeed be impossible of execution if in the treble, but this sort of writing came in later in the eighteenth century and was essentially harpsichordic or pianistic. There is one series of treble sixths and no series of treble thirds in the whole of Bach's *Sinfonia*, music which may be

taken as indisputably clavichordic, and only a very few times have
two notes above the treble stave to be struck or held simultaneously.
I am however not adducing this in proof of anything, only to say that
I do not think the prevalence of *gebunden* clavichords at any time or
place necessarily means that tuning in equal temperament was not
practised.

Eventually, however, clavichords were made with one string to
each tangent, and they were called *bundfrei* clavichords. The next
step in evolution was the Silbermann clavichord. Silbermann was
the German inventor of the Italian-originated pianoforte and the
supplier of grand pianofortes to Sans Souci, on which J. S. Bach played
when he visited Frederick the Great nearly half-way through the century. Silbermann did away with the dampers by causing each tangent
to strike exactly in the middle of each string, both portions could then
vibrate, doubling the quantity of the sound and improving its quality,
while the *bebung* (the power of singing legato as explained) and the
heightened pitch were just as possible as on the older models. In the
problem of heightened pitch, it is obvious that the tangent always had
increased the tension in both sides of the string, but in the old damped
models part of this tension was unheard.

The clavichord-making industry of Germany reached, about the
time of Bach's visit to Potsdam, great heights of activity. The decades of birth of the pianoforte saw the clavichord made in hundreds
from one factory alone, and exported as far as Archangel, the Arctic
port of Catherine the Great. Its compass was being continually
expanded, and the late Carl Engel, writing in *The Musical Times*, in
1879, gives the following for an instrument made near Hanover in
1780: the lozenge shapes denote the compass of Bach's Chromatic
Fantasia, music written at Cöthen in 1723 or before.

By 1800 clavichords were being made with two strings to each
note, but there progress ceased. Pianoforte touch can be eased or
strengthened at will: it has nothing to do with the stringing or tension
of the instrument itself. If a pianoforte had a keyboard with a very
hard touch, a different keyboard with a very easy touch could be fitted
instead. For all the key has to do is to sling the hammer upwards.
This is far from being the case in the clavichord, where the tangent is

part of the key, going up at the other side of the fulcrum when the finger presses it down. Two strings and deep notes (entailing long wires, and consequently long tangents) require a heavy touch, while the treble notes would have something like the old light touch. On a pianoforte keyboard, touch is uniform, for it has nothing to do with the length of wire which the hammer will eventually hit.

Clavichords made in the twentieth century usually go back to Bach's days: they are *bundfrei* but not Silbermann, have one string to a note, and a comfortable compass of about four octaves, just enough to play the Chromatic Fantasia, and ample for the *Sinfonia* and most of the "forty-eight" of *The Well Tempered Clavier*. Real late eighteenth-century freaks like clavichords with two manuals and four-feet and sixteen-feet couplers were rarely made and need not now be more than mentioned.

Germany was the country of the clavichord. The instrument was known in other lands, and no doubt even played, but no music was specially written for it, and it was treated as a cheap and indifferent substitute for a virginal. It just was not understood.

Germany is a loose word, never meaning much in particular, and even less before 1806 when the Holy Roman Empire crumbled. But either I say Germany or the Holy Roman Empire, and the one is shorter than the other.

In this huge patchwork of big and little kings, from rulers of European Powers like Frederick to tiny little towns like Celle, nominally directly under the Emperor but a very long way from Vienna, there were patches of hopeful modernism. These places were the free towns like Hamburg and Leipzig; Hamburg, where the opera attracted Handel and the organ-playing attracted J. S. Bach; Leipzig, where J. S. Bach reared his large double family and was *in loco parentis* to so many students; Leipzig, from which a dispersion of Bachs took place on the death of the old man in 1750, a dispersion which has fructified music almost to this day; Leipzig, in which the greatest of publishing firms was started, Breitkopf and Hartel.

In this confusion of great, middling and small countries; with Courts trying to rival Versailles; with military Courts; with Courts like that of the Duke of Wurtemberg whose "passion for music was carried to such excess as to ruin both his country and people, and to oblige his subjects to remonstrate against his prodigality at the diet of the empire" (Burney in 1772); with teeming merchant cities; with Lutheran preachers and Catholic priests; and with the Imperial Court itself at Vienna; there was much room for a middle class to grow. There were preachers, priests, school teachers, writers of theological books (and how many there seem to have been!), indifferent poets like Bach's own Neumeister and Franck, gentlemen capable of addressing the deity in terms of erotic endearment, organists like all the Bachs, barber-surgeons like the elder Handel and new publishers like Breitkopf. The whole Empire was far less centralized than the kingdom of France, the Emperor was far less of a sun than Louis XIV, and in Germany there may have seemed a prospect of a middle class arising, so diverse in religion, profession, ideas and business as to form a body of immense value to a state. Only in England was there to be found anything similar.

In Bohemia, part of the Empire, Dr. Burney found a school, typical of the country, "full of little children of both sexes, from six to ten or eleven years old, who were reading, writing, playing on violins, oboes, bassoons and other instruments. The organist had in a small room of his house four clavichords. . . ."

When a schoolmaster of Leipzig wrote out keyboard lessons for his eldest son they were for the clavichord. When the local publisher put out a book on tuning, the clavichord was mentioned first. *Anweisung wie man Claviere, Clavecins und Orgeln nach einer mechanischen Art in allen zwolf Tonen* . . . etc.; a long title.

Much could be written in a sentimental vein of the varied middle classes of the Empire and their love for their national instrument, the gentle and musicianly clavichord.

I wish to make the point that the clavichord is an introvert instrument, and the spinet an extrovert, without appearing too far-fetched. In both Germany and England the middle classes were increasing in numbers and in wealth. But in Germany the rulers could pursue the most fantastic caprices unchecked by any definite action of their subjects. The singularly unpleasant father of a not likeable son, King Frederick William I of Prussia, required a regiment of tall men, and H. N. Gerber, a student at Leipzig University, was over six feet. He was a pupil of J. S. Bach for music, who considered it wiser for him to hide his talents in an obscure organistship in the country than to risk the closer attentions of the King's recruiting sergeants. So Gerber retired to the organ console of a country church and devoted his leisure to making clavichords.

In England the powerful Nonconformist conscience has never admitted any gap between art and life. Beauty in art should induce beauty in living. Noble music should induce noble action. This ideal never has been the case, and sometimes the English middle class drape their heroes, Handel, Mozart, Mendelssohn, Beethoven, in clean togas and newly plucked laurel, and sometimes (as recently) indulge in hurt iconoclasm. The sneers at "Bloomsbury" have exactly the same motive as the deification of Shakespeare at Stratford. Art and life should be one. Meanwhile the individual in his actions will try and make them one. The spinet player seeing a woman dying of fever with a child at her breast would, if he were a Squire Allworthy, bury the mother decently and adopt the child. Were he (or she) a Mrs. Jukes, he would hire stout fellows to haul the woman off and smother the baby. But there would be action, and action to keep the surface of things clean, for the Nonconformist conscience has not always taken to the little bit about whited sepulchres and the outside of the platter.

But the organist of Bohemia with his four clavichords, and the schoolmaster of Leipzig with at least as many, what would they have done? If the history of central Europe helps us at all, with its pattern of a patient middle class allowing every sort of horror and wickedness to happen unrebuked around them, my answer is, that these musicians retired to their clavichords, went on setting their sanctimonious texts, and the woman went on dying outside, for art is art and life is something quite different, and there is no cause and effect between them.

The clavichord is a lonely instrument, of most sufficient sound for the player, but useless for concerted music. But the spinet player looks forward to having a harpsichord, and playing sonatas for flute or violin, or adding the figured bass to a quartet of two violins and viola da gamba, or flute and violin and viola da gamba, or accompanying a singer, or going to the opera and hearing there the harpsichord holding the orchestra and stage together. While the clavichord is a lonely instrument, the harpsichord family are social. Art and life are the same thing, and if they are not, they had better be made so, the harpsichordists seem to say.

It follows that while virginals, spinet, and harpsichord cases were often of valuable polished wood or painted by artists of the calibre of Rubens, the poor clergymen, scholars and village schoolmasters of Germany were content with cases of plain deal stained black or dark brown. Some, of course, were painted. Nuns forced to the clavichord by a desire for secular music but a fear of being overheard might paint the lid in spare time, but usually the case was as plain as the binding of the volume of theological poetry which lay upon it.

2. The Composers

Although such composers as Froberger and Pachelbel wrote music for keyboard instruments, some of it very lovely, it was usually the organ which was in their minds. Their Toccatas, Canzonas, Capriccios, Ricercares, Fantasias, Choral Preludes and Ciaconas are not clavichord music, though possibly their Suites are. These little works, on the whole shorter and a good deal less vigorous than the Suites of Purcell, are somewhat dull, one or two melodious Sarabandes apart.

Kuhnau is more important to us: he was the predecessor of J. S. Bach in Leipzig. This city seems to have gone through three phases in the eighteenth century. In Kuhnau's time there was an Opera in being during the famous Leipzig Fair, an Opera, it is true, inferior to that of Dresden, but still, an Opera enticing enough to make the elder choir boys restless. One or two even ran away to join it. There was also a secular musical gathering, the equivalent of the public concerts which for a generation had been held in London. Coffee, too, had recently been introduced and something of a metropolitan social musical life was developing. Kuhnau came up against this. The city fathers, as uncouth, tactless and slow as any other specimens of an unpolished race, appear to have trodden on everybody's toes impartially, but Kuhnau felt only the pain in his own corns. What with teaching Latin, punishing disobedient boys but not punishing them too hard (Article 9), attending morning and afternoon at the singing class, asking the burgomaster politely if he might go to Halle on business, and finding new scruffy urchins for his choirs, Kuhnau's life was that of an overdriven usher.

And one fears that the life of J. S. Bach would have been little better had it not been for his tumultuous household, his genius and his ability to ignore petty officialdom—much to the annoyance of the petty officials. He did, however, put up with it, a thing which you feel Handel would never have done: but then Handel was a harpsichordist and after his childhood perhaps never touched a clavichord, not even the one at Maidstone, reputed to be his on doubtful authority. During Bach's term of office in Leipzig the Opera waned and vanished.

Telemann went to Hamburg. There was a pietetic religious revival which J. S. Bach disliked but which nevertheless may have influenced some of his music through the texts he set. On his death and after the dispersal of his household a third period of Little Metropolitanism set in, and this is the Leipzig we meet when reading Goethe.

Eighteenth-century composers all have their moonlight anecdotes of childhood: J. S. Bach copying music locked from him by his elder brother, Arne playing the clavichord in the King Street garret, and Handel also playing a clavichord in his Halle bedroom, smuggled into him, Sir Newman Flower suggests,[1] by his kind Aunt Anna. We do not know what the boy George Frederic could have played, for a little later when the Duke of Saxe-Weissenfels began to take an interest in his musical education, Handel seems to have been but a beginner. After all, he may not have been more than seven at the time.

J. S. Bach came to Leipzig to take up his varied and onerous duties of Cantor at the School of St. Thomas with a new wife and several children. He was to father many more children, and to have in his household many pupils as lodgers, and to be daily visited, not only by his own pupils of St. Thomas, but by many university students. In his quarters by the church were beds, chairs, tables, kitchen utensils, theological books, pile upon pile of manuscripts, either his own compositions or copies of the music of others—manuscripts written by himself, by his wife, by his sons and by his pupils, full scores and parts. In the midst of all this were all kinds of musical instruments, leaning on barrels of wine, hung up by nails from the wall and used when suitable as tables. They included perhaps as many as nine clavichords (i.e. he had five at his death and he gave four to his youngest sons), a spinet, a harpsichord with pedals, two *lautenclaviere* or clavichords fitted with lute strings to produce a lute tone, one *lautencymbal* or harpsichord with three manuals fitted with lute strings (this instrument was got rid of before his death), and as many violins, violas and cellos as his large family and pupilage needed for concerti grossi. The cupboard containing his silver plate must have often been inaccessible to Anna Magdalena because of the instruments piled on the black leather chairs, though no doubt Bach himself saw to it that his flat-topped writing desk was kept clear. Of all the households known to history I wonder if any excite more curiosity and sympathy than the

---

[1] *George Frederic Handel*, Cassell, 1923.

Bach one in Leipzig? If one could spend a day as an historic ghost it would be the house next to the Thomaskirk that I should choose, even before Gough Square. How on earth were all the adults, children, instruments, books, manuscripts and household utensils fitted in? How did they all get out of bed, perform such morning toilets as Leipzig society demanded, and gather for breakfast?

J. S. Bach said in a letter written from Leipzig in 1730, "I can already form a concert in my own family," and by this term he may have embraced his pupils, too, numbering among them the seventeen-year-old Krebs, Agricola, Doles who afterwards became Cantor himself, and Kirnberger. We may imagine this musical team, strengthened by Bach's own sons, Friedemann, Emanuel and Christian especially, and any musician who happened to be passing through the town and who was certain of an invitation to Bach's hospitable board, sitting down to the concertos for one, two, three or four claviers, with strings. Whether spinet tone was mingled with clavichord we do not know, but the two tones, so very distinct, do form an agreeable contrast to one another, and the antiphonal effects often to be found in these concertos, often indeed to the extent of repeating identical notes in what, if the works are played upon pianofortes, appears to be in a pointless manner, may be arguments for the probability of a spinet-clavichord effect being intended.

These family concerts were doubtless conducted by Bach himself from a harpsichord, filling in the figured bass even of keyboard concertos, and doing so, as one of the pupil's (Mizler) himself wrote later, "in such a way that one imagines that it is a concertino part and that the melodic line played by his right hand had been specially composed beforehand". We may imagine that those of the household, like Kirnberger and Doles, who also attended lectures at the university, were both unable and unwilling to tear themselves from the concert to retire to their rooms quietly (if quietness was possible in that household) to prepare their drier studies for the next day.

As Bach grew older his household did not, for childish sons and pupils grew up to take the place of departing youth, and Bach himself was still in the midst of them, though inspiring more and more awe. Fetis is the authority for a charming story of one of the latter-day pupils who became himself a teacher, and when any student had done exceptionally well he would be placed before a curtained portrait, and the cords would solemnly be pulled to reveal the heavy features of a man in a big wig—J. S. Bach himself.

Much more startling than the move of the Byrd household, only two of them and perhaps with one pair of virginals, from Lincoln to London, was the move of the Bach family, so many of them and so many instruments, from Cöthen in Anhalt to Leipzig, not that it was far. Twenty miles took the family to Halle, where they possibly staged, and the next day another twenty miles to Leipzig. What did John Sebastian do? Play the organ of the Liebfrauenkirche with its sixty-three stops and let the family go on ahead to get the new place warm for him?

Many years later his visit, accompanied by Wilhelm Freidemann to Sans Souci to meet his son, C. P. E. Bach, who must have already bewildered the old gentleman with his clavichord sonatas, was his last long journey. His reception by Frederick is famous, but belongs to the history of the harpsichord. The clavichord may have been the instrument for which his Court musician, C. P. E. Bach, preferred to write his new sort of music, but it was the aristocratic harpsichord which Frederick required him to accompany on when Royalty played the flute.

C. P. E. Bach was not altogether comfortable in his work at Sans Souci, and on the death of his father, which took place only three years after his visit, he applied for the vacant Cantorship at Leipzig. His marriage had added to his expenses, one may suppose, at a greater rate than increments in salary and regular promotion had done in that very official and military Potsdam Court. We are told that Frederick was difficult to accompany, as he took such liberties with the time. It was not even as if Frederick condescended to interest himself much in C. P. E. Bach's clavichord sonatas: Graun, and especially Quantz, his flute tutor, wrote music much more to his taste. It is difficult to assess the exact degree of Frederick's musicianship, but I do not think he was equal to an ordinary amateur chamber music player of to-day, for it was not chamber music which he played, but solo flute music with an obsequious accompanist. By the way, the evidence shows that C. P. E. Bach did what music students are warned not to do, and what his father strictly forbade; he composed on the clavichord.

Anyhow, he did not please the Leipzig selection committee. Perhaps they felt unwilling to have another Bach in office after the intransigeance of the last office-holder of that name. He later competed for an organistship at Zittau, a small town on the borders of Saxony and Bohemia well over a hundred miles from Berlin. His fellow applicants were old Leipzig scholars, his brother W. F. Bach and Altnikol, his father's last pupil, and J. L. Krebs, "the best crab in the brook" (an atrocious German pun). But not one of these four students of the great Bach secured the post. So C. P. E. Bach had to return to the flute-playing martinet of a king whom he served, sitting nightly at the harpsichord; while the fiddlers stood like sentries on each side, the cello breathed down his neck to look at the bass line, and Frederick stood apart, as an officer should, from the mere musicians, and played the easy passages quickly and the difficult passages slowly until it was time to move to the next section of his self-appointed time-table.

But 1753 is a year marked in C. P. E. Bach's life for an event to us much more important than the meeting of four ex-Leipzig dispersees to compete in Zittau, for his book *Versuch uber die wahre Art das Klavier zu spielen* was published. This is probably the single most important text-book published on the way to play the clavichord, and is something of the German equivalent of Couperin's *L'Art de toucher le clavecin*. Like Couperin, Bach dwells much on ornamentation, and quotations from the *Versuch* will be found in the next section of this chapter, which deals with clavichord music rather than its composers.

It was not until seventeen years after his father's death that C. P. E. Bach managed to find suitable employment out of reach of Frederick, when he went to Hamburg to succeed Telemann, who had just died. Bach was escaping from a reluctant Greatness who, however, was possibly the less tenacious as advancing age made his wind for the flute less capacious and he entertained thoughts of taking up the harpsichord. As an accompanist C. P. E. Bach was not so essential. Here in Hamburg he was visited by Dr. Burney.

The instant I entered, he conducted me upstairs, into a large and elegant music room, furnished with pictures, drawings, and prints of more than a hundred and fifty eminent musicians: among whom, there are many Englishmen, and original portraits in oil, of his father and grandfather. After I had looked at these, M. Bach was so obliging as to sit down to his Silbermann clavichord, and favourite instrument, upon which he played three or four of his choicest and most difficult compositions, with the delicacy, precision, and spirit, for which he is so justly celebrated among his countrymen. In the pathetic and slow movements, whenever he had a long note to express, he absolutely contrived to produce, from his instrument, a cry of sorrow and complaint, such as can only be effected upon the clavichord, and perhaps by himself.

After dinner, which was elegantly served, and cheerfully eaten,

I prevailed upon him to sit down again to a clavichord, and he played, with little intermission, till near eleven o'clock at night. During this time, he grew so animated and possessed, that he not only played, but looked like one inspired. His eyes were fixed, his under lip fell, and drops of effervescence distilled from his countenance. He said, if he were to be set to work frequently, in this manner, he should grow young again. He is now fifty-nine, rather short in stature, with black hair and eyes, and brown complexion, has a very animated countenance, and is of a cheerful and lively disposition . . . .[1]

Wilhelm Friedemann, J. S. Bach's eldest son, ranks second only to his younger brother C. P. E. as a composer for the clavichord. The reason why he ranks second is not because of any deficiency in talent for composition, for many, among whom I would wish to number myself, prefer his music to that of his brother. But he is not so important, nevertheless, partly because he wrote no *Versuch* and partly because the music for which he is best known, fugues and polonaises, did not initiate the classical sonata of the Viennese period. As C. P. E. Bach has definite claims to be the John the Baptist of Haydn, he inevitably ranks high in musical history, while W. F. Bach can be passed over, for he forms no link in any ascertainable chain.

About the time of his visit with his father to Potsdam he secured an appointment at the Liebfrauenkirche in Halle, an office called by some, "musical director", and which may have meant presiding at the harpsichord, for that instrument had made its way in some churches into the organ loft, where it supplanted the organ in the filling-in of the figured bass. Fourteen years before, he had been organist of a church in Dresden, and the interval had been spent at home in Leipzig as his father's closest friend and companion. It was he, for instance, who went to Halle on behalf of his father to meet Handel to invite him to Leipzig. Handel, who had been travelling to Italy to see his old mother and was on his way back to London, felt disinclined to turn on his tracks.

On his father's death W. F. went to Leipzig for the funeral and returned to his duties in the church where, a generation before, the boy Handel had been taught the organ.

J. S. Bach did not leave much property, either in cash or in kind, and all the family desired to turn as much as they could, instruments,

---

[1] Present State of Music in Germany, the Netherlands and United Provinces, 1773.

snuff-boxes and the like, into cash. C. P. E. Bach sold the stereoplates of *The Art of Fugue*, and W. F. Bach tried to auction the manuscript of this work. Most biographers have said, shame on them! That is because we are wise after the event. This is not to say it is not pathetic: the Leipzig dispersal and all it suggests was most sad, and anyone reading the details of the Will and a list of the goods and how they were divided as set out in the third volume of the monumental Spitta will surely be moved to think of the vanity of human effort. Biographers have also blamed both sons of the first marriage for not helping to support their stepmother, but a little note on the gift of three clavichords to the youngest son seems to hint a rift between the children of the two marriages.

Anyhow, W. F. Bach seemed already to be in financial difficulties which perhaps culminated in the loss of his position in Halle and his removal to Berlin in 1764. In the Prussian capital he taught for a living and had among his pupils Sara Levi, the grandmother of Mendelssohn. He still composed, and six clavier fugues written in his sixty-ninth year were dedicated to Princess Amalia, one of the King's sisters of about his own age. However advanced in years these elderly people were, it did not prevent Friedemann from being jealous and unhappy when the princess also favoured Kirnberger, his old Leipzig comrade. Friedemann is supposed to have been drunken and dissolute but, if so, it is surprising that he lived to be over seventy, that he enjoyed the friendship of an elderly and very Prussian princess and had among his pupils the daughter of a wise and wealthy Jewish banker.

We must now turn to Joseph Haydn. This boy had come to Vienna from a village lower down the Danube to sing in the cathedral choir. He was turned out at the age of seventeen to fend for himself in the great capital, and was befriended by another ex-choirboy whose voice had not failed him so badly as Haydn's had, for it had matured into a tenor of sufficient quality as to get him work in the choir of another church. Haydn's pleasant and gentle nature made him other friends, and a timely loan from a tradesman and some modest pupils enabled him to have his own *menage*, a garret in Vienna a hundred years before Rudolfo's in Paris but, one gathers, very similar. Here was his clavichord and we picture him playing to himself the first six sonatas of C. P. E. Bach when the weather was not too cold or when he had a fire. These sonatas had recently been composed and a copy had been sent from the Composer at Potsdam to old J. S. Bach (who was still alive: we tend to think of Haydn as belonging to a much later epoch), who no doubt thought little of them. But Haydn thought much of them, and took C. P. E. as his model. Haydn grubbed about in Vienna for a little more than a decade in this manner, when he came under the patronage of Prince Esterhazy and began to spend most of the year in the country where "he was forced to become original" (i.e. to develop from C. P. E.) and later became pianistic and forgot the clavichord. I think it is of use and of importance to differentiate between the early keyboard styles of Haydn and of Mozart: Haydn was a clavichord player by birth, disposition and taste: the courtly and fiery Mozart was from his earliest years a harpsichord player. Later on of course they both turned to the pianoforte. Very possibly during the period of his poverty in Vienna Haydn had to play the harpsichord for Porpora, the titular Kappelmeister to that King of Poland who was also Elector of Saxony: this distinguished and various musician was in the decline of his life engaged in writing violin sonatas for which one assumes the tone of the clavichord would have been too weak. But Haydn's mind was not turned outwardly to vocal or chamber music, but inwardly towards the development of this wonderful new dramatic and harmonic form, the sonata of C. P. E. Bach.

Vienna, however, was too much under Italian influence to be a great clavichord centre, which was essentially a German instrument, and indeed the times in general were growing hard for this quietly impassioned predecessor of the already growing pianoforte. Only in Bonn, at a time when Haydn was already becoming a great man and had turned to the new instrument with no less a youth than Pleyel for his pupil, might the clavichord be heard by an imaginery spirit of history, for the child Beethoven was driven to it hours upon hours every day by a father who saw in himself a second Leopold Mozart.

3. The Music

Clavichord music had essentially as short a life and as confined a geographical environment as virginal music. From the works of Kuhnau to about Haydn's Op. 14 is about as long as the earlier virginal compositions of Byrd to the death of Orlando Gibbons. The clavichord and its music was confined, as far as artistic importance went, to

Germany, and the virginals and its music was confined, with the same modification, to England.

Like virginal music, clavichord music is very diverse, ranging from a five-part fugue to a simple tune and accompaniment, from a little Prelude for teaching to a long piece of programme music.

Unlike virginal music, however, the method of classification is not by forms, but by composers. Kuhnau, J. S. Bach, W. F. Bach, C. P. E. Bach and Haydn had their own individualistic styles to such an extent that it is the composer that counts, not the nominal form in which the piece was written. General considerations of ornamentation are, for instance, useless: J. S. Bach used far less ornament than his son C. P. E., whose *Versuch* can only be applied to his own music and not to that of others. While the French school rose to Couperin and fell away from Couperin, leaving that great composer as the classic by whom the others are to be measured, the German clavichord school fell from great artistic heights to an experimental period, rising in turn to very different but equally great heights, while before the peak was reached, progress was diverted to another instrument. There is therefore no single great clavichord classic, but the music flows backwards and forward like a tide between J. S. Bach's *Sinfonia* and Haydn's Op. 14, two such very different works that it is amazing that the two men lived eighteen years as contemporaries.

Kuhnau, Bach's predecessor at the Thomasschule, has much the same effect on a writer of music, on this writer on music at any rate, as a lost sheep scripturally has on the shepherd. This minor master is usually represented as an early Richard Strauss busy depicting the flight of the stone from David's sling to Goliath's forehead by a parabola of semiquavers.

His *Clavierubung*, first part published in 1689 and second part in 1692, gives us Suites in the traditional forms, Allemande, Courante, Sarabande, galanterien and Gigue. The movements are about as long and as evolved as in J. S. Bach's French Suites, and are similar in their melodious approachableness. They are not particularly ornamented, and anyone who has played and enjoyed the French Suites will like Kuhnau's *Clavierubung* provided he does not expect J. S. Bach's genius thrown in. There is nothing in it whatever of a descriptive nature, any more than there is in the French Suites.

The baroque title-page of Kuhnau's 1696 publication may lead us to expect something a little more unusual.

JOHANN KUHNAUENS
FRISCHE CLAVIER FRUCHTEN
oder
SIEBEN SUONATEN
von guter Invention ured Manier
auff dem Clavier
re zu Spielen
Leipzig Anno 1696

The "fresh fruit" referred to in the title clutters up the above title-page to such an extent that the logical flow of the lettering suffers. In a very small space left by the apples, pears and grapes and by the hideous curliwigs of the lettering, is suffered to appear a meek clavichord with the usual and conventional oblong score, this one indeed with a mere three staves per page.

These sonatas, however, although they show something new, do not do so in any programmatic way. It is merely that Kuhnau has adapted the *sonata da chiesa* to the clavichord. The *sonata da chiesa* is distinct from the *sonata da camera*: the first was originally meant for the church, the second for the chamber; the first was a series of movements, slow, quick, slow, quick, as made familiar to us in the violin sonatas of both J. S. Bach and Handel, the other started the Suite in its colourful career. But for some reason while *sonata da camera* were applied to solo keyboard instruments, the *sonata da chiesa* usually was not. But Kuhnau did so, and may have been the first to have done so. The *sonata da camera* suits the pianoforte admirably and may be presumed to have suited the clavichord. Both instruments can sustain a melody and give importance to a bass, diminishing the middle harmonies to less importance. Now a spinet can do none of this and a harpsichord only two of the three things. And this is perhaps the reason why it was in clavichord Germany that the *sonata da chiesa* was adapted to the keyboard solo, and not in Italy. Sometimes Kuhnau includes a fugue with plenty of air in the parts, so it is effective on a keyboard. The D minor Suite of Arne is very nearly a Kuhnau *sonata da chiesa*, and the J. C. Bach harpsichord sonata in C minor starts off like one, but lacks the third slow movement. Kuhnau was the only man, however, to do the job thoroughly in no less than seven sonatas, and I think the clavichord was the only instrument really to do it with.

Kuhnau's music in the "Fresh Fruits" is graver and less obviously tuneful (but not less melodious) than in his *Clavierubung*, and these seven sonatas perhaps represent his best work for the clavichord.

Lastly come his "Bible Sonatas", published in 1700, of which the David and Goliath is usually dwelt upon by historians. But musically the Saul sonata is both better and more typical. The adagio recitative which builds up to a noble fugue is not spoiled by its programme, but is enjoyable as pure music. David's harp is expressed in *arpeggii* and Saul's melancholy in the subject and the development of the fugue, which is interrupted from time to time by *arpeggio* passages in thirds and sixths, representing the unsubdued harpist. It is not until the second movement that David begins to succeed, his patient grumbling in the tenor register from time to time, while David at last manages a melody—rather a short-winded one it is true. In the last movement Saul expresses his joy at recovered sanity in a strange piece in dotted rhythm, which by most of the conventions of the time should be played in a stately manner with the semiquavers short and the dotted notes long. This rhythm is associated with the regal state, with the opening of operatic overtures, with the introductory symphony of cantatas for ducal birthdays, and the like. Saul was a king once more, and no longer a muttering imbecile, Kuhnau seems to say. Played to some-one unacquainted with the programme, the first movement would sound like an eccentric but extremely effective grand toccata and fugue, the second like a pleasing insipidity and the third like a first movement for some odd reason played last. But the musical value is far greater than the eccentricity due to the programme, and the G minor fugue is one of the finest pre-J. S. Bach clavichord fugues ever written.

When we come to J. S. Bach there is the difficulty of splitting his music up into that intended for the clavichord and that for the harpsi-chord. Both instruments have their partisans. Some say that when Bach in a title-page used the word "clavier" he meant the clavichord, but I do not see how this contention can be sustained in view of some of the contents of the *Clavierubung*, a work published in four parts which was partly designed to follow in the tradition of Kuhnau but which broke new ground as well. There is in Part III, for instance, the series of Chorale Preludes known as the "Catechism Preludes" which are organ music, though for manuals only. J. S. Bach, like many other composers of his times, used the word clavier at large, to mean, in fact, nothing in particular, and it is the internal evidence to be found in a composition which should guide us as to the instru-ment to be chosen.

The partisans of the harpsichord are led by Madame Wandowska, who, it seems to me, disregards the clavichord as a sort of kitchen instrument unfitted altogether for such aristocratic music as Bach's, all of which she seems to think playable on the harpsichord, and actually so plays most of it.   All of it is, of course, playable on the harpsichord, though not all of it is equally effective thereon.   But not all of it is playable on the clavichord, for there are passages in such works as the "Goldberg Variations" which can only be properly managed on an instrument with two manuals.

If we put on one side all such obviously harpsichord music as this, and on the other the teaching pieces written mainly for W. F. Bach as clavichord music, we have remaining to us a quantity of music which might be played on either.   And perhaps too daringly I would wish to defend the proposition that this music is aesthetically equally suitable for either clavichord or harpsichord, but this does not mean that it should be played on either instrument in the same manner. There are some who regard the C major Prelude of the First Book of *The Well Tempered Clavier* as clavichord music, to be played slowly with the minims held and to be heard through the *arpeggio* figure, everything quiet, harmonic and mystic.

But others regard this Prelude as a series of brisk arpeggio chords, clear and dashing, and even (some go so far) as to imagine "echo" effects, though personally I can imagine nothing so monotonous as each chordal repetition played on a manual with *piano* registration.

If, therefore, this Prelude is played on a pianoforte it appears to follow that it can be played quietly and slowly with some use of both pedals (the damper pedal is the nearest the pianoforte can get to a *Bebung*), or quickly and with clarity, with some difference of quantity of tone at the chordal repetitions and with no use of either pedal.   In other words, there is no right and wrong way to play quite a good deal of Bach, provided each interpretation is logical within itself and does not mix quasi clavichord style with a quasi harpsichord.

It is indeed a mystery of our art that some music can be interpreted in two quite different ways, slowly and quietly, even (as in the F minor Prelude and Fugue from the Second Book, with its either solemn or comic passages made so by context and by either slow or fast playing) to the extent of giving contradictory impressions.

 from the Prelude

 from the Fugue

There is no equivalent to this in any other art except perhaps in Moslem mosaic, when the same pattern and gorgeous colour might suggest the majesty of Allah when adorning the ceiling of a mosque, and the eroticism of the *Arabian Nights* if found in a pasha's palace.

The essential clavichord music of J. S. Bach to be played in no other way but quietly and easily and with perfect vocal phrasing and such use of either pianoforte pedal which artistry needs, is to be found in the Inventions and *Sinfonia*, music written for the education of his son Friedemann but nevertheless music which has an absolute value as of the greatest beauty needing extremely finished technique if its quality is fully to be realized.

J. S. Bach's fingering for his son does not strike one as any obvious advance on that of Couperin in *L'Art de Toucher*. Here, for instance, are right- and left-hand scales in C, taken from the *Clavier-Buchlein* in a sort of exercise introduction preceding the two part Inventions.

J. S. Bach later wrote an explanatory title to a manuscript of the Inventions written out later, in which he said that the manuscript was "a true guide, in which Amateurs of the Clavichord, and in particular beginning Amateurs, will find clearly expressed rules for playing in two and in three parts . . . and, most important of all, a *cantabile* touch. . . ."

It is indeed this *cantabile* touch which renders the clavichord different from and superior to all other keyboard instruments.

Other undoubted clavichord music is one of his two "family" pieces, called, in Italian, *Capriccio sopra la lontananza del suo fratello dilettissimo*. The other, with passages indicating I think equal suitability for clavichord or harpsichord is in Latin, *Capriccio in honorem Johan Christoph Bacchii*. Kuhnau, by the way, had equally felicitous deviations into Italian, his Saul and David sonata being entitled *Saul malinconico e trastullato per mezzo della Musica*. But to return to the Capriccio for Bach's brother bound for Sweden as an oboe player. After an Adagio representing his friends trying to persuade him not

to leave cosy Thuringia, there is a movement in which they make out
that the journey will be full of difficulties and dangers, and the theme
of this fugue (for such it is) is the most heavily ornamented subject
that Bach ever wrote.

Commentators say that the ornaments represent the difficulties and
dangers! Only the treble line is ornamented, the alto tenor and bass
entries are plain. Whether this is intentional and has some programmatic meaning, or whether it was a species of musical shorthand,
it being taken for granted that the ornamentations should be inserted
in all voices I have no idea: the more ornamented the lower voices the
greater the difficulties and dangers, no doubt! This Capriccio is
remarkable for a figured bass in the succeeding movement, one in
which the friends weep *Adagiosissimo*, for the clavichord is not a figured
bass instrument, and the presence of figures under a ground bass with
no treble at the first enunciation suggests quick writing and musical
shorthand. When the right hand enters it is with such a typically
clavichord "weepy" figure that it must be given here, first as written
and secondly as the convention of the time required it to be played.

The ensuing three movements are of no particular clavichord
interest, the last two indeed, *Aria di Postiglione* and *Fuga all' Imitazione
della Cornetta di Postiglione* being equally effective on a harpsichord.

We can perhaps now leave the clavichord music of the greatest
master of this instrument who ever lived, provided just a few words
are given to the subject of ornamentation. J. S. Bach's keyboard
ornamentation in general is dealt with in the third section of the chapter dealing with the flugel (i.e. harpsichord) in Germany. There
appears to have been no difference in his use of signs for either instrument. There therefore merely remains here to be discussed the
question of what ornaments should be used when playing clavichord
music on the pianoforte. Many authorities say few, or none, but my
own opinion is that they should all be played, so as to induce the

player to take the music (I mean the clavichord music) slowly and intimately.   It is obvious that the sound will be ugly if, for instance, the G minor "dangerous travel" fugue quoted above is taken fast and loudly.   By the pianist putting in all the ornamentation he will be driven to imagine he is playing the clavichord.   And this means that I think a professional pianist should not play clavichord Bach on a modern grand concert pianoforte in the Albert Hall.   The result would be a worse transcription than the late Sir Henry Wood's astonishing orchestration of the F minor "Friends' Lament" quoted above.

The clavichord music of W. F. Bach is masterly and beautiful. It is not historically important, for this composer did nothing to extend sonata form, neither did he occupy a central social position like the London Bach.   Consequently the musical beauty of his work is often ignored.   Possibly too much is made of "form" in music, by "form" meaning the arrangement of keys and sequence of melodies.   Texture and emotion have more immediate effect on the ear.   If a string band strikes up some music, music which is unknown, it is not whether it is in sonata form which is the question, but the impact on the ear, that is to say, its texture, which determines the guess "Haydn" or "Bach" or whatever it may be.   While sonata form bulks very large in all histories of music, the quite as fascinating and important question of texture is sometimes not alluded to at all.   The difference in this aspect of music between the work of J. S. Bach and his son C. P. E. is so great that nothing can be learned from comparison.

But in W. F. Bach we are furnished with a stepping-stone, one leading away from his father even if it does not quite allow you to reach the younger son.

So, first, his clavichord fugues.   Their subjects are often melodious. Just as W. F. Bach awaits his English monographist, so The Fugue awaits its non-technical artistic historian.   I feel such an historian would make much of the increased melodiousness of fugue subjects after the death of J. S. Bach, especially subjects by the minor masters (if I may call them so in relation to Mozart and Beethoven) like Mendelssohn and Schumann.   Then, as modern days approach, fugue subjects become less melodic and more rhythmic and contrapuntal, even though the counterpoint is much more free.   And I think it was W. F. Bach who started this melodious subject movement.

Here is a snippet of a subject: there are three or four semiquavers after, but W. F. treats them very cavalierly.

"La Leçon de clavecin". From an etching by Fredeberg, about 1768, the year in which young Erard (the future piano maker) first came to Paris as an apprentice, and in which Taskin took over Blanchet's business as the best of clavecin makers. Thus at the time of this etching the clavecin attained its greatest prosperity and development. Within fifty years the Erard piano superseded the Taskin clavecin.

Courtesy of Bibliothèque Nationale, Paris.

The private clavichord (above) and the public flugel (below), the one from
J. W. Hasler's *Clavier-und Singstucke* (Erfurt 1782) and the other from an
engraving by Chodowiecki in J. B. Basedow's *Elementarwerk*.

This slowish tune is even more typical in its sense of decadence and particularly in the fact that it is incomplete: it is as though W. F., having created a "speaking" series of notes, would tie them up with other material by any quavers that lay handy.

Here we have a counter-subject, or, the second subject of a double fugue, whichever nomenclature is preferred.

Here again there is no end: the B natural I have chosen is as good a point as any, as it creates W. F.'s characteristic wistfulness and is also a note when the clavichord would doubtless yield the cry which Burney thought possibly only C. P. E. could create.

In keeping his parts clear and precise W. F. is as strict as his father and much stricter than the equally melodious Mendelssohn, who from time to time seems to have forgotten he was engaged upon a fugue. Where W. F. allows himself romantic licence is in the use he makes of his subjects. For instance, the dramatic centre of the F minor fugue whose counter-subject is quoted above is neither that nor the subject itself, but is when the bass enters towards the end of a sort of development section. At this point both subjects are inverted and played by the right hand when the bass enters (with the tenor silent and two octaves below the alto) with a most telling sentence hitherto and afterwards unheard. This music is classical in its restraint, romantic in its melody and feeling of decadence. It is remarkable and beautiful music, but W. F. cannot be numbered among the great men because this autumn feeling pervades all his work: it is monotonous in atmosphere.

His Polonaises are as remarkable as his Fugues. It will be remembered that by what in this context might be called a Holy Roman accident the King of Poland was also the Elector of Saxony, holding his court in the operatic capital of Dresden. Thus the Polonaise, or what passed for that "smooth and fluent, though majestic" movement, became known in Germany. J. S. Bach himself wrote one or two

N

examples, as, for instance, in the E major French Suite. But the
Polonaises of W. F. Bach are very different affairs, subtle, syncopated
and as wistful as ever, while the ornamentation, as well as the rhythm,
seems to show us, not so much the shadow of the old Bach, as that of
Chopin himself.

This phrase opens one of the Polonaises, which strain is then repeated *in toto* a fourth higher. What extraordinary music for the
eighteenth century! But how suited to the clavichord, the only
instrument which can make the treble line pathetic enough.

W. F. Bach is a real curiosity in music: a drunkard who lived to a
ripe old age; a reprobate friend of austere princesses; a romantic son
of a great classic; a romantic composer, indeed, ignored by the
Romantics who discovered his own father.

When we turn to Carl Philip Emanuel Bach we see a figure much
written about in his own times, but less since. In his own times a
great modernist, then the thin son of a ripe father, and now? Perhaps
the dullest of all the classics.

His music is his ornamentation: it is as inseparable from his texture
as is the ornamentation of Chopin. Of these ornaments the most
individual was the *Bebung*, a way of alternating and retaining the
pressure on a clavichord key so as not only to sustain the note but to
give it those tiny alterations in pitch and quality which no other keyed
instrument can do. The "cry" (the word used by Dr. Burney) was
denoted thus:

and whole sections of his music are liberally besprinkled with these
dots. For instance, in the F major sonata from the 1779 set:

After the *Bebung* perhaps it was the *Pralltriller* which exercised his attention most. This is, of course, merely our old friend, ∿

played ♩ ♪ | ♩ ♫♩♪ and it may be felt it has never bothered
anybody else before or since. But Clavichord Bach (if this is a
mild pun on his first initial, it has at least the merit of providing a
mnemonic), in his *Versuch* says, "But while I write of the proper
playing of this kind of shake, it is very important for me to point
out that at a cadence—where it usually occurs—the tone should be
diminishing, and it is very hard to play a *Pralltriller* delicately
on a pianoforte. The very rapidity of the notes implies a certain
degree of force, and in the pianoforte increased force means increased
tone. . . . The difficulty is greater when this shake occurs together
with a cadential turn."

But I do not think we should be pleasing Clavichord Bach if we
omitted his *Pralltrillers*, for he says elsewhere in the *Versuch*, "Nobody
doubts the necessity of ornamentation. We can all see for ourselves
how essential it is if we open any score at random : we find signs for
ornaments scattered in profusion. These ornaments bind the notes
together into phrases, though sometimes they do the opposite, and
single out special notes for solitary emphasis: above all, they keep
the music vocal, and so help to hold the ear of the listener, and
they make the player cause his melody to sing. A poor piece
of music will be enriched by ornamentation, while a beautiful
melody played with no ornaments, will be but unfurnished and
uninteresting."

I wonder to what extent our modern ear agrees with this ? The
melodies of J. S. Bach are frequently played without ornamentations,
as are many of the more popular slow tunes of Handel. Indeed, did
we hear the "Largo" of the latter sung by a male castrato and heavily
ornamented, I think many in the audience would feel compelled to
leave their seats in a sort of religious disgust. This habit of listening
unadorned may be merely the result of generations of laziness. But
while it is undoubted that J. S. Bach and Handel can make magnificent
effects without ornament, it is hardly true of C. P. E. Bach, whose
music really does require it as much as he says, perhaps with egocentric
exaggeration, all music does.

So it may be that a pianist unable to control his fingers to the exact degree of singing nicety to execute a shake at a cadence, should not omit the shake, but contrive to afford to purchase that not expensive and not unobtainable instrument, the clavichord, where he will enjoy something essential to the music and not to be found on the piano-forte, namely a *Bebung* effect.   His chief initial difficulty will un-doubtedly be the smallness and narrowness of the keys, their shallow drop and very easy touch.   The best way of becoming accustomed to them is to play exercises, very slowly, of the usual pianoforte sort: depressing one finger at a time; depressing three or two while two or three free fingers play, playing slow *legato* scales, and so on.   After a while the transition piano-clavichord, or clavichord-piano, can be made almost at will.   It is perhaps no greater than the transition violin-viola, or, in wind instruments, treble and descant recorders. Touch is all, and any touch can be got used to with some expenditure of nervous concentration on simple exercises of the five-finger school.

The other ornaments of C. P. E. Bach, the turns which occur in the middle of a melody and give it additional grace, the trills and the tiny notes present no unusual difficulties in actual playing.   And in interpretation, it is quite clear and definite in C. P. E. Bach what is only conjectural in the music of most other composers, that the small note steals its value from the note or notes coming after: as

As to the music itself, Clavichord Bach wrote Rondos and Sonatas. The Rondos, having no "link" value in the history of Sonata form, are rarely alluded to in the histories, but the pianoforte or clavichord player wishing to begin serious acquaintance with this Bach may reasonably be directed to the Rondos first, as clearer in outline, with sturdier tunes and rhythms and, if only because of the constant re-entries of the main theme, without that bugbear of the lover of minor eighteenth-century music, the great opening which leads merely to arid passage work.   Further, these Rondos are individual, and as un-like the essays in this form of either Mozart or Haydn as well can be imagined.

His Sonatas often open really magnificently, as this by the eight-eenth-century Brahms:

Yet though this opening movement of the F minor sonata of 1781 does not continue with the fine vigour of the opening, it is at least always coherently progressive, and not experimentally stationary, as is too often the case. And the actual visual appearance on the page of such subsequent bars as

must have been as bizarre to the old contrapuntal organists of J. S. Bach's generation still surviving at the age of eighty or so as atonal music in score is to us. Completely meaningless at first glance, that is to say.

When we turn to Haydn we turn to the only really great clavichord composer besides J. S. Bach. Not all his fifty-two sonatas, the earliest of which were published when he was first introduced to the Esterhazy family but probably were written during his Vienna poverty and apprenticeship, are for the clavichord. It is clear from his correspondence that he forsook the clavichord for the pianoforte when establishment at Esterhazy enabled him to do so. But his earlier sonatas bear unmistakable influences of C. P. E. Bach and the calvichord. This, for instance, from the A major of the 1776 set might be by either, except for its greater grip and the masterful way in which Haydn pushes the music to the dominant, whereas C. P. E. would have watched his pen modulating in bewilderment.

Haydn never specifies *Bebung*, but all his early slow movements call for this effect. The impassioned and baroque melody of the

Partita (though it is strictly a sonata) in B flat, one of his earliest clavichord works to come down to us, certainly requires this particular clavichord "cry". This B flat Partita, by the way, is numbered forty in one Breitkopf and Hartel edition: this Leipzig firm whose origin has been noted in this chapter, number it two in their collected edition.

No more varied master than Haydn (we must always except Mozart in anything we say) ever lived. Haydn was not a simple soul given to feeble practical jokes who had the honour to be the incompetent teacher of Beethoven for a while until the young lion pawed him away. Haydn, as far as his clavichord music is concerned, is young, passionate, revolutionary. His music is both bold and tender, his slow movements are voluptuous, warm, almost heated. Do not approach him backwards from Beethoven, approach him forwards from C. P. E. Bach. Then it will be realized how Burney hailed him as the joy of his old age.

It is a commonplace that music is, in a sense, a universal language. Suppose just by patient listening and the knowledge of the Latin alphabet alone it were possible to read Shakespeare, Cervantes, Dante, Tolstoy and Goethe, in fact all the literatures of Europe. After the works of the great writers mentioned, would there not be plenty of room for other great geniuses, from Milton to Proust, from Balzac to Pushkin? Yet in music we think that, so crowded must the scene be and so few must be the Truly Great, that because Haydn lived in the great Beethoven epoch he must necessarily be somewhat secondary. In my view he is one of the greatest European artists who has ever lived, and in no aspect of his art is he greater than in his clavichord writing. Quite on the same plane, though totally different in his texture, as J. S. Bach himself.

SHORT BIBLIOGRAPHY TO CHAPTER V

Fuller-Maitland: *The Age of Bach and Handel*, OXFORD HISTORY OF MUSIC, VOL IV (Oxford University Press).

C. Sandford Terry: *The Music of Bach* (Oxford University Press 1933).

Philipp Spitta: *Johann Sebastian Bach*, trans. Bell and Fuller-Maitland (Novello 1885, 3 vols).

Johann Nikolaus Forkel: *Johann Sebastian Bach*, trans. by C. S. Terry
(Constable 1920).

Albert Schweitzer: *J. S. Bach*, trans. E. Newman (A. & C. Black 1911,
2 vols.).

Carl Engel: *Some Account of the Clavichord*, MUSICAL TIMES, VOL XX,
1879.

Arnold Dolmetsch: *Interpretation of the Music of the 17th and 18th
Centuries* (Novello).

Karl Geiringer: *Haydn* (Allen & Unwin 1947).

CHAPTER VI

THE HARPSICHORD IN ENGLAND

1. The Instruments

AMONG the illustrations to this book, there is an instrument
photographed from above. The comparison between the virginal and the clavecin was made in Chapter II, and as for the harpsichord, it is just the English name for the French clavecin. The
instrument depicted facing p. 209 is a harpsichord, of Handel's time,
in the Victoria and Albert Museum, in South Kensington. This
noble, beautiful and very workmanlike instrument is, as we see, a
two-manualled harpsichord. Some harpsichords were made with only
one manual, while three or even four manuals have been known.
But two manuals was the most common arrangement for the large
and powerful instrument used in the opera house and in the concert
hall. Differences in sound were produced by the quills plucking the
string near or further from the bridge, by plucking the string with a
leather plectrum instead of a quill, or by plucking a string shorter or
longer than that usually available by depressing a given key so as to
sound its octave, above or below according to whether this string
was shorter or longer. The timbres of the two manuals could be
arranged before or during playing (for instance, at the repeats so common in all Suite movements) so that, just as on an organ, each manual
had its own tone quality and orchestral effects could be produced.
We can observe the two stops for the left hand above the bass and one
stop for the right hand above the treble upper keyboard. Sometimes
harpsichords were fitted with pedals with which to operate the registers, and there were also arrangements so that the knee, pressing a
lever to the left below the keyboard, could command the registration.

It is usually maintained that the harpsichord of Handel's era was a somewhat insensitive instrument, quite incapable both of gradations of tone and the sustaining of notes. Just as in his orchestration Handel would select his timbres, perhaps a soprano voice, and oboe, and the usual strings, and then keep to them throughout the aria, so in his harpsichord playing he would register, as on an organ, and keep to his selected stops throughout. The blending of colours, in fact, it is said, was something not known to composers of his day.

There is some truth in this, but we must remember that the blending of musical colours was very well known in vocal music, and had been known for hundreds of years. Handel, however far he may be from the delicate colours of Byrd, shows in, for instance, the "Darkness" chorus of *Israel in Egypt* what a master of shading he was. Then again, modern harpsichordists, like for instance Lucille Wallace, show that phrasing of quite a pianistic kind, of a kind quite different from any organ, can be made effective. In fact, it is surprising that there has ever been any doubt on this head. Writers have maintained that the plucking of a string was a means of making sound not subject to gradation, but you can pluck a string slowly or quickly: the vibrations per second are not altered, but the measure of sway of the string is broadened on a quick pluck, and the sound is correspondingly louder. Then as to sustaining power, once the string is vibrating, it will give off sound, but of course it eventually comes to rest and the sound ceases, just as does the pianoforte string. Owing to the great tension, measured in tons, and the girth of string in modern concert grand pianofortes, their sustaining and inflective powers are many times greater than Handel's harpsichord, but it does not mean that this old instrument was incapable in these particulars, or that Handel intended his music to be played without phrasing and at a constant *forte* or *piano*.

Later on, after Handel's day, swells in the shape of Venetian blinds, like those fitted to organs, were introduced, allowing formidable *crescendi* to deafen those romantic folk open to such influences.

Handel was an essentially harpsichord rather than clavichord composer, his music fitting the dignity, grandeur and architectural quality of his instrument. He wrote nothing intimate and poetical such as Bach's clavichord music. Consequently it is with surprise that one reads here and there of "Handel's clavichord" in the museum at Maidstone: one does not know what Handel would have done with a clavichord. The flap is inscribed with the maker's name and the date, 1726. This date allows the possibility, but just as there is a tendency to consider every virginal or collection of virginal music to have belonged to or at least been associated with Queen Elizabeth, so Handel seems to attract all musical instruments and musical legends, however without foundation, of the first half of the eighteenth century.

Between the close of the virginals era and the opening of the harpsichord era, there was a penumbra which gave rise to writing of this sort.

> Up betimes, and by coach towards White Hall, and took Aldgate Street in my way, and there called upon one Hayward, that makes virginalls, and did there like of a little espinette, and will have him finish it for me: for I had a mind to a small harpsicon, but this takes up less room, and will do my business as to finding out of chords, and I am very well pleased that I have found it.

Thus Pepys, on the 4th of March, 1668, seems to have considered it all just a matter of size. Whether there were any virginals for sale in John Hayward's shop in Aldgate we do not know, but to the instrument smaller than a "small harpsichon" he gives the name "little espinette".

We have three nouns in our sentence. Did Pepys write carelessly, using "virginalls", "harpsicon" and "espinette" indifferently for any domestic keyboard instrument?

As the years went on, the word harpsicon became harpsichord: Johnson in his *Dictionary* (1747–55) gives the modern spelling without equivocation: not so precise, however, is the definition, "A musical instrument, strung with wires, and playing by striking keys." By this, a virginal, a clavichord and a pianoforte would all be harpsichords. To this day the dividing line between virginal and spinet, and between spinet and harpsichord has not been defined. In a recent exhibition a spinet was labelled harpsichord, presumably by its own modern maker. The most recent book by Ernest Closson, says the difference lies in whether there are one or two keyboards.[1]

To my mind there is no real difference between the virginal instrument and the spinet instrument. The different name is largely a matter of usage, date and fashion. It was the fashion in Tudor times to encrust the little instrument in costly, ornamented, box-like, oblong cases. In the days of Hepplewhite and Sheraton the fashion

---

[1] *History of the Piano*, 1947.

was for plain wood, what we might call a functional shape of case, which was therefore a sort of rounded triangle, like the wing only of a grand pianoforte. So on seeing an unadorned triangular wing-like instrument, we might say "spinet", and on likewise noticing a coloured and enormous glove box on stilts, we might say "virginal".

A harpsichord looks quite different, it is a long instrument with one long straight side to accommodate longer and deeper strings than a spinet ever has, and with one or more keyboards at right angles to the strings. There is, surely, no mistaking a harpsichord. The difficulty may lie, if the flap is down, and if there is only one manual, in distinguishing it from an eighteenth-century pianoforte. If the touch does not give it away, notice if there are any hand stops, though even this is not certain, as pianoforte damper and *una corda* registers were sometimes hand-operated in early models. No, the only thing to do is to open the flap, and see if the strings are plucked or knocked. If knocked by a felt-covered hammer head you are, of course, in the presence of a pianoforte.

The fingering of the harpsichord required bent fingers, clawlike, with the nail joint vertical: some said the fingers should release the keys by flicking under the palm, not by raising. By 1740 the modern way of fingering seems to have come largely into its own: a book of this year, *The Harpsichord Illustrated and Improved* gave the present Continental system of numbering the thumb 1 and the other digits 2 to 5, and this for both hands. Certainly this shows a definite change from the instructions for fingering to be found in the 1696 edition of Purcell's posthumous *Choice Collection of Lessons for the Harpsichord*, in which numbering went by the left in each hand, the little finger of the left hand being 1.

The smaller instruments, virginals and spinets and perhaps some smaller harpsichords, were made in England in the seventeenth century, and sold by their makers and also sold retail. In the shop of Purcell's publisher, Playford, were all sorts of things.

At Mr Playford's shop is sold all sorts of ruled paper for musick and books of all sizes ready bound for musick. Also the excellent cordial called "Elixir Proprietatis" a few drops of which drank in a glass of sack or other liquors is admirable for all coughs, consumption of the lungs, and inward distempers. . . . Also if a person desires to be furnished with good new Virginals and Harpsicons, if they send to Mr Playford's shop they may be furnished at reasonable rates to their content.

But many instruments had always been imported, especially the more costly as to their cases, or large as to their number of manuals. This situation was radically altered in the eighteenth century by a foreign incursion of the greatest benefit. Experienced craftsmen came from Switzerland and Bohemia, or were more or less and quite kindly kidnapped from Italy when boys, and set up shop in London, with the result that instruments for the greatest composers, such as Haydn, and the most powerful monarchs, such as Frederick the Great, were bespoken from and executed by Londoners.

These craftsmen set up outside the City, in the new residential area to the north of the then chaotic ground between Piccadilly and the Strand. The area now bounded by the squares of Leicester and Trafalgar was once very different. Soho Square was perhaps one of the two centres of the new "estates" as we would call them: Bedford Square, north-east across the junction of Hog Lane and the Tottenham Court Road was another such centre. Bloomsbury is still with us, beautiful and dignified: we must imagine Soho like Bloomsbury if we are not to be shocked at learning it was the home of the harpsichord, both makers and players. Some eighteenth-century houses still exist to help us; there is a terrace, sordidly hemmed in, in Meares Street: there is a house at the corner of Soho Square and Carlisle Street. From here to the west, getting towards Bond Street, in the streets rising at the back of noblemen's gardens fronting on to Piccadilly, dwelt at one time or another manufacturers like Shudi; Broadwood, Shudi's journeyman, son-in-law, partner and then founder of the modern pianoforte business; Kirkman; Clementi the manufacturer of both harpsichords and pianofortes and an important composer; J. C. Bach, son of J. S. Bach, and his fellow Leipzig student Abel; Handel (in Brook Street); Haydn and Mozart on their visits and others whose acquaintance we have yet to make in this chapter, such as the organist of St. George's, Hanover Square, Thomas Rosengreive. There was, it is hardly necessary to add, no Regent Street arbitrarily to divide Soho from what is now Mayfair.

These immigrant craftsmen became men of property, they seem to have absorbed considerable musical culture and attained a social position similar to that, perhaps, of professional men. By far the most famous was one of the latest, Clementi. As a boy in his teens in Rome, he attracted the attention of Peter Beckford, cousin of the author of *Vathek*, and was taken back to England and supported and taught in his country house. His patron was himself an author, his *Thoughts*

Upon Hunting has indeed proved "immortal", that is to say a modern edition was brought out not so many years ago, and there was a good library in which Clementi is reported to have come across the fugues of J. S. Bach. But the life of a virtuoso harpsichordist, in which later Clementi rivalled Mozart, did not interfere with the more commercial activities to which the boy felt drawn as he grew up. He became a publisher and retail seller of music and a manufacturer of harpsichords and pianofortes, writing, as it were in his spare time, pianoforte sonatas (for harpsichord or pianoforte, as the title-page invariably said) which in texture and layout are the most pianistic of all Beethoven's predecessors. What Clementi did in such a large way, others did in a small. Dussek (there are many Dusseks, not all related, but here the reference is to the composer, J. L. Dussek) joined Clementi and led the same sort of life. Kirkman, the earlier harpsichord maker, was also organist of St. George's, Hanover Square. The Swiss friend of Handel, Shudi, would only make his instruments to order and required to know what was wanted, and would make instruments to any specification and taste, but in his own time and mood. Shudi also had Broadwood as his assistant, and so gave a chance for another name, as well known as Clementi's, to come down to us.

But if Shudi had Broadwood as his assistant and enjoyed the patronage of the Prince of Wales with the plume of feathers as a sign, his rival Kirkman had Charles Burney for his assistant and enjoyed the patronage of the King himself, and flourished the King's arms. To us, it is his connexion with Burney which may reasonably interest us most. Young Charles Burney had been brought to London by Arne, the composer, and (he was not yet of age) indentured as an apprentice. He put himself at Kirkman's disposal to help sell his harpsichords: it would appear that Kirkman, less aristocratic than Shudi, made instruments as a speculation and not to order, a speculative builder rather than an architect. Not that it would appear that Burney was particularly good as a salesman, according to his daughter's account.

On one occasion it was arranged that he should "shew off the several instruments that were ready for sale, to a gentleman who was disposed to purchase one of the most costly.

"Young Burney, with no other idea than that of serving Kirkman, immediately seated himself at an instrument, and played various pieces of" Italian violin composers, one of whom was resident and popular in London. Quite how Burney did this is not clear, perhaps he played the solo violin line on one manual, filling in the figured bass on the other. His choice of music was however surely strange. Perhaps Fanny Burney was wrong.

The customer "coldly and proudly walked about the room: took snuff from a finely enamelled snuff-box, and looked at some prints, as if wholly without noticing the performance". Burney, finding the customer inattentive, tried many harpsichords, one after the other until "coming at length to keys of which the touch, light and springing, invited his stay, he fired away in a sonata of Scarlatti's, with an alternate excellence of execution and expression, so perfectly in accord with the fanciful flights of that wild but masterly composer" that the haughty customer, attracted at last "softly drew a chair to the harpsichord, and listened, with unaffected earnestness, to every note" which, we may surely agree, was exceedingly good of him.

"To be easily pleased, however" (Fanny Burney adds) "or to make acknowledgment of being pleased at all, seems derogatory to strong self-importance: Mr. Greville, therefore, merely said, 'You are fond, Sir, it seems, of Italian music?'

"The reply to this was striking up, with all the varying undulations of the crescendo, the diminuendo, the pealing swell, and the 'dying, dying fall', belonging to the powers of the pedal, that most popular masterpiece of Handel's, the Coronation Anthem."[1]

We must pause here for breath. The haughty Mr. Greville, filled with strong self-importance and not indisposed to purchase one of the more costly instruments, this eighteenth-century "Mr. Salteena", was a Fulke Greville, though neither the poet who lived before him nor the diarist who lived after.

Fanny Burney's last paragraph is muddled: granted that the harpsichord had its registers and Venetian swell acted upon by pedal stops, and granted that "pealing" alluded to the quill instead of the buff (or leather) plectrum, there is still tautology, the crescendo and the swell, the diminuendo and the dying, being the same thing. But at least Fanny Burney, who was not really musical, avoids the commonest of literary faults; she does not confuse modulation with undulation. Lastly, we notice the popularity of arrangements of Handel.

But Shudi, and Broadwood after him, hired out as well as sold harpsichords, and, it would appear, perhaps purchased second-hand instruments for the purpose. Our Appendix B will contain more information about the Ruckers instruments which were so much in

---

[1] *Memoirs of Doctor Burney*, by Fanny Burney (Moxon 1832, pp. 26 *et seq.*).

demand, and which the Shudi-Broadwood combination found it advisable to acquire. Often of great value and age, perhaps repainted and fitted with new keys, these harpsichords had a silvery and sweetly true tone, and the account books of the firm show that such leaders of fashion as the Duchess of Richmond, Lady Pembroke and Lady Catherine Murray, spelling the instruments indifferently as Ruckers, Rukers, Rookers or Roukers, frequently hired them. Of the Shudi-Broadwood new instruments the prices were, single harpsichords thirty-five guineas, the same but fitted with an octave stop forty guineas, the forty-guinea model if fitted with a swell became fifty guineas, but a double harpsichord with a swell and an octave stop was as much as eighty guineas. I notice, to make a modern comparison, that two-manualled harpsichords, new, may be had from a Suffolk maker for 137 guineas, whereas a new virginal costs only forty guineas.

We may imagine one of the long, powerful, two-manualled instruments being carried out of Shudi's or Kirkman's by "sturdy rogues", laced on a dray and lumbered eastward to Drury Lane or south to the Haymarket, and arrived there, lugged out and placed in position inside the theatre. Later it would be tuned, and later still its keys would move to the fingers of a Pepusch, a Handel or a Gluck, who directed the performance of the music he had written from its keyboard, another and subaltern harpsichord with its attendant player filling in the figured bass from the side for the songs.

But sometimes the dray would lumber much further east, to Clerkenwell, or even south-west to St. James's, or it might be dispensed with altogether, and the instrument carried along a few steps or a few streets into Carlisle House near Soho Square. Not that Clerkenwell and St. James's were always to be approved of, indeed, one concert was "established under circumstances that tended rather to degrade than to recommend such an entertainment" as it was "being set on foot by a person of the lowest class in a suburb of the town and in a room that afforded them scarce decent accommodation when they had escaped the dangers of getting at it". So much for the worthy efforts of a coalman to help the art of music by affording accommodation in his Clerkenwell Green house, where he offered coffee at one penny a cup. More robust people than the knighted nice attorney, Sir John Hawkins, just quoted, however, often went to hear Handel himself play in the first few years of his arrival in London from the Continent.

But the first concert harpsichord was perhaps that instrument which we may imagine to have stood in "Mr. John Banister's house, now called the Musick-school, over against the George Tavern in White Friars" as an advertisement in *The London Gazette* for 30th December, 1672, announces, going on to proclaim that there "will be musick performed by excellent masters, beginning precisely at four of the clock in the afternoon, and every afternoon for the future".

The harpsichord in Hickford's Great Room off the Haymarket, a room which stretched, it would appear, between the streets of Panton and James, with two exits, was however the most fashionable. Only the really musical among the wealthy, such as the Earl of Winchilsea, ventured to Clerkenwell Green, but anyone, even a snobbish attorney, might be seen at Hickford's, and consequently the type of recreation offered became less musical and more merely fashionable, more a showing-off of personalities. Yet this harpsichord too was honoured by the hands of Handel, and not only Handel, but Domenico Scarlatti as well, for we may surely deduce that mysterious master's personal presence at this harpsichord during his 1724 visit to London from the notice of a benefit concert, "in which a Pastoral Cantata for two voices, accompanied by all sorts of instruments, composed by himself on this occasion" would be performed.

At Carlisle House, however, the gathering was even more select; five guineas was the subscription; the tea, that aristocratic, indeed regal, beverage was to be had below stairs and ventilation was to be had above. The five guineas expected for only six concerts so far from driving people away attracted those who desired to form part of a genteel assembly, and so the harpsichord, sounding under the fingers of the great Bach's son, John Christian, lately come to London, was later transferred to the more commodious Almack's in King Street, St. James's.

As for royalty, many harpsichords were admitted to their presence, sometimes hired. Charles I wanted a new instrument; for the famous Dutch family was still at work in 1638, when Sir F. Windebank, described in Grove curiously as the "private secretary" to the King (monarchs did not have official "private secretaries" until Victoria, until then such an official as the Keeper of the Privy Purse did the work) wrote to Antwerp about purchasing a good harpsichord. His correspondent, a painter, replied with the information that a Ruckers with two manuals might be had for £30, and that Rubens himself had painted a portion of the decorated cover. This instrument was

Upper, the harpsichord at home (Gainsborough, who drew this, may be turning over) and, lower, the harpsichord in public, at the oratorio (Handel is
standing on the right). Note the cello player looking over the harpsichordist's
shoulder to double the figured bass.

The upper picture shows the printed paper decoration often used by Ruckers in harpsichords that family exported to England. The lower shows Handel's Ruckers photographed from above.

The detail from a Vermeer is by courtesy of the Lord Chamberlain's Office, and the Handel by courtesy of the Victoria and Albert Museum.

accordingly ordered to be sent over, but did not meet with approval when it arrived, owing to its limited compass. The reason why Windebank wrote to a painter was, that painters, or so I understand the position, purchased instruments in plain cases from Ruckers, and embellished the wood themselves, selling at as great a profit as possible. We notice the increase in price between about 1640 and about 1740, a greater proportional increase than happens between 1740 and now, two hundred years later.

All our monarchs had harpsichords in their palaces, possibly the last being George IV, but there is a charming story of Charlotte of Mecklenburgh and a harpsichord in a ship carrying her over from Cuxhaven to Harwich to marry King George III. The voyage took ten days owing to calm weather, and she occupied some part of those mild September days of 1761 in playing English music: perhaps *Musick's Handmaid*, perhaps even from an old copy of *Parthenia*? Let us hope our music inclined her to the country which she was (though only nominally) to rule, and in which she was to bear many children, including two kings-to-be, George IV and William IV.

In royal and aristocratic houses during the eighteenth century the harpsichords often sweated under the palms of infant prodigies. King George III personally, it would appear, placed before "our invincible Wolfgang" . . . not only the works of the Vienna composer Wagenseil, but also of the London residents J. C. Bach, that composer's old fellow student Abel, and of Handel himself. The proud father goes on to report to his Salzburg correspondent that his little son accompanied the Queen on the harpsichord while she sang an aria: the same Queen who had played English music on the ship's instrument. Little Wolfgang Mozart and his slightly older sister played often in London, both in public and a sort of odious semi-private, when between twelve o'clock and three o'clock visitors could come individually to test their powers at the Frith Street lodging. The Hon. Daines Barrington, moved by a spirit of scientific curiosity and with a paper for the Royal Society in mind, was one such visitor. He was enchanted with Wolfgang, admired much his instrumental powers, but even more his unaffected boyishness when a cat came into the room who simply had to be hugged, and when Wolfgang, tiring of figured basses, jolted round the room on a stick like a man on a horse.

Of minor prodigies there were many. The harpsichord in the

o

theatre in the Haymarket was touched by Cassandra Paradies, aged
five and a half.   The harpsichord in a clergyman's home had a tune
played on it "readily and in just time and always with a true bass to it"
by the three-year-old son of the Rev. Charles Wesley.   In the public
pleasure gardens of Vauxhall a boy named Thomas Busby played the
harpsichord, and then the Rev. Charles Wesley produced a second
prodigy, though three-year-old Samuel was not quite the equal of his
older brother Charles at the same age, for though he could play a tune,
he was weak when it came to adding a bass.   After the Wesley couple,
a Norwich carpenter by name of Crotch put forward his son William,
able at the classic age of three to play both the harpsichord and the
organ.   There were others.   In general, it is not fanciful to assume,
looking at any old instrument, that one or two children have in its
time been hoisted level with the keyboard, and have plucked out a
tune with a bass, the latter more or less appropriate.

But the growing wealthy middle class also afforded many homes
for harpsichords.   There is a pathetic little story to be gleaned from
the pages of *Evelyn's Diary*.   John Evelyn came at the very beginning
of the harpsichord period, and was a country gentleman of means,
looked up to by Pepys in the latter's struggling days.   Evelyn says
(20th November, 1679): "I dined with Mr. Slingsby, Master of the
Mint, with my wife, invited to hear music, which was exquisitely
performed by . . . Signor Bartholomeo, an Italian, on the harpsichord. . . ."   Later this harpsichordist became the teacher of his
daughter Mary.   But Mary Evelyn died in March, 1685, and we find
the entry, "My daughter Mary . . . died the 14th to our unspeakable
sorrow. . . .   She had an excellent voice, to which she played a
thorough-bass on the harpsichord, in both which she arrived to that
perfection, that of the scholars of those two famous masters, Signors
Pietro and Bartholomeo, she was esteemed the best."   This girl was
only nineteen when she died so tragically of smallpox.   When we
look at pictures showing a harpsichord incidentally as part of a seventeenth-century interior composition, we mark the neat rooms and
evidences of what seem to us a calm and settled society, and we contrast those times with our own.   But those times were far from
calm, and in every clear interior painted after the manner of the
Dutch school, all sorts of diseases lurk round the fresh young woman
sitting at her instrument.

The increased sustaining powers of the harpsichord as against the
spinet are hinted at by Dr. Delaney, Dean of an Irish cathedral, when

he wrote of his wife, "The harpsichord was a new instrument when she played upon it, and the notes sounded under her hand in a combination of harmony, as if they had been naturally connected." When a girl, Mrs. Delaney had practised on a spinet. But it was as late as 1731 when Dr. Delaney first met his future wife, and it is an error to write that the harpsichord was then a new instrument. However, this all shows that it was a new instrument to the households visited by beneficed clergy. As wealth increased, and as the price of the instruments did not rise in proportion to the average cost of living, they spread abroad out of palaces and opera houses and concert platforms into rooms where "we all adjourned . . . I was placed at the harpsichord, and after jangling a little Mr. Wesley took his fiddle and played", as the widow wrote to her sister, and implicitly thus contradicting her future husband's opinion of her powers of extracting legato from the harpsichord.

"So back again home, and there my wife, and Mercer and Tom and I sat till eleven at night, singing and fiddling, and a great joy it is to see me master of so much pleasure in my house, that it is and will be still, I hope, a constant pleasure to me to be at home. The girle plays pretty well upon the harpsicon, but only ordinary tunes, but hath a good hand; sings a little, but hath a very good voyce and eare. My boy, a brave boy, sings finely, and is the most pleasant boy at present, while his ignorant boy's tricks last, that ever I saw. So to supper, and with great pleasure to bed." Thus Pepys, while only Clerk of the Acts. The girl with the good hand but who could play only ordinary tunes on the harpsicon is to us a disappointment, for the time of this diary entry was only four years after the last reprint of *Parthenia*, and it would have been pleasant to have heard Pepys on Byrd's *Pavane: The Earle of Salisbury*, or upon a publication he might have preferred, *Musick's Handmaid, New Lessons and Instructions for the Virginals or Harpsychord* published the same year of 1663 by Playford.

And so, with this glance into the familiar and certainly picturesque household in the City, noting with pleasure the central position in the family enjoyed by the "harpsicon", we may leave the instruments themselves and turn to the men who composed music for them.

2. *The Composers*

Eccles, Barrett, Piggott, Blow, Clarke, Croft . . . a string of English names.   Eccles we have met: fanatical Solomon Eagles.   Barrett and Piggott are names we may pass over.   Dr. Blow we must pause at, for all that we may find his music dull.   He was one of the teachers of Purcell, became organist of Westminster Abbey, gave up his seat in the organ loft to his great junior, and replaced himself when that great junior had prematurely died.   Clarke, now Mr. Jeremiah Clarke, Mr. Jerry Clarke as his contemporaries called him, is known for a trumpet tune with which orchestral concerts start when their pro-moters wish to include some music at once both classical and English into the programmes.   He was a fellow pupil of Purcell's under Blow, became Master of the Choristers of St. Paul's, and in 1707 musical London was shocked by his suicide.   It is supposed to have been a mysterious love affair which caused him to take his own life: one can imagine the morbid interest taken in the affair among the many music sellers of St. Paul's Churchyard and neighbourhood.

Croft is perhaps musically the greatest (though "great" is too strong a word for him) of these six minor names.   He also was a pupil of Blow and also eventually became organist of Westminster Abbey, after the Blow–Purcell–Blow sequence had finished.   Croft is known to all readers of musical histories for his remark in the Preface of his Burial Service, "In that service there is one Verse composed by my predecessor, the famous Mr. Henry Purcell . . .   The reason why I did not compose that Verse anew is obvious to every Artist; in the rest of that service composed by me, I have endeavoured as near as I could, to imitate that great Master and celebrated Composer . . ." and we may now turn to "the famous Mr. Henry Purcell" himself.

Whenever I think of Purcell I think of Westminster, in which city he was probably born, where he practised his art, and died.   He may have been born in one of the streets to the back of the Abbey: the great church dominated Westminster architecturally far more than it does now, even though since Purcell's time the two western towers have been added.   For one thing, although no doubt larger than when we imagined Byrd riding in from Harlington, it was still a small cathedral city.   Purcell's life seems to have been spent between his home (when he married he remained in the locality), the organ loft of the Abbey, the Chapel Royal in St. James's Palace, the Duke's

Theatre in Dorset Gardens (near the Thames, about where Salisbury Square now stands), the Temple Church and, let us harmlessly suppose, with Dryden in Will's Coffee House near Covent Garden, having repaired thither after a performance at the Duke's Theatre for which Dryden wrote the words and Purcell the music, the latter having also presided at the harpsichord over the twenty-four royal violins and the bass lutes.   Perhaps he went with the court on its Royal Progressions, but he usually seems to have remained behind to compose welcoming songs against their returns, welcoming impartially Englishman and Dutchman, Anglican and Catholic.   Purcell seems not to have worried over the political vagaries of the time, not even those of James II, though that monarch caused him worry in another connexion.

Purcell had been left an orphan at an early age, and in his teens had begun to collect "offices of employment under the Crown", offices which, once collected, he seems to have taken good care to retain, in this way becoming one of music's most noted pluralists.   At least two of these offices were connected with the care, tuning and general supervision of the household musical instruments, including the harpsichords.   Pay under the Stuarts was usually in arrears, and we see Purcell in 1687 asking for, among other items, a financial grant to cover an estimated portage and tuning of a harpsichord to a concert before the King four times a year, which was the minimum number of "songs" he expected to be commanded to, using, I think, the word "songs" to denote a concert.   Here again we find the player on the harpsichord was also its tuner, and, in this case at least, the man who also supervised its getting into position, and who was paid for all these jobs.   So here we have another instance of the lack of specialization in the seventeenth century.

Purcell was a very busy practising musician, composing for Church and State, for Westminster Abbey, the Chapel Royal and the theatre in Dorset Gardens: in between times he wrote a little chamber music. His actual solo harpsichord music is small in quantity, though he would have had the instrument much more habitually in mind than, say, Mr. Benjamin Britten, a similarly active composer of our own day, would have the pianoforte.   The figured bass for harpsichord sustained the theatrical recitatives, and would have sounded through the orchestra of strings in the smallish theatre.

On the eve of St. Cecilia's Day, 1695, he died, perhaps of a lung sickness.

When we turn to Handel we turn to a more robust figure, though not to a more vital one. Handel landed on these shores for the first time in the autumn of 1710, aged twenty-five. It would be satisfying to know which particular shore it was, but the biographers are beautifully vague upon the point. Even Hawkins who knows most things, right or wrong, contents himself as to Handel's reception by saying that it was in the open arms of the manager of the Queen's Theatre in the Haymarket. Here he presided at the harpsichord for his first London opera, with, perhaps, the really beautiful manager, a youth of his own age, sitting beside him. Handel left England once, and then again, and perhaps three times, but each period away was shorter and shorter: at first he left because he was in the employment of the Elector of Hanover; when that imperial nobleman became also King of England, Handel sweetened his presence by placing his harpsichord upon a gilded barge, and with his strings, trumpets and drums about him, serenading His Majesty as he was rowed up the Thames to Westminster Stairs, a procedure by no means so original as it sounds to-day. When Handel left England subsequently it was to find singers, to revisit his native Halle (but purely as a visit), or to take the waters of a Continental spa when, as an old man, he seems to have had a nervous breakdown, or something very like, one of the symptoms being an apparent inability to compose unless he started off with a quoted idea. These quoted ideas, which hardly occur in his harpsichord music, are no more diminutions of his genius and originality than a splash of petrol on a carburettor plug testifies to anything wrong with the engine: it just set the machine in action. In the end, Handel honoured us by becoming a naturalized Englishman, perhaps the greatest naturalized Englishman in our whole history.

Active, attractive, not a woman's man, a good eater and drinker, a bad linguist, a kind, generous, even benevolent soul, there was something of the Dr. Johnson about him—devout, learned, matter-of-fact, striving in his work for clarity and power. His household, like Dr. Johnson's, was unorthodox, and seems to have consisted of protégés: there was a man named Smith from Anspach who looked after his financial affairs for him to some extent. Smith's son, named John Christopher, caught Handel's fancy, and was taught the harpsichord by the master in person. When he grew up he became Handel's copyist as the portrait by Zoffany shows, perhaps even his filler-up of figured basses and general bottle-washer when Handel was in the heat of composition and too aware of what he wanted to say next to

correct and fill out what he had already written.   J. C. Smith eventually became Handel's concert organizer, and was at length bequeathed
the harpsichord whose photograph is reproduced in the illustration facing
p. 209.   This instrument he gave, in gratitude for the continuation
of a pension, to George III, whence it comes into public view at the
Victoria and Albert Museum.   Another musician lived with him, a
cellist who also sang and who, if we may believe a painting of him
sitting with his cello and the famous harpsichord near, was fond of
beer and smoking: this amiable musician was his cook named Waltz.
He too, perhaps, was called in to help Smith finish off manuscripts.
Who wrote some of the passage work in the well-known harpsichord
Fantasia in C, Waltz or Smith?   Certainly not Handel.   Smith
actually wrote an opera.   Indeed, Handel's helpers were not to be
sneered at, and when the master declared that Gluck, who visited
London and presumably directed his opera from the harpsichord in the
King's Theatre in the Haymarket, knew no more counterpoint than
his cook, it was no great abuse.

It was almost certain that Handel knew Arne.   When Handel's
setting of the pastoral by Gay, *Acis and Galatea*, had its first performance in the Duke of Canons theatre on his estate near Edgware, young
Arne was at the harpsichord and this boy's sister sang the part of Galatea while Waltz sang Polyphemus.   May we imagine them dining
together, not at the Duke's table, but at the second one?   Along with
the Duke's chaplain, his secretary and the gentlemen who supervised
his stables, his garden and his estates.   Was such a position so very
humiliating, so much worse than that of a Walton or Britten in need
of being "sponsored" by some Government departments?

All three monarchs under whom Handel worked, Queen Anne
and the first two Georges, were kind to him and liked his music,
facts enough to make all music-lovers kind to the memories of these
not always respectfully treated crowned heads.   Not that such kindness was not sometimes embarrassing.   I am indebted to Miss Gladys
Scott Thomson for permission to quote from a letter written by the
aged Duchess of Marlborough to her grand-daughter, the Duchess of
Bedford, 24th June, 1735:

> I never in my life heard so strange a thing as happened at
> an opera not long before the King left England.   Mr Seymour,
> who is member of parliament for Marlborough, at a great
> distance from His Majesty, was in some box over the stage, or
> somewhere high, and His Majesty observed that there was

a man in a hat, at which he was very much offended; and after speaking of it with some warmth he sent my Lord Carlo up to him, and he told Mr Seymour as civilly as he could, that His Majesty would have him pull off his hat.   Mr Seymour answered that he was ill, and could not do it for fear of catching cold.   Several curious messages followed, but all in vain; for Mr Seymour said that he had paid for his place and he would not prejudice his health. And a great deal passed that is not to be written; but Mr Seymour stood to his point.

Another extraordinary thing happened of much the same nature.   The famous dancing woman (I do not know her name) in the opera, the audience were so excessive fond of her that they hollered out "encore" several times to have her dance over again, which she could not do, because as she was coming on again, the King made a motion with his hand that she should not.   At last the dispute was so violent that to put an end to it, the curtain was let down, whereby the spectators lost all after the third act.

I forgot to give an account in this great struggle concerning the hat, His Majesty ordered the guard to go up and take it away; but his servants in the box prevailed with him not to do it, saying he was an ill-bred country gentleman but was of a great family and had many friends, and it would make a noise which was better not to do.   Mr Seymour agreed with those that carried the King's message that he had chosen to sit in a place that he thought would give no offence, on account of his ill health, that he should have thought it very wrong to have done anything of that sort in the King's palaces, but there was no kings at operas or playhouses where everybody might sit as they pleased.

Meanwhile we may imagine Handel directing the music amid the din of the audience yelling for the dancer, the shuffles and conversations as the messages went backwards and forwards between the King and Mr. Seymour, and no doubt wondering if he gained or lost by Royal Patronage.

Often when Handel was thus at the harpsichord he would improvise.   In Armida's aria at the end of Act II in this first opera of *Rinaldo* there is a pause and blank staves on which the word "cembalo" is printed, meaning not so much a cadenza, as a free improvisation bringing the music forward, while a cadenza is dynamically and often emotionally static.   And so the opera audience would listen to "nervous, exalted and harmonious" music from the harpsichord before the players adjusted their violins once more under their chins.

Piracy as well as royalty worried Handel in connexion with harpsichord music: of course, in his larger spheres of activity he had many more worries still—a prima donna in tears, an impresario scheming with a nobleman, a debt—which seem always in the background. In the Preface to the first volume of his *Suites de Pieces pour le Clavecin* (why, one wonders, written in French?) "printed for the Author and are to be had at Christopher Smith's and by R. Mears engraved and Printed at Cluer's Printing-Office in Bow Churchyard Cheapside 1720", Handel himself writes, "I have been obliged to publish some of the following Lessons, because Surrepticious and incorrect copies of them have got Abroad. I have added several new ones to make the Work more usefull, which if it meets with a favourable Reception; I will still proceed to publish more, reckoning it my duty, with my Small Talentt, to Serve a Nation from which I have receiv'd so Generous a Protection."

It is a curious thing that when we read of Handel playing the harpsichord in private houses to amuse himself or others, for instance at Mrs. Cibber's where he played the Overture to his opera *Siroe*, that he did not usually play his Lessons, but his operatic or oratoric overtures and even choruses. One or two of his printed harpsichord fugues are such choruses rearranged. Burney played such orchestral arrangements in Kirkman's warehouse in Soho before Fulke Greville. Yet surely Handel's string music, with trumpets and drums and perhaps bassoons and oboes, is not really effective on a keyboard, nor on an organ, on which instrument such arrangements are still to be heard. Burney, to whom we owe the Mrs. Cibber story, goes on: "his hand was then so fat, that the knuckles, which usually appear convex, were like those of a child, dinted or dimpled in, so as to be rendered concave; however, his touch was so smooth, and the tone of the instrument so much cherished, that his fingers seemed to grow to the keys. They were so curved and compact, when he played, that no motion, and scarcely the fingers themselves could be discovered."

One of Handel's particular friends at one time was Greene, the organist of St. Paul's, with whom he used to hobnob at the organ, repairing to a tavern in the Churchyard afterwards. Later there was an estrangement because Greene also liked an imported operatic rival of Handel's. Greene wrote some harpsichord music, perhaps more than Handel did, but his music has died with him.

Not so Nares's, for a somewhat insipid three-movement Lesson in B flat is reproduced in full and with fostering parental pride by Fuller-Maitland in the fourth volume of that somewhat curious work, the

1902 Oxford History of Music.   Nares was organist and composer to
the Chapel Royal, following on Greene in that post.

Arne we have already met, at Canons, in the performance of *Acis
and Galatea*.   He is the man whose music is next after Handel's in the
early and middle eighteenth century for modern remembrance.   Who
would come third, J. C. Bach?   And fourth?   Well, no one, just
possibly the Nares aforementioned.   There is no fifth.   Arne, with
J. S. Bach and Handel, is one of the group of boys about whom similar
legends exist: the garret, the smuggled spinet or clavichord, the moonlight, and the irate father or guardian.   To the eighteenth century
such a legend was as necessary to their conception of a composer as
two loves, one good and the other bad, is necessary to the Hollywood
artist.

Arne's father was an upholsterer and maker of coffins in the Covent
Garden area, and young Thomas was in due course, the family pros-
pering, sent to Eton, a school which has had the honour of producing
two of our best composers between Purcell and Elgar, that is to say,
of producing Arne and Parry.   Arne overcame the dislike of his
father for a musical profession, in fact his father eventually came
blundering into things by producing, without Handel's permission, a
performance of *Acis and Galatea* in the Haymarket Theatre (indifferently called the King's or the Queen's Theatre according to the sex of
the reigning monarch).   There should be no surprise at an upholsterer
starting as impresario.   This particular upholsterer had in his daughter,
Sussanah Maria, later Mrs. Cibber (Handel's hostess when he played
in *Siroe*), one of the greatest singers of the time.   He also had a ready-
made maestro to direct from the harpsichord in his son.   Other im-
presarios were amateurs; the Handel-welcoming manager of the
Haymarket himself had been a dabbler in pills and was to end his life
distilling whisky in a small town of the Highlands of Scotland.

Thomas Arne was a drinking and wenching example of eighteenth-
century manhood, facts which did not prevent him from writing some
charming and tender music for the harpsichord.   Like Purcell, he
was essentially a Londoner, but while the older and greater master
was rooted in Westminster, Arne was centred in the district north of
the Thames and between the two cities: Covent Garden, Lincoln's Inn
Fields and Drury Lane.

In Thomas Roseingrave we not only meet a man interesting in
himself, but through him we also meet one of the greatest harpsichord figures of the times, the equal of Handel himself, in Domenico

Scarlatti, who was a friend of Roseingrave's, and who visited London. As for visits to London, a city which then occupied much the position that New York now does, I would say, as a sort of challenge to be proved wrong, that every great composer of the eighteenth century visited London except J. S. Bach.

In 1725 the post of organist to St. George's famous and fashionable church in Hanover Square was vacant, and applicants were invited to furnish compositions to a tribunal consisting of Greene, organist of St. Paul's, Pepusch, already perhaps at work with Gay on the tunes and figured basses which were to make him immortal, and one un-known, with the charming name of Galliard. The winning entry was from the Irishman Thomas Roseingrave, who thereupon set himself up in fashionable London as a teacher, with his organistship to give him background—perhaps, indeed, a background of respecta-bility. But Archdeacon Coxe in his *Anecdotes of George Frederick Handel and John Christopher Smith* tells a sad story. Roseingrave submitted to the temptation which must assail all true men who also teach the ladies. But the girl he fell in love with had a wealthy and ambitious father, who showed Roseingrave the door. This "showing the door" was no empty formula: in those days the masters of music more often visited at their pupil's residences than their pupils came to them. Roseingrave lost not only the girl, as such, but the girl in her quality of pupil, and the father saw to it that he lost other pupils, too. Archdeacon Coxe goes on to say that the disappointment affected Roseingrave's brain, but he must surely have been a rather unimaginative man not to have anticipated just such difficulties. His teaching practice fell away the faster as he brooded the more, and the time came when he had to depend upon his organist's stipend of fifty pounds a year— quite a handsome sum when paid in gold and without income-tax deductions. However, the Archdeacon seems not to have considered the salary sufficient, for he adds that Roseingrave "was often in indigence". In this unhappy state he took refuge in the country, in Hampstead. He became mentally unbalanced, and comforted him-self, it is said, by writing out passages from Palestrina and sticking them on the wall: a charming madness. Besides Palestrina, he occupied himself with Scarlatti, and edited *Forty-two Suites of Lessons for the Harpsichord by Domenico Scarlatti*, introducing the whole by a lesson of his own. This edition, one of the first in Europe, was successfully published by a music-seller of Cheapside. Perhaps it was during his Hampstead retirement that Roseingrave wrote his other harpsichord music, *Eight Suites for Harpsichord or Spinet*.   Burney was later to call his music "intolerably harsh and ungrateful" and alludes to "a licentious and extravagant modulation, and a more frequent use of the sharp third and flat sixth, than any composer with whose works I am at all acquainted, not excepting Dr. Blow. . . ."

Roseingrave was born in Dublin and to this city he seems to have returned after his London adventures; in Dublin he was able to act as host to Domenico Scarlatti, who stayed with him several months before continuing his journey from Spain to London, leaving Roseingrave behind.   Mrs. Delaney says in a letter: "Mr. Roseingrave, who was sent away from St. George's Church on account of his mad fits, is now in Ireland, and at times can play very well on the harpsichord." Then the *Dublin Journal* of the 3rd February, 1753, carried this advertisement showing what was to happen between the acts of a forthcoming opera by "Mr. Roseingrave [who] will perform Scarlatti's *Lessons on the Harpsichord*, with his own additions, and will conclude with his celebrated *Almand*".   Anyone who had been permitting himself to become fond of the errant late organist of St. George's, Hanover Square, will feel the "with his own additions" a greater indictment than anything the bishops and curates could have committed to his charge.

John Christian (to anglicize a little) Bach was born of the great John Sebastian and Anna Magdalena in Leipzig.   When he grew old enough to notice things, he found that a boy surnamed Abel was living in his home, being one of the several and sometimes many pupils or apprentices of his very busy father.   Later in life, both middle-aged men, Abel and J. C. Bach met each other in London.   Abel had been teacher and harpsichordist to Queen Charlotte for two or three years when J. C. Bach arrived to write opera and to teach and compose for the harpsichord.   These two attractive Germans lived together in a street very near Soho Square on terms of bantering affection, and the painter Gainsborough was one of their circle.   Gainsborough, who was very musical, but by no means a musician, would dare to attempt to play the harpsichord at the Bach-Abel's, his hosts trying in vain to stop the awful noise.   From their house it was an easy walk to see Kirkman or Shudi, Carlisle House concerts were very nearly literally next door, and surely commissions could be picked up quietly by discreet professional gentlemen.   A pupil wants a harpsichord, an attender at the Carlisle Concerts wishes to learn the instrument: nothing easier, dear lady.   Dr. Johnson made one of his deliberate coat-trailing faux pas in his question to his old friend Dr. Burney as to whom Bach was, "is he a piper?"

Little Mozart when he came to London with his family, met the "English" Bach, as he was called, and admired him. His childish music was copied from him: it even looks like his. This, for instance,

for violin or flute with harpsichord accompaniment, the left hand executing an Alberti bass. As Mozart grew older the J. C. Bach influence dwindled to nothing, for all that some commentators say that their music is similar, and that J. C. Bach at his best is like and equal to Mozart at his not so best. But the facts are, as I see them, that when J. C. Bach is at his most impressive, he leans back towards his father, as in his harpsichord sonata in C minor Op. 5 No. 6, published as late as 1770.

J. C. Bach was one of the first composers, Abel perhaps being his only rival, to write early examples of what we would nowadays recognize as symphonies. The harpsichord was still necessary for their performance, as the cello and double bass line was invariably fitted with a figured bass.

Towards the end of the century Haydn visited us to give his twelve last and (as is usually thought) greatest symphonies under the auspices of an impresario named Salomon in the Hanover Square Rooms. A keyboard instrument was still considered an essential, but it was by then a pianoforte, not a harpsichord, and Haydn certainly did not trouble to write 6/4 5/3 at the end of a cadence. Haydn wrote some keyboard music, one slow movement a sort of love song for his Buckingham Gate widow, but it was designed for the pianoforte rather than the harpsichord. Haydn was never much of a harpsi-chordist: as a youth he had loved the clavichord, and graduated to the early and not dissimilar pianoforte. For all that, the opening move-ment of his best-known keyboard concerto, that in D, is clearly harpsichord music.

In fact, the victory of the aristocratic, straight-sided, long and lean grand pianoforte was complete before Haydn, Mozart, Clementi, Dussek and Beethoven had ceased to allow their publishers to inscribe title-pages of collections of sonatas with "for harpsichord or piano-forte" (it was usually in French, "pour le clavecin ou le piano forte"), and Clementi was building harpsichords as late as 1803, though his music was essentially pianistic.

So the harpsichord composers in England split into two groups: the first, the smaller, is entirely English, is Stuart, grouped round the Court and Westminster Abbey, and is headed by Purcell. The second, larger, is almost entirely foreign, Hanoverian, grouped round Soho and Covent Garden, and is headed by Handel. Members of both these groups led most active and pluralistic lives: taking in pupils for harpsichord lessons, tuning and repairing the instruments, even building them, helping in harpsichord warehouses, printing and publishing harpsichord music, accompanying singers and holding together orchestras and, from the keyboard, controlling operatic performances. All this in addition to other and great musical activities, writing and rehearsing opera and oratorio, the duties of the organ loft, collecting and writing anthems and services, and constant attendance on "the Great", which included dedications like: "a son Altesse Serenissime Monseigneur le Duc Ernest Duc le Mecklenbourg . . . et Major General des Armees de S. M. Britannique . . ." This typical dedication shows the national mixtures: French words imported by Charles II, German men imported by George I, and English offices because it was in England these things happened. As has been said a few pages back, the nearest modern equivalent is New York.

Some writers are unhappy at the foreign influence which crushed English music during the eighteenth and nineteenth centuries, and blame Handel, merely, as far as I can make out, because he was the greatest genius among them. But he was just one of many foreigners, and it is his virtue that he was the greatest. If our own greatest, Arne, was completely Handel's inferior, that is our fault. There is now no danger at all from as many visits from as many Honeggers and Hindemiths as the Continent cares to send us. In just the same way, the Elizabethans and early Jacobeans could have faced any competition: Palestrina and Monteverdi themselves would not have dwarfed Byrd, Morley and Dowland, to name only three.

3. The Music

In the first place, the music of the time does not come down to us in beautiful manuscript, as is the case with the sixteenth century. It is almost all printed, often rather badly printed. After *Parthenia*, and published when that Byrd-Bull-Farnaby anthology had not lost its vogue, came *Musick's Hand-maid, New Lessons and Instructions for the Virginals or Harpsychord.* Playford was the publisher, and in the shop near the Temple selling patent medicines and harpsycons he offered it for sale in 1663, and reprinted it in 1678. It is a small oblong quarto with a pretty vignette on the title-page showing performers on the virginal and the violin, engraved by one William Vaughan. The music in this collection is spare and dull, a great drop from *Parthenia*.

However, a second part to *Musick's Hand-maid* was added in 1689, and this second part contains some of the harpsichord music of its editor, Purcell himself. "The Virginal," says Playford, "is strung with one single course of strings; the Harpsichord with two or more, and is fuller and louder." But the difference between virginal and harpsichord music does not lie in its fullness and loudness.

Firstly, the type of melody is quite different. Byrd, Bull, Farnaby and Gibbons were influenced by ecclesiastical chants, by madrigal-like "points", by folk-song and folk-dances and by "courtly masquing airs". Purcell was influenced by the opera and the sort of singing Charles II sent Pelham Humfreys to Versailles to bring back, even into religious music. Charles liked music he could beat time to, and used, not even very good-humouredly, to ask if he had not ears as well as anybody else when some brave enthusiast played Elizabethan music before him, music too rhythmical to be metrical.

Purcellian melody then is clear metrical and direct, usually unsuited for contrapuntal treatment: it follows it had a quite different sort of ornamentation, derived, indeed, it is not too much to say, from the coloratura of *castrati* like Sefauchi (or Siface) for whom Purcell wrote an harpsichord "farewell" in D minor, a short piece which certainly requires the vocal line, the treble, of course, in this case, to be fully ornamented.

Songs and dances and Act Tunes were used in the harpsichord collections, or borrowed from them for the stage. One of Purcell's most moving Grounds comes from the 1683 St. Cecilia Ode. In his music include as much dramatic ornamentation as can be managed:

a good deal can be managed on a harpsichord and quite a lot on an early pianoforte, such as one of the square type, pre-Victorian instruments preferably, which seem to be coming into favour again. On a modern instrument with its tension to enable as much legato as possible, such ornamentation is difficult, for it sounds clumsy, and indeed much music for the harpsichord sounds thin on it. The Purcell Suite in G minor seems almost to consist of delicious double wobbles, presumably executed before the beat, the Almand, Courante and Saraband seeming to vie with each other as to how many can be fitted in. Typically the last movement, a Chacone, also forms material for the possibly earlier "Curtain Tune" which finishes off *Timon of Athens*. It is almost as though Purcell had a stage with a *castrato* on it in his mind's eye as he wrote: an unpoetic conception to that school of musical appreciators who prefer a composer to entertain the fairies at the bottom of his garden.

Playford was the great musical business man in the Stuart era, Walsh took his place in the Hanoverian, and was Handel's man of business. Handel had quarrels with him from time to time: not surprising, considering that Walsh had a quite Levantine strain of rather nasty cunning. For instance, he would pirate words and not bother to correct proofs, and when a half-mad composer saw his reputation about to be ruined because of the misprints, Walsh would inquire if he, the composer, thought it worth his while to pay a handsome sum for their removal, thus acknowledging the piracy. Walsh must, however, either have had no rivals, or some virtues, for not only Handel but almost all the other composers in London did business with either father or son Walsh, to whom there are over thirty references in the index of Burney's *History*. And Hawkins is very bitter. "Their publications were in numberless instances a disgrace to the science and its professors; but they got money, and no one complained." This is not quite true: Handel did complain, and gave some other publisher a chance, but these rivals found themselves unable to stand their ground, thereby, as Hawkins adds, "leaving a son of Walsh in possession of almost the whole trade of the kingdom".

Most of the harpsichord music printed by Walsh and others was written by Londoners, native or immigrant; only a few Continental residents' work became known. We have seen how Roseingrave introduced Scarlatti; Mattheson, an inferior contemporary of Bach's, was known for one publication in two volumes, but Bach himself was known only by reputation, and a somewhat limited reputation at that.   Rameau does not seem to have been played, either.   It was in fact an insular London, content with itself and only admitting Scarlatti.

Of its old virginal music this London was sometimes contemptuous: it was considered "too common and vulgar to afford pleasure, or even to be heard with patience, by fastidious judges of modern melody"—such a fastidious judge being, of course, the writer, Dr. Charles Burney.   The same critic says of Mattheson that his pieces are "not only composed by one of the greatest masters of the age, in a taste altogether Pleasing and Sublime, but are peculiarly adapted to that Instrument" (i.e. the harpsichord).

In the passage of two centuries the music of the old virginal composers has become more and more modern, and so too has the harpsichord music of Purcell.   The very forms of Purcell, the ground bass for instance, has come again into prominence in the hands of such composers as Rawsthorne and Britten, while the false relations which so pained Burney on finding them even in the works of Dr. Blow lend, in our ears, peculiar poignancy to the music of Purcell and his predecessors.   The G minor Chacone of Purcell which also forms the Curtain Tune in *Timon of Athens* when played on the harpsichord must have formed one of those "lively and trickling Movements" whose perpetual false relations between E flat and E natural "thrill in the Ear", as old Avison describes it.

Lessons were, as we have seen, usually Suites, and quite different from Tutors, but as these became more popular the word Lesson was dropped, until it reappeared with a new and modern meaning.   Thus Walsh in 1712 put out Babell's *Suits of the most Celebrated Lessons*, music which was in fact arrangements from the operas, chiefly from Handel's *Rinaldo*.   Nearly fifty years later came *The Compleat Tutor for the Harpsichord or Spinnet, wherein is shewn the Italian manner of Fingering*.   And by 1800 we have the modern usage: *Progressive Lessons for Beginners on the Harpsichord or Piano-Forte for the Use of Schools*.   But as this title says, the pianoforte was by then in mind, and in the rapid survey of harpsichord music in England the word Lesson can be taken as interchangeable with the words Suites or Pieces as the case may be.

The Suite in its full form was a work consisting of at least four movements, each named after a dance, but the music was no more written for dancing than the Minuets and Trios of the Haydn symphony.   In the Suite the four-movement cycle familiar to orchestral

P

concert-goers is the rule, but it is the symphonic form in which the
Scherzo comes before the slow movement, not after it.   The string
quartet is after all nearer in spirit to this music than the symphony, and
Debussy's quartet is the thing to remember the arrangement of the
movements by, even to their shortness and to the use of themes in
more than one movement.

The opening *allegro* then, was the Allemande, a flowing movement
in even quavers or semiquavers and in rather square time, often very
majestical.   The *scherzo* was the Courante, a quicker triple movement
often based on the melody of the Allemande.   The Italians used a
Corrente in simple triple time, but the French Courante had cross
accents, the 3/2 time tending to break up into 6/4 at the cadences.
The slow movement, the *andante*, was the Sarabande, a grave slow
dance in triple time in this metre

$$\frac{3}{4} \, \quad \text{♩ ♩. ♪ | ♩ ♩}$$

or any of its obvious variants.   Sometimes it was the most highly
ornamented because the most vocal of the movements: there is no
musical difference between several of the well-known Handel arias
in slow triple time (for instance, the well-known one in *Rinaldo*) and
his harpsichord Sarabandes.   Lastly in place of the *rondo allegro* came
the Gigue, a movement in 12/8 or 6/8, which had two forms, a
simpler one in which the quavers and dotted crotchets went
swimmingly along, sometimes too long, and a more complex, fugal
form, in which the initial theme in 12/8 or 6/8 was worked out in
double counterpoint reversed at the double bar, sometimes inverted
as well.

Between the Sarabande and the Gigue the composer was free to
insert any *galantieren* he liked, a minuet, a piece with an echo effect,
a caprice, or what he wished.   To introduce the whole came an
opening movement, usually called a Prelude.

All the regulation movements were in binary form; that is to say,
a double repeat bar splits the movement in two, the music from the
opening key moves into the dominant, after the double bar there may
be a touch of subdominant and so leading back to the tonic.   If the
composer starts off with one idea and develops a part of it so as almost
to convey a new melody in the dominant, and if, after the double bar,
there is a short development, then we are on the threshold of one aspect
of sonata form.   Only one aspect, however, because the texture of

the music in Suite movements remains homogeneous throughout, like the orchestration in a concerto grosso movement. In playing these regulation movements with repeats it is supposed that the harpsichord players used different registrations, perhaps different manuals. In playing them upon the pianoforte different tone values or different touches or, more intellectual, different parts may be brought out.

In the non-regulation movements, the Preludes were rarely in this binary form, but were like free improvisations. Sometimes, however, they were full Overtures of an orchestral nature, slow-quick-slow, with the quick middle often fugued, and sometimes both slow and quick repeated. The *galantieren* was almost always in binary form, the so-called Airs not being popular tunes at all, but simple melodious flowing movements.

Purists say that when this music is played on the pianoforte romantic stresses should be disallowed. Provided one does not play Handel as though he were Chopin, there are these considerations to be borne in mind. Firstly, the voice remained the most important musical instrument, some Suite movements were transcriptions from vocal music, many Suite movements were modelled on it. Musical stresses, such as the usual phrasing $<$ $>$ of a phrase, especially a phrase with an upward contour, are modelled upon the natural rise and fall of the human voice. Such stress therefore as is necessary to make a part sing is essential in playing this old music. However impossible such singing may be on the organ, it is possible on the harpsichord, though this instrument has not the responsiveness of the pianoforte or clavichord. Secondly the music of the times was full of emotion; the age in which "He was despised" from *Messiah* was written, in which *Clarissa* was the best selling novel and in which Gray was the coming poet (not to mention Cowper a little later) was full of sensibility. The wonder is, that the glories of the nineteenth-century romantic movement should ever have obscured the stronger, but no less tender, glories of the eighteenth-century romantics. Gray, by the way, could play well enough to amuse himself—J. C. Bach was his favourite. To go back a hundred years, we must not forget the wind music that made Pepys recall the days when he was sick for the love of his wife.

None of Purcell's Suites contain the full regulation movements: that in C major is as complete as most. After a fugal and spirited Prelude we have an Almand full of subtle part writing, a vocal Courante richly ornamented, and both this movement and the subsequent

Saraband shows Purcell's almost, at times, undue delight in syncopation.   One wonders if the *castrati* practised swing, like muted modern
trumpeteers?   Then follow the voluntary movements, a Cebell (a
sort of Gavotte), Minuet, Rigadoon, a piece with no name in 3/4
time and a March which closes the work—there is no Gigue.

Handel, who in length and breadth is to Purcell as Beethoven is to
Haydn (but the larger building is not always the more beautiful),
has written some monumental Suites.   The first set of eight, *Suites
de Pieces pour le Clavecin*, are very free, contain some magnificent
introductory fugues and their dance movements are sometimes labelled
simply Allegro or whatever it is, though the dance origin of the subsequent movement is clear.   The second set of eight with the same
title, the words *Second Volume* only added, contain on the whole
stricter Suites with Allemande, Courante, Saraband, Gigue following
in due order, but this fact coupled with the quality of some of the
music makes one wonder.   Some of them consist of only three movements and these movements are shorter and somewhat glib.   One
might almost suppose that in the case of one or two of the Gigues,
Handel had hastily written out the tune, added a few remarks as to the
way the piece was to be developed, added the two most important
cadences, the one at the end of the first part and the last one of all, and
handed the sheet to Waltz his cook or to J. C. Smith his protegé to
finish.   Further, this second set lacks those magnificent fugues which,
in the first set, studded the music like diamonds.   The F sharp minor,
the E minor, the D minor and the F minor are among the greatest
keyboard fugues ever written: there is nothing of comparable workmanship in the second set pirated by Walsh.

But instead of differentiating between the great Handel and
Waltzing Handel, so to speak, many writers have written detractingly
of Handel's whole keyboard output.   Walker, in his *Music in England*
exaggerates a good deal the number of pages in which Handel's writing
is admittedly perfunctory.   Grove is of the opinion that "all Handel's
music written for the harpsichord or clavichord suffers from one
defect.   In comparison with J. S. Bach, Domenico Scarlatti, Couperin
or Rameau, it is angular without gaining character, hard without
brilliance. . . .   It is probable that his own playing, which is known
to have been of the highest order of technical accomplishment, was
largely improvisational".   So the great Suites in D minor, G minor
and F minor are "angular and hard"?   But they are nothing of the
sort, they are to me full of character, and brilliant, to which one may

add, dramatic and expressive, exciting and tender, and, generally speaking, to be numbered among the finest Suites in the literature of the domestic keyboard instruments.

Samuel Butler would have gone much further in this. But nowadays the merits of Handel as a keyboard writer are hardly controversial for there seems a general ignorance on the subject, few people apparently caring, after their pupil stage of learning a few pieces from an Handel Album for the Young or some such compilation, to inspect a complete edition of Handel's keyboard music. Many teachers of the pianoforte seem not to be aware that Handel himself wrote variations on the theme in B flat chosen by Brahms more than a hundred years later for his well-known set.

Consider for a moment the monumental greatness of the set of pieces called *Three Lessons*, consisting of

> Prelude in B flat ("Erewhon"),
> Air and variations in B flat ("Brahms"),
> Minuet in G minor,
> Chaconne in G major.

These four pieces (the first and second consist of Lesson No. 1) form a coherent whole.

The Prelude is improvisatory, and has little intrinsic musical importance, but it leads to the announcement of the theme which so interested Brahms that he had to treat it anew. Handel's own variations are strong and flowing, but the musical plane is only one step higher than the Prelude.

The Minuet introduces us to the relative minor, and is a sweetly pretty little tune: it closes, without a *tierce de picardie*, in G minor, and with the first chord of the ensuing Chaconne we are in another world; in the tonic major of the Minuet, in G major. The strong, swinging tune and the virile variations are in the mode of the "Brahms", and as eight variations run their course they become less musically interesting, because we are about to experience the second dramatic crisis, the eighth variation, Adagio, in the tonic minor—the G minor of the Minuet and the relative minor of the Prelude and "Brahms" Variations. We now are in the core of the whole work, and with the last of the G minor variations, Variation No. 16, we have the climax itself, passionate and singing: the following five variations lessen the musical interest, return us to G major, but keep the tremendous momentum attained thundering along in a simplified version of the tune laid out in spread chords. This is Handel at his most masterful:

extrovert, sweeping, large, disdainful of ornamentation so long as he gets his proportions and his key relationships right: of all composers, one of the most architectural.

The Sonatas of Scarlatti were things quite different from the Suites of Handel and of Purcell except that they were mostly in binary form and some of them have some similarity to dance movements. Most of them, however, are quite different in both spirit and texture. As to the spirit, Scarlatti was a Neapolitan, as we have seen in Chapter III. As an Appendix will explain, he spent many years in the Iberian Peninsula. Therefore his difference in spirit from those Londoners, Purcell and Handel, may well be allowed. But the difference in his texture is more baffling. It is partly due to the Spanish and Neapolitan use of the guitar, and Scarlatti does make the harpsichord sometimes sound like a guitar, a thing it is well able to do. His genius, however, was much freer than that of his contemporary harpsichordists, and no wonder proper little Fanny Burney says of him that he was "wild but masterly". After Roseingrave's introduction of Scarlatti's harpsichord music into London by the two volumes published in 1739, not much seems to have been added until the great Longo edition. His operas and other works have been allowed to lapse and have excited no interest. Few of Domenico Scarlatti's complete operas have ever been given in London: indeed, it would appear that after Handel and before Weber descended on us, most opera was made up of *pastiches* from any scores lying around handy, including Domenico Scarlatti scores. Scarlatti is quite different in every way from Chopin, why therefore couple them? For this reason: both are now known only for their keyboard music. One may have put his whole heart into it, writing other things without a heart, the other had no heart even to try other things. At least let us give full credit to Roseingrave for introducing this most civilized and individual composer to the London of Handel.

The sonata was not a harpsichord form. Sonata texture (let us forget the first subject, second subject, development and recapitulation theory, a theory rarely borne out by actual living music) is the great thing about the sonata, but I cannot explain its difference from Suite texture, though it is very obvious. The Suite is, within each movement, homogeneous: the Sonata heterogeneous. How far does this take us? The opening two bars of Mozart's Serenade, *Eine Kleine Nachtmusik* is so similar to the equivalent two bars of the second movement of Handel's Concerto grosso No. 1 in G, that if the cello parts got mixed, I don't think there would be any harm done. Yet the one is as clearly sonata music as the other is suite: I have heard someone (a German, of course) explain it that one is the music of sensibility and the other is baroque. But labels do not teach us why and how the two styles are different.

Anyhow, the point here is, that sonata form does not agree with the harpsichord. It requires the clavichord or the pianoforte, because it was built up on the string quartet (of which the clavichord is the ghost) and the orchestra (of which the pianoforte is the mocking ghost). Arne called his works Sonatas. They are, rather, hybrids, and though they suit the pianoforte they must often have been played on the harpsichord when they were published in 1762.

The Sonata in D minor containing the vigorous fugue is deservedly famous, while several movements from the others have an agreeable appeal. But Arne, like other second-rate composers of the mid-eighteenth century, often began better than he could continue. Thus the opening Andante of the first Sonata, in F, starts with an interesting phrase, which is duly answered in the second bar, but which then degenerates into meaningless scale passages in triple semiquavers until a modulation into the dominant brings the first section to a close. The second section opens with the initial phrase in the dominant, but with a different answering phrase. Then the triplets in C major scales occupy a few bars until we have another cliché of the times— repeated notes, usually sixths. At last, however, the initial phrase reappears in the tonic with such development as may be attained by a sequence, until five or six bars more of triplets brings the movement to two bars of cadenza, after which an Allegro almost entirely innocent of any idea whatever concludes the sonata.

The Adagio of the E minor work is short and affecting, but the next Sonata, in G, is perhaps the most disappointing of all. The *Preludio, quasi improvisazione* is very poor improvising indeed, and the stirring opening of the succeeding Allegro is treated in the usual Arne manner of bridge passages of considerable dullness leading to the theme in the dominant, which in turn leads back to the theme in the tonic.

That Arne can think continuously is, however, shown by his Sonata in D minor, with its Andante, conceived as a whole, and on quite a large scale; its short but expressive Siciliano, the Fugue already alluded to; and a pleasant brisk Allegro with some (if not much) pretence at fugal entry. There is no need to dwell on his other harpsichord music, for we have examined the best and the worst; but what a drop from the standard of the second volume of *Musick's Handmaid*!

When Charlotte of Mecklenburgh, who played old English music on her voyage over, arrived in England and became Queen, she chose as her harpsichord master the organist of St. Martin's in the Fields, an accomplished player who used to draw Handel himself, it is reported, into the congregation to hear him. Now in middle age, this organist had also behind him a reputation for neatness and rapidity in the execution of the music of Scarlatti, another pointer to the popularity of Roseingrave's edition. Queen Charlotte therefore continued the patronage of music given by the Hanoverian line of monarchs who, though often stupid and boorish in regard to the other arts ("I hate boetry and bainting," growled George II when confronted with plates by Hogarth), loved music, and loved with a taste and discretion which passed gradually with the years into loving with obstinacy and conservatism.

To return to J. C. Bach, whose opera *Orione* was the first fruits of his appointment to the position of composer to the King's Theatre. The first two performances of this opera were attended by the King and Queen, and *Orione* ran for three months, something which very few operas can do nowadays. Queen Charlotte then appointed J. C. Bach to be one of her musicians, and perhaps she liked his music as much as Scarlatti's, for Burney says that J. C. Bach's compositions for the clavier were "such as ladies can execute with little trouble". Some have said that J. C. Bach himself was a poor player, but we have to remember that Queen Charlotte was used to the tuition of a man who excelled in playing the difficult music of Scarlatti, and was not really likely to have favoured a decidedly poorer player. Further, one doesn't quite see the justice of Burney's remark as to the ease of performance of J. C. Bach's Sonatas. The early sonatas of Haydn are, for instance, a good deal easier. What is perhaps the grandest of the Sonatas of J. C. Bach, that in C minor, is decidedly difficult. It consists, in effect, of a Prelude and Fugue followed by a lighter movement in binary form. It harks back to the Leipzig style, and is as difficult as it is effective. J. C. Bach's more sparkling and more shallow works are yet difficult enough, certainly not easier than the works of his brothers, or indeed much of the harpsichord writing of Handel. He only appears simple when compared with Scarlatti (ignoring the English Suites of J. S. Bach as they were, perhaps, completely unknown in London and to Burney).

The harpsichord in England was nothing like such a fugue-playing instrument as it was in the Empire, let alone such a zealot of counterpoint as was the clavichord or organ of those parts. But it did have some fugues: Handel inserted some magnificent examples in his Suites, and in 1735 published through Walsh a set of fugues by themselves, not even with Preludes. *Six Fugues or Voluntarys . . . Troisième Ovarage.* This set included the one which four years later was used in the chorus "They loathed to drink of the water" in *Israel in Egypt.* There are also isolated examples by J. C. Bach in C minor and Arne in D minor which have already been alluded to.

The harpsichord was also used as a solo instrument in concertos, which were usually played by harpsichord and strings. The title-pages of the collections usually giving the option of harpsichord or organ, the concertos still played are almost always done so on a perfectly deafening organ against a huge body of strings. Most London readers may remember these gigantic affairs at the Promenade Concerts. But the word organ was introduced into the title-page rather to give added appeal than to name the more suitable instrument. In the eighteenth century few organs had pedals, perhaps only that in St. Paul's Cathedral was so fitted, and as the manuals and stops of both harpsichord and organ bore some relation to each other, the music written for one could be played on the other. Wanda Landowska has recorded one of Handel's least interesting harpsichord concerti with a smallish body of strings. But if concert promoters fight shy of the right instrument, could they not at least try the effect of a modern concert grand pianoforte? This is always done for J. S. Bach's D minor and F. minor concertos: no one ever plays them on an organ.

The first set of six was published by Walsh in 1738, and a second set in 1751, while Walsh scraped together a third set from various material after Handel's death. These twelve authentic, to which may be added four truly Handel Concertos, even if transcriptions, form one of the great sets of music in the relevant repertoire. The sublime opening of Op. 4 No. 1 in G minor (I had better explain that Handel or Walsh gave the Opus No. 4 to the 1738 set, and Op. 7 to the 1751: operas, oratorios and cantatas were not given opus numbers until the time of Beethoven), the heart-easing *larghetto* of the F major Op. 4 No. 5, adapted from a flute sonata, and the extreme vigour of the last movement of the one in D come instantly to mind. One trouble

is, however, that no Köchel and Einstein has arisen to work on Handel:
the thematic table in use to enable me to refresh my memory in the
last paragraph appears to omit the D major concerto, while a standard
biography then consulted alluded to the Op. 7 set in the index as Op.
6 and stated that the Op. 7 set was pirated by Walsh from the *concerti
grossi*, though the twelve *concerti grossi* and the six harpsichord concerti
Op. 7 contain no movements in common as far as I can trace.   But
then the number of the *concerti grossi* has never been fixed, and I have
seen listed as many as twenty-eight, some of which certainly duplicate
some of the last, the third collection of harpsichord concertos, which
third set, not Op. 7, may have been pirated by Walsh.

   Improvisation was a great point with Handel and just as in the
opera the orchestra would be silent to allow Handel to proceed alone
at the harpsichord, so in these concerti.   But, as in opera, these improvisations probably bore no relation at all to *cadenzas*, but were actual
bricks and mortar of the whole fabric, not ornaments stuck on afterwards.   Their loss to us is a real loss.   Nor are these concerti symphonic in style, the solo instrument may or may not play all the
time, but its music is of the symphonic sort, contrasted with the body
of the orchestra, usually allotted to the *concertino* strings as against the
ripieno strings in a *concerti grossi*.   Here again it is a question of texture,
a question which eludes me.   Lastly, I must apologize for the seeming
affectedness of "concerti" instead of "concertos".   One naturally
says "the pianoforte concertos of Mozart", but then, he did not write
works whose plural might then logically be the surely appalling
"concertos grossos": it is this plural which seems to me to require
the "i", which then has to be carried to the harpsichord concerti,
for they and their string relations are all the same sort of music.

   Both Arne and J. C. Bach also wrote harpsichord concerti: the
publishers (not Walsh) said of the first: "those Amateurs and Professors who witnessed the astonishing effect of these Concertos, when
they were so successfully performed under the masterly execution and
direction of the doctor's son, the late Mr. Michael Arne . . ."   This
perhaps illegitimate son of the better known Thomas Adolphus en-
dured a miserable life of debt and madness, and was at one time
imprisoned in Dublin, but managed to smuggle in a spinet to console
himself.

   In spite of this talk of Suite, Sonata, Fugue and Concerto, we are
not to suppose the young ladies of the eighteenth century usually
played music in these forms by Purcell, Handel, Arne, Scarlatti and

J. C. Bach. To judge from the music published, "the most Favourite Aires and Song Tunes, with their Symphonys Collected out of the latest Operas for the Harpsichord or Spinnet" were the thing.

Why did the harpsichord die? It was well established, it was judged essential to the opera and to the orchestral concert, it was the support of chamber music, it had a fine literature for the solo player, and in its spinet form was sufficiently inexpensive for most middle-class houses to be able to afford it.

The growth of symphonic music, which is essentially a matter of texture rather than form, eliminated it from the opera and the concert hall. This did not happen at once. What occurred was that the pianoforte took its place for a while, though the essential thing which banished the harpsichord was not so much the intrusion of the piano-forte but the absence of a figured bass in symphonic scores. For a time in London there were two rival sets of concerts, one performing music in the old style, mainly Handel, and using a keyboard instrument as an essential ingredient of the orchestra, the other, the new Philharmonic Society, playing Haydn and Beethoven and with no use for any keyboard instrument, though, as a vestigial remain, it was placed on the concert platform.

The same thing happened in chamber music, which had hitherto been written essentially in contrapuntal parts. Perhaps only two parts, one would be executed by the harpsichordist following a figured bass line, the other by a violin or flute. Perhaps it would be in three parts, the harpsichord again having the one bass part, the right hand filling out the harmony according to the figuring, and the two solo instruments, two violins perhaps, playing the other two parts. The quite common addition of a 'cello or *viola da gamba* did not alter the number of parts: it merely meant that the 'cello also played the bass line as well as the left hand of the harpsichordist.

But sometimes three-part music was played by two instruments, the treble and bass lines would be for the right and left hands of the harpsichord player, he filling up intermediate harmonies when he could from the figured bass, the solo instrument playing the third part. It was Haydn with his purely string quartet with no keyboard or figured bass, or his pianoforte trio with its independent writing, who altered all this. His music was popular in England towards the end of the century. Burney first came across his name in 1763, and by 1789 his feelings were "the admirable and matchless Haydn! from whose productions I have received more pleasure late in my life, when tired of most other Music, than I ever received in the most ignorant and rapturous part of my youth, when every thing was new".

Burney also explains the decay of solo harpsichord music: according to him "it gave way, about the middle of the century, to the more elegant and expressive compositions of C. P. Emanuel Bach. . . ." Now as we saw in Chapter IV, this son of Bach, and Haydn in his earlier days, was a clavichordist. And it might even be denied that the pianoforte killed the harpsichord; it might be said that the clavichord in its projection called the pianoforte killed its centuries-old rival. This theory is based on what I consider to be the fact that, although the eighteenth-century grand pianoforte was indistinguishable from the harpsichord when the cases of both were closed, it was much nearer the clavichord in tone. In both instruments something came up from below and struck the string, and in neither case was the string plucked. In the pianoforte the strings were longer and the tension greater and the blow was sudden and the hammer fell back: in the clavichord the strings were shorter, the tension less, and the tangent did not automatically fall back whether the key was released or not. Consequently the clavichord made less noise and had a shorter compass and had nothing in the nature of a sustaining pedal. However, I think it can be maintained that the clavichord was the ancestor of the pianoforte, and that the harpsichord was a completely different instrument. People preferred, as a matter of taste, the music of C. P. E. Bach, and Haydn to that of Purcell and Handel, and so the instrument and its successor for which C. P. E. Bach and Haydn wrote became popular and flourished, while the instrument for which Purcell and Handel wrote, died. As to why Haydn became more popular than Handel in professional musical circles, is another story; it would take us into the nineteenth century Romantic movement.

Lastly, and as a fitting concluding paragraph to this, I fear, inadequate study, the reason why the harpsichord is reviving is that the course of nineteenth-century romanticism has been run, and while we love Haydn, we love Handel too: the seventeenth and eighteenth centuries are now classical in the sense of containing antique composers of the first rank. We admire them all and love them because of their differences from one another.

SHORT BIBLIOGRAPHY TO CHAPTER VI

Charles Burney: *A General History of Music*, vols. 3 and 4 (the modern reprint by Foulis, vol. 2).

Newman Flower: *George Frideric Handel* (Cassell 1923).

William Coxe: *Anecdotes of G. F. Handel and J. C. Smith* (Cadell & Davies 1799).

John Mainwaring: *Memoirs of the Life of the Late George Frederic Handel* (Dodsley 1760).

Wanda Landowska: *Music of the Past* (Bles 1926).

Fuller Maitland: *The Age of Bach and Handel* (Oxford History of Music, vol. 4).

William Dale: *Tschudi, the Harpsichord Maker* (Constable 1913).

John Hawkins: *General History of the Science and Practice of Music*, vols. 4 and 5 (the modern reprint by Novello, vol. 2).

Grove's *Dictionary*, under HARPSICHORD.

John Evelyn's Diary (Everyman edition).

Samuel Pepys's Diary (Bell—ed. Wheatley).

A. J. Hipkins: *History of the Pianoforte* (Novello 1896).

Ernest Closson: *History of the Piano*, (——, 1947).

The Letters of Mozart and His Family, translated by Emily Anderson (Macmillan 1938, vol. 3).

Ernest Walker: *A History of Music in England* (Oxford 1922).

Daines Barrington: *Miscellanies on Various Subjects* (1781).

Wyzewa et Saint-Foix: *W. A. Mozart; Sa Vie Musicale* . . . (Paris 1912, vol. 1).

C. S. Terry: *J. C. Bach* (Oxford 1929).

DOMENICO SCARLATTI IN THE IBERIAN PENINSULA

Iɴ the chapter dealing with the cembalo in Italy we have seen the parentage and early years of Domenico Scarlatti. We have seen him, too, during at least one visit to Naples from his work in Spain, and we have seen him in his old age. In the chapter on the harpsichord in England we have met his Irish friend Roseingrave, and met Domenico when he visited London. All that needs to be done in this Appendix is to provide a sufficient linking narrative of his years in Portugal and in Spain, linking his early middle age when he left Italy to his old age when he returned.

Now all this information is to be found in the only monograph on our composer in the English tongue, that of Sacheverell Sitwell, published by Faber in 1935. The difficulty is, that little is known, and the distinguished *litterateur* gives the Iberian scene in a colourful, appreciative, mannered and, I hope, accurate, short book.

Domenico Scarlatti visited London in 1719 and in 1721 is found in Lisbon, whose king had summoned him to teach the princesses. One of these, the Infanta Barbara, was ten years old at the time. After a not long visit, Scarlatti returned to Italy, and the Infanta Barbara grew up and became, on her marriage, Princess of the Asturias and, in due course, Queen of Spain. Scarlatti was summoned to her to take the position of music master in 1729, and did not leave her service until twenty-five years later, returning to Italy in 1754 when he was nearly seventy years old. These twenty-five years were spent in a Court which usually settled in the palace named La Granja outside Madrid, and also attached to the Court was a fellow countryman, the *castrato*, Farinelli, with whom Domenico (always, as his friendship with Handel and with Roseingrave shows), ready to be companionable, became sufficiently intimate for the great singer to help his old friend's family when he died in 1757, impoverished by gambling.

The princely and royal household was obviously a curious one. Farinelli, for instance, sang just four songs every evening, and always the same four, chosen from operas famous in their day, but like their composers, Hasse, for instance, extinct equally in music and in fame. Scarlatti may have had a good deal of time on his hands: he became acquainted with Spanish native songs and customs, and affords one of the first examples in some of his Sonatas of the *genre* which became popular less than a hundred years ago and unfortunately still exists: that of writing music to describe a country, using the folk-tunes and rhythms of that country. I say unfortunately, because few of Scarlatti's successors have had his genius, or his tact to be quick about it.

THE RUCKERS HARPSICHORDS OF ANTWERP

IN the various chapters of this book we have dealt with the greater instrument manufacturers, Taskin of Paris, Kirkman and Shudi of London, have mentioned Cristoferi of Florence, and mentioned also that Vienna was more famous for its early pianofortes than for harpsichords. What the plan of the book has forced us to omit is mention of perhaps the greatest harpsichord-manufacturing family of all, the Ruckers of Antwerp, whose instruments were prized by the nobility of both France and England; so much so, that at the Revolution the confiscated clavecins of the aristocracy were more often Ruckers than Taskin, while, in London, Kirkman and Shudi themselves made a considerable income out of keeping old Ruckers in tune. It was their tone which was especially prized: time seemed to have had an improving effect upon them.

The Ruckers came from Malines early in the sixteenth century to settle in Antwerp, the first maker of European reputation being Hans the Old as he was called, working about 1570. Hans the Young and Andre the Old were brothers and worked together and signed their instruments together. Andre the Young was working in 1640, and a later date in which a Ruckers was made is 1667. The harpsichord shown photographed from above in this book—Handel's harpsichord —is a Ruckers.

A curious fact about the Ruckers in Antwerp is that they were not considered as makers of musical instruments, but belonged to the Guild of St. Luke, and belonged in their capacity of painters, for the painting on the cases was not only beautiful but attracted artists of the quality of genius of Rubens himself to the work.

The virginals (for these smaller instruments were made as well as harpsichords) were not usually painted unless to the order of a wealthy man, as we have seen in our Carolean anecdote in the first chapter.

The ordinary bourgeois virginals were usually decorated with patterned paper, as in the well-known picture by Vermeer of a girl standing and playing her instrument.

More about the Ruckers can be found by reading a remarkable article in Grove, written by A. J. Hipkins with additions by Francis Galpin. These two authorities produced, by consecutive work, a masterpiece of concise information. Other sources are:

Lion de Burbure: *Recherches sur les Facteurs de Clavecins et les Luthiers D'Anvers* (Brussells 1863).

Ernest Closson: *La Facteur des Instruments de Musique en Belgique.*

INDEX OF COMPOSERS MENTIONED

Abel, Carl Friedrich, 157, 204, 209, 220, 221.
Agricola, Johann Friedrich, 180.
Alberti, Domenico, 115, 118, 120.
Altnikol, Johann Christoph, 182.
Anglebert, Jean Henri d', 61, 73, 82.
Arne, Thomas Augustine, 106, 179, 205, 215, 218, 222, 234.
Ashton, Hugh, 39.

Bach, Carl Philipp Emmanuel, 138, 150, 181, 182, 183, 186, 194-97, 236.
Bach, Christian, 180.
Bach, Emanuel, 180.
Bach, Friedemann, 180, 190.
Bach, J. C., 124, 157, 161, 204, 208, 209, 218, 220-21, 227, 232, 234.
Bach, J. N., 138.
Bach, J. S., 14, 17, 36, 38, 45, 50, 53n., 75, 80, 81, 82, 85, 86, 88, 91, 106, 112, 115, 125, 126, 134, 138, 139, 141, 146, 149, 151, 153, 154, 155, 157, 167, 174, 178, 184, 186, 187, 192, 195, 197, 198, 218, 219, 224, 228.
Bach, Wilhelm Friedemann, 155, 181, 183, 186, 192-93, 194.
Barrett, John, 212.
Beaumarchais, Pierre Augustin Caron, 90.
Beethoven, Ludwig van, 55, 87, 122, 124, 146, 150, 161-62, 167, 177, 192, 198, 221, 235.
Begue, M., 73, 82.
Berlioz, Hector, 91.
Blitheman, Mr. 39.
Blow, Dr., 212, 225.
Brahms, Johannes, 162, 168.
Britten, Benjamin, 137, 213, 225.
Bull, Dr. John, 34, 35, 36, 37, 38, 41, 42, 43, 44, 46, 53, 72, 74, 223.
Busby, Thomas, 210.
Busoni, Ferruccio, 149, 150.

Byrd, William, 17, 21, 24, 27, 28, 29-33, 34, 35, 37, 38, 40, 41, 42, 43, 44, 45, 46, 53, 63, 72, 74, 119, 120, 126, 185, 201, 212, 222, 223.

Cambert, Robert, 80.
Campion, Thomas, 24.
Chambonnières, Jacques Champion de, 73, 80, 82.
Champion, Jacques, 73.
Cherubini, Luigi, 72.
Chopin, Frederic, 91, 150, 194, 230.
Cimarosa, Domenico, 112, 113, 119, 123, 124, 125.
Clarke, Jeremiah, 212.
Clementi, Muzio, 109, 204-5, 221, 222.
Clerembault, Louis Nicolas, 73.
Cohen, Harriet, 46.
Corelli, Archangelo, 101, 102, 105, 116.
Corrette, M., 73, 89.
Corsini, Ottavio, 101.
Cosyn, Benjamin, 43.
Croft, William, 129, 212.
Couperin, François, 65, 68, 69, 72, 73, 74, 76, 77, 79, 82, 83, 84, 85, 86, 87, 88, 89, 91, 112, 125, 146, 157, 182, 186, 228.

Dagincourt, François, 73.
Daquin, Louis Claude, 73, 77, 126.
Debussy, Claude, 72, 91, 150, 168.
Desaides, M., 89.
Dieupart, Charles, 153.
Dohnanyi, Erno, 89.
Doles, Johann Friedrich, 180.
Donizetti, Gaetano, 124.
Dowland, John, 24, 36, 53, 222.
Duphly, Dornal, 73, 89.
Durante, Francesco, 118.
Dussek, J. L. 205, 221.

Eccles, Solomon, 26, 212.
Edelmann, Johann Friedrich, 71.

Farinelli (Carlo Broschi), 103, 109, 115, 239, 240.
Farnaby, Giles, 37, 38, 44, 48, 53, 55, 72, 223.
Farrant, John, 39.
Ferrari, Wolf, 97.
Fischer, Johann, 157.
Frescobaldi, Girolamo, 118, 119, 128, 140.
Froberger, Johann Jacob, 118, 140, 141, 178.

Gabrieli, Giovanni, 119, 125, 126, 127, 130.
Galliard, Johann Ernst, 219.
Galuppi, Baldessare, 107, 120, 125.
Gasparini, Francesco, 105, 106, 107, 113.
Gerber, H. N., 176.
Gibbons, Christopher, 27, 141.
Gibbons, Orlando, 37, 41, 43, 44, 46, 49, 53, 54, 72, 118, 120, 185, 223.
Gluck, Christophe Willibald, 69, 71, 72, 134, 215.
Gossec, François Joseph, 72.
Graun, Johann Gottlieb, 181.
Greene, Maurice, 217, 219.
Gretry, Andre Ernest Modeste, 69, 72, 91.

Handel, G. F., 37, 72, 75, 80, 81, 85, 88, 101, 103, 104, 105, 106, 109, 112, 115, 117, 119, 120, 124, 128, 129, 134, 143, 146, 177, 178, 179, 187, 195, 201, 202, 204, 207, 208, 209, 214-17, 218, 224, 227, 228, 229, 234, 236, 239.
Hasse, Johann Adolph, 106, 114, 240.
Haydn, Joseph, 72, 91, 112, 124, 134, 135, 144, 146, 151, 162, 184-85, 186, 196, 197-98, 204, 221, 235, 236.

Jomelli, Niccolò, 100.

Kirnberger, Johann Philipp, 180, 184.
Krebs, J. L., 155, 180, 182.
Kuhnau, Johann, 138, 141, 178, 185, 186, 187-88.

Lalande, Michel Richard de, 73.
Loed, Leonaro, 118.

Liszt, Ferencz, 97.
Lotti, Antonio, 107.
Lully, Jean Baptiste, 69, 73, 76, 80.

Marcello, Benedetto, 107.
Marchand, Louis, 73, 75, 139.
Martini, Padre, 102, 103, 109, 117, 147
Mattheson, Johann, 137, 224, 225.
Mehul, Étienne, 71, 72.
Mendelssohn, Felix, 177, 192, 193.
Mizler, Lorenz Christoph, 180.
Monsigny, Pierre Alexandre, 89.
Monteverdi, Claudio, 222.
Morley, Thomas, 32, 33, 34, 35, 49, 222.
Mozart, Leopold, 66, 102, 103, 144, 146.
Mozart, W. A., 38, 66, 69, 72, 77, 80, 81, 89, 90, 91, 100, 101, 102, 103, 104, 109, 112, 113, 119, 124, 134, 135, 139, 144, 147, 149, 151, 153, 157, 161, 162, 167, 177, 192, 196, 204, 209, 221.
Muffat, Georg, 143.
Muffat, Gottlieb, 143, 144, 149, 158.
Munday, Mr., 55.
Mysliweczek, Josef, 147.

Nares, James, 217, 218.

Ottoboni, Cardinal, 101, 102, 116.

Pachelbel, Johann, 178.
Palestrina, Giovanni Pierluigi da, 24, 98, 119, 222.
Paradies, Domenico, 118, 120.
Parry, C. H. H., 124, 155, 218.
Pasquini, Bernardo, 102, 116, 118, 125, 128, 129, 130.
Pergolesi, Giovanni Battista, 76.
Philidor, François, 89.
Phillips, Peter, 36, 55.
Piggott, Richard, 212.
Porpora, Niccola, 135.
Poulenc, François, 80.
Puccini, Giacomo, 99.
Purcell, Henry, 37, 64, 80, 81, 146, 212-13, 218, 222, 223, 225, 234, 236.

Rameau, Jean Philippe, 63, 68, 69, 72, 73, 74, 76, 78, 79, 81, 88, 89, 125, 224, 228.

Ravel, Maurice, 168.
Rawsthorne, Alan, 225.
Redman, Mr. 39.
Roseingrave, Thomas R., 106, 204, 218–19, 220, 224, 230, 239.
Rossi, Michal Angelo, 118.
Rossini, Gioacchino, 90, 124.
Rousseau, Jean Jacques, 67, 69, 71, 76, 90.
Rutini, Giovanni Maria, 100, 119, 120, 125, 161.

Salieri, Antonio, 135, 156.
Salomon, Johann Peter, 221.
Scarlatti, Alessandro, 102, 103, 104, 105, 107, 113, 114, 116, 118, 127, 128
Scarlatti, Domenico, 80, 85, 91, 101, 103, 104, 106, 109, 112, 113, 114, 118, 119, 120, 121, 123, 124, 125,

128, 130, 146, 208, 219, 220, 224, 228, 232, 234.
Schobert, Johann, 72.
Schubart, Daniel, 133.
Schubert, Franz, 24.
Schumann, Robert, 192.
Smith, John Christopher, 214–15, 228.
Strauss, Richard, 35.
Tallis, Thomas, 21, 26, 28, 29, 30, 32, 39, 44.
Telemann, G. P., 179, 182.

Vittoria, Tommaso, 24.
Vogler, Abbé, 139, 147.
Wagenseil, Georg Christophe, 144, 209.
Wagner, Richard, 162.
Wallace, Lucille, 69, 149, 201.
Weber, Carl Maria, 147, 230.
Zipoli, Domenico, 129.

INDEX

Abel, Carl Friedrich, friend of Bach, 157, 204, 209, 220, 221.
Abergevenney, Lord Edward, 40.
Abt Vogler, 147.
Agricola, Johann Friedrich, pupil of J. S. Bach, 180.
Alberti bass, the, 120, 121, 122, 124, 125, 221.
Alberti, Domenico, 115, 118, 120.
Album of Selected Pieces, 56.
Allemande, The, 80, 85, 226, 228.
Alman, The, 49.
Altnikol, Johann Christoph, 182.
Anne of Cleves, Queen, 22.
Andrews, Miss Hilda, 40, 41, 46.
Anglebert, Jean Henri d', 61, 73, 82.
Aprile, Giuseppe, Viennese singer, 135.
Arcadians of Italy, 102.
Arne, Susanah Maria, 218.
Arne, Thomas, 106, 179, 205, 215, 218, 222, 234.
Harpsichord concertos of, 234.
Sonatas of, 231.

Compositions by: Suite in D minor, 187.
Fugues in D minor, 233.
Ashton, Hugh, 39.
Attaignant, Pierre, 80.
Augier, M. d', 115.
Augsburg, 140.

Babell, William, author of Suites of the most Celebrated Lessons, 225.
Bach, Anna Magdalena, 179.
Bach, Carl Philipp Emanuel, 138, 150, 181, 182, 183, 186, 194–97, 236.
Music of, compared with J. S. Bach, 192.
Ornamentation of the clavichord, 148.
Rondos of, 196.
The Art of Fugue, 184.
Six clavichord sonatas, 184.
Sonata in F Major, 194.
Sonatas of, 196.
Pralltriller, 194–95.
Bebung of, 194, 196, 197.

Bach, Carl Phillip Emanuel—*con.*
  Versuch uber die wahre Art das Klavier zu spielen, 182, 186, 195.
Bach, Christian, 180.
Bach, Emanuel, 180.
Bach, Friedemann, 180, 190.
Bach, J. C., 124, 157, 161, 204, 208, 209, 218, 220–21, 227, 232, 234.
  Fugues in C minor, 233.
  Harpsichord Concertos of, 234.
  Harpsichord sonata in C minor, 187.
  Orione, 232.
  Sonatas of, 232.
Bach, Johann Nikolaus, 138.
Bach, J. S., 14, 17, 36, 38, 45, 50, 53n., 75, 80, 81, 82, 85, 86, 88, 91, 106, 112, 115, 125, 126, 134, 138, 139, 141, 146, 149, 151, 153, 154, 155, 157, 167, 174, 178, 184, 186, 187, 192, 195, 197, 198, 218, 219, 224, 228.
  Bach, W. F., music written or, 189f.
  Cantabile touch of, 190.
  Cantor at Leipzig, 179.
  Clavichord, music of, 188–89, 190, 201.
  Death of, 183.
  Duel with L. Marchand, 139.
  English Suites of, 232.
  Family concerts of, 180.
  First wife dies, 142.
  Flugel, method of playing, 149.
  French Suites of, 186.
  Fugues of, 155.
  Harpsichord music of, 188–89.
  Income of, 142.
  In prison, 142.
  Inspiration of, 151.
  Italian Concerto of, 163, 164.
  Letter of, from Leipzig, 180.
  Marries again, 143.
  Move to Leipzig, 181.
  Musical director to the Prince of Anhalt, 141.
  Musical instruments in the household of, 179.
  Musical shorthand and, 150.
  Music of C. P. E. Bach compared with, 192.

  Ornamentation of the clavichord, 148, 191.
  Partita, Preamble and Overture, 153.
  Sarabandes, comparison with those of Couperin, 158–59.
  Sinfonia (first movement of a Partita), 153.
  Sonatas of, 159.
  Toccata (first movement of a Partita), 153, 155.
  Visit to Carlsbad, 142.
  composition by:
  Allemandes, 50.
  Aria di Postiglione, 191.
  Arrangement of sixteen concertos by various composers, 163, 164.
  Brandenburg Concertos, 142, 163, 166, 167.
  Cantata No. 51, 152.
  Capriccio in honorem Johan Cristoph Bacchii, 190.
  Capriccio sopra la lontananza del suo fratello dilettissimo, 190–91.
  "Catechism Preludes" (from the *Clavierubung*), 188.
  Chromatic Fantasia, 154, 155, 174, 175.
  Chromatic Fantasia and Fugue, 142.
  Clavierubung, 132, 188.
  Concerto for Flute, Violin and Flugel in A minor, 166–67.
  Concertos for two flugel, 165.
  Concerto for three flugel, 165, 233.
  Concerto in F minor, 233.
  Concerto No. 4 in G minor (transcription from Vivaldi), 163.
  Concerto No. 14 in G minor (transcription from Telemann), 164.
  Concerto No. 16 (transcription from Vivaldi), 164.
  "Dangerous Travel" fugue in G minor from *Capriccio sopra la lontananza del suo fratello dilettissimo,* 191–92.
  D minor sonata, 159.
  English Suites, The, 142, 153.
  Fantasia in C minor, 115, 154.
  Flugel concerto in A minor, 138.
  Flugel concertos, 164.

BACH, J. S.—*continued.*
"Friend's Lament" in F minor, as played by Sir Henry Wood, 192.
Fuga all' Imitazione della Cornetta di Postiglione, 191.
Fugue in E flat for the Lautenclavier, 155.
Gigue of the B flat partita, 115.
Gigue of the first partita, 158.
"Goldberg Variations," 149, 155, 156, 189.
"Inventions", 190.
Italian Concerto, 122.
Lautenclavier Suites, 158.
Lautenclavier Suites, 158, 159.
Polonaise from the French Suite in E major, 103-4.
Sarabandes from the Partitas and English Suites, 157.
Sarabande of the G minor English Suite, 152.
Sinfonia, 173, 175, 186, 190.
Suite No. 1 in A major, 153.
Trio Sonatas for flugel, 138.
Well Tempered Clavier, The, 154, 155, 175, 189.
Bach, Wilhelm Friedemann, 155, 181, 183, 186, 192-93.
Auction of manuscript of *The Art of Fugue,* by J. S. Bach, 184.
Clavichord music of, 192.
Fugue in F minor, 193.
Meeting with Handel in Halle, 183.
Musical director at the Liebfrauenkirche in Halle, 183.
Polonaises of, 193-94.
Balbastre, M., 64.
Baldwin, scribe to W. Byrd, 40.
Bantock, Sir Granville, 47, 52, 53, 56.
Barbiere di Siviglia, 90, 124.
Barley Break, The, 50.
Barrett, John, 212.
Barrington, Hon. Daines, 209.
Bartholomeo, Signor, 210.
Beaumarchais, Piette Augustin Caron, 90.
"Je Suis Lindor," 90.
Beckford, Peter, author of *Thoughts Upon Hunting,* and patron of Muzio Clementi, 109, 204-5.

Beethoven, Ludwig van, 55, 87, 122, 124, 146, 150, 161-62, 167, 177, 192, 198, 221, 235.
Affinity to Handel, 162.
C major pianoforte concerto, 151, 162.
"Moonlight Sonata," 158, 161, 162.
Sonata Op. 101, 161, 122.
"Vittoria," 55.
Ornamentation and, 151.
Begue, M., 73, 82.
Berlioz, Hector, 91.
Berlin, 140.
Bie, Herr Oscar, 84.
Birley, Juliana, 27.
Blanchet, François Etienne, 64.
Blitheman, Mr., 39.
Blount, Thomas, 27.
Blow, Dr., teacher of Purcell, 212, 225.
Bold, Mr., 31.
Bologna, Italy, 93, 102, 103, 109.
Bolt, John, 36.
Bonn, 139.
Borde, Jean Benjamin de la, 63.
Borren, van den, author of *Sources* of *Keyboard Music in England, The,* 46.
Bourbon, Duchesse de, 78.
Brahms, Johannes, 162, 168.
Sonata in F minor, 197.
Brandenburg, Margrave of, 142.
Breitkopf and Hartel, publishing firm of Leipzig, 175, 176, 198.
Britten, Benjamin, 137, 213, 225.
Rape of Lucretia, The, 137.
Broadwood, partner of Shudi, manufacturer of musical instruments, 204, 205, 206-7.
Brun, visited by Mozart, 145.
Bull, Dr. John, 34, 35, 36, 37, 38, 41, 42, 43, 44, 46, 53, 72, 74, 223.
Alman (Duke of Brunswick), 50.
"Dr. Bull's Jewel," 36, 49.
Fitzwilliam Virginal Book No. 51, 55.
Fitzwilliam Virginal Book No. 262, 50.
"King's Hunt," 51.
"My Selfe" (Fitzwilliam No. 189), 50.

Bull, Dr. John—*continued*.
  Pavan (Fitzwilliam No. 34), 49.
  Salvator Mundi (Fitzwilliam No. 45), 52.
  Toye (Fitzwilliam No. 262), 47.
  "Walsingham," 48.
  Flees to Flanders, 35.
  Organist of Antwerp Cathedral, 36.
Burney, Dr. Charles, 38, 40, 64, 99, 100, 103, 104, 106, 109, 114, 115, 133, 134, 176, 182, 198, 205–6, 225, 235, 236.
  Plays Handel's Coronation Anthem to Mr. F. Greville, 206, 217.
Burney, Fanny, *Memoirs of Doctor Burney*, by, 206.
Busby, Thomas, 210.
Busoni, Ferruccio, 149, 150.
Byrd, William, 17, 21, 24, 27, 28, 29–33, 34, 35, 37, 38, 40, 41, 42, 43, 44, 45, 46, 53, 63, 72, 74, 119, 120, 126, 201, 212, 222, 223.
  Friendship with Thomas Tallis, 28, 29, 30, 32.
  Granted lease by Queen Elizabeth, 29.
  At Harlington, Middlesex, 30.
  Lawsuits of, 32.
  Marriage of, 27.
  Move of family, 181.
  Organist of Lincoln Cathedral, 29.
  Organist of the Chapel Royal, 28.
  At Stondon Place, Essex, 31.
  Teacher of Lady Nevell, 40.
  Teacher of Thomas Morley, 32.
  Use of *canti fermi*, 53.
  compositions by:
  "All in a garden grine" (Fitzwilliam No. 104), 51.
  Ave Verum, 52.
  "Battell," 55.
  "Bells, The" (Fitzwilliam No. 69), 54.
  "Callino Casturame," 51.
  Fitzwilliam Virginal Book No. 66, 50.
  Fitzwilliam Virginal Book No. 155, 49.
  Fitzwilliam Virginal Book No. 158, 51.

  Fitzwilliam Virginal Book No. 181, 50.
  "Ghost, The," 30, 55.
  "Jhon come kisse me now" (Fitzwilliam No. 10), 51.
  Miserere (Fitzwilliam No. 177), 52.
  MyLadye Nevell's Booke, No. 6, 50.
  "O Mistris Mine," 50.
  Pavan, 49.
  Pavan, Sir William Petre, 49.
  Pavane, The Earl of Salisbury, 211.
  "Sellenger's Round" (Fitzwilliam No. 64), 50.
  Set of variations on "*Will You Walke The Woods Soe Wylde*," 41, 51.
  "Sir Jhon Graye" (Fitzwilliam No. 191), 49.
  "Ut, mi, re" (Fitzwilliam No. 102), 47.
  "Wolsey's Wilde" (Fitzwilliam No. 157), 51.
  "Woods so Wild, The" (Fitzwilliam No. 67), 47.

Cambert, Robert, 80.
Campion, Thomas, 24.
Canzone, the, 126.
Carlisle House, 208.
"Carmens Whistle, The," 51.
Cassel, 140.
Cavaliere servante, 96, 97.
Cello, the, 91, 235.
Cellos, in Dresden orchestra, 136.
Cembals, the, 15.
Chabot, Duchesse de, 78, 80, 89.
Chaconne, the, 81.
Chamber Music, 166.
Chambonnières, Jacques Champion de, 73, 80, 82.
  "La Verdinguette," 81.
Champion, Jacques, 73.
Charlotte, Princess of Mecklenburgh, 209, 232.
Cherubini, Luigi, 72.
Chiqulier, M., 64.
Chopin, Frederic, 91, 150, 194, 230.
Christoferi of Florence, 241.
Christofori, Bartolommeo di Francesco, 110, 119.

Cimarosa, Domenico, 112, 113, 119, 123, 124, 125.
  At the Court of Catherine of Russia, 112.
  Il Matrimonio Segreto, 113.
  Death in Naples, 113, 115.
Civita Castelonia, 102.
Clarke, Jeremiah, Master of the Choristers of St. Paul's, 212.
Clavecin, The, 15, 97, 140, 145, 149, 161, 200.
Clavicembalo, the, 110.
Clavichord, The, 13, 16, 17, 18, 22, 61, 98, 122, 132, 134, 143, 148, 149, 161, 167, 202.
  Comparison with pianoforte, 170–72.
  Music composed for by Haydn, 144.
Clavicymbal, the, 109.
Clavicymbolum, The, 16.
Clavicytherium, The, 15, 109.
Clavier, The, 17, 132.
Clementi, Muzio, 109, 204–5, 221, 222.
  Sonatas for pianoforte, examples of, 163.
Clerembault, Louis Nicolas, 73.
Closson, Ernest, *History of the Piano*, 202.
Cohen, Harriet, 46, 49.
Compleat Tutor for the Harpsichord or Spinnet, wherein is shewn the Italian manner of Fingering, The, 225.
Concertos for Two or More Flugel, 165.
Concerts Spirituels, 71, 72, 74, 77.
Coranto, The, 49.
Corelli, Archangelo, 101, 102, 105, 116.
Corrento, The, 49.
Corrette, M., 73, 89.
Corsini, Ottavio, 101.
Cosyn, Benjamin, 43.
Couperin, François, 65, 68, 69, 72, 73, 74, 76, 77, 79, 82, 83, 84, 85, 86, 87, 88, 89, 91, 112, 125, 146, 157, 182, 186, 228.
  Organist at St. Gervais, 74.
  Sarabandes, comparison with those of J. S. Bach, 158–59.

compositions by:
"La Bandoline," 87.
"La Bourbonnoise" (Gavotte), 86.
"La Coquéterié," 87.
"La Fidélité, 87.
"La Frénesié," 87.
"La Jalousie taciturne," 87.
"La Laborieuse" (Allemand), 85.
"La Langeur," 87.
"La Majesteuse" (Sarabande), 86.
"L'âme en peine," 87.
"La Milordine" (Gigue), 86.
"La Persévérance," 87.
"La Pudeur," 87.
"L'Ardeur," 87.
L'Art de toucher Le Clavecin, 74, 83, 84, 86, 182, 190.
"La Tenebreuse" (Allemande), 85, 88.
"La Triomphante," 88.
"L'Auguste" (Allemande), 85.
"La Favorite," 86.
"La Virginité sous le Domino couleur d'invisible," 87.
"L'Enchanteresse," 87.
"Les Canaries," 86.
"Les Coucous bénévoles sous des Dominos jaunes," 87.
"Les Fastes de la grande et ancienne Menestrandise," 88.
"Les Folies Francaises, ou Les Dominos," 87.
"L'Esperance," 87.
"Les Petits Ages," 88.
Les Tours de passe-passe, 65.
Minuets, 86.
Musete de Taverni, 82.
Ordres, 82, 85.
"Ornemens pour diversifier la Gavotte précédente sans changer la Basse" (Gavotte), 86.
Passacaille in B. minor, 86, 87.
Passepieds, 86.
Pieces de Clavecin, 74, 83, 85.
"Premiere Courante, Dessus plus orne sans changer la Basse," 85.
Rondeau, 81, 82.
"Seconde Courante," 85.
"Soeur Monique," 87, 88.
Couperin, Marguerite Antoinette, 69.

Courante, The, 49, 80, 85, 226, 228.
Coxe, Archdeacon, author of *Anecdotes of George Frederick Handel and John Christopher Smith*, 219.
Creutz, Comte de, 69.
Croft, William, 129, 212.
Crotch, William, 210.

Dagincourt, François, 73.
Daquin, Louis Claude, 73, 77, 126.
Dances, 157.
Debussy, Claude, 72, 91, 150, 168.
  Quartets of, 226.
Delaney, Dean, 210–11.
Demler, M., friend of Mozart, 166.
Desaides, M., composer of *Opera comique Julie*, 89.
Dieupart, Charles, author of *Six Suites de clavessin*, 153.
Dohnanyi, Erno, 89.
Doles, Johann Friedrich, pupil of J. S. Bach, 180.
Dolmetsch, Arnold, on Bourreés, 158.
  On how to ornament music, 149–150.
Donaldson Museum, Royal College of Music, 20.
Donzetti, Gaetano, 124.
  Don Pasquale, 124.
Double basses, in Dresden orchestra, 136.
Douglas, John, author of "Select Works, 66.
Dowland, John, 24, 36, 53, 222.
  Lachrymae, or Seven Tears, 49.
  Pavan, 49.
Dresden, opera orchestra at, 135, 136.
Drums, The, 154.
  In Dresden orchestra, 136.
Duet Sonatas, 162.
Duphly, Dornal, 73, 89.
Durante, Francesco, 118.
Duras, Madame de, 70.
Dussek, J. L., 205, 221.
Dusseldorf, 139.

Easte, Mr., 32.
Eccles, Solomon, 26, 212.
Edelmann, Johann Friedrich, 71.

Edward IV, King, 18.
Elizabeth, Queen, 22, 23, 28, 48, 202.
Engel, Carl, 174.
Epinay, Madam d', 78.
Epinette, 59.
Erard, firm of, 65, 72.
Ernest, Prince of Hanover, 105.
Eschiquier, 18.
Espinette, 22, 25.
Evans, Dorethie, 42.
Evelyn, John, 210.

Fantasia, The, 52, 54, 125, 153.
Farinelli (Carlo Broschi), 103, 109, 115, 239, 240.
Farinelli, Prime Minister of Spain, 99.
Farnaby, Giles, 37, 38, 44, 48, 53, 55, 72, 223.
  "Conceit," 55.
  "Dreame," 55.
  Fitzwilliam Virginal Book No. 55, 55.
  Fitzwilliam Virginal Book No. 270, 50.
  "Humour," 55.
  "Rest," 55.
  "Tower Hill" (Fitzwilliam No. 245), 52.
  Triumphs of Oriana, The, 37.
Farrant, John, 39.
Fellowes, Dr., 32, 46, 55.
Ferrari, Wolf, composer of *The School for Fathers*, 97.
Firmian, Count von, Governor of Milan, 117.
Fischer, Johann, oboeist, 157.
Fitzwilliam Virginal Book, 21, 30, 43, 44, 49, 56.
Fitzwilliam, Viscount, 43.
Florence, Italy, 93, 103, 104, 119.
Floriani, Benedetto, 110.
Florio, author of *New World of Words*, 25.
Flower, Sir Newman, 116.
Flugel, The, 15, 163.
Flute, The, 68.
Franck, poet, 176.
Frederick the Great, 133, 181, 204.
Frescobaldi, Girolamo, 118, 119, 128, 140.

Frescobaldi, Girolamo—*continued*.
  Partita No. 1 in D minor, 128.
  Partita No. 2 in A minor, 128.
  Partita No. 3 in F, 128.
  Partita No. 4 in G minor, 128.
Froberger, Johann Jacob, Court
  organist in Vienna, 118, 140, 141,
  178.
  and Westminster Abbey organ,
  140, 141.
  Suites of, 178.
Fugue, the, 127, 128, 155.
Fuller-Maitland, J. A., 149.

Gabrieli, Giovanni, 119, 125, 126,
  127, 130.
  Ricercari, 126.
Galliard, Johann Ernst, 219.
Galliard, The, 41, 49.
Galpin, Canon, 18, 173.
Galuppi, Baldessare, 107, 120, 125.
Gasparini, Francesco, 105, 106, 107,
  113.
Gavotte, the, 86.
Genoa, 93.
Gerber, H. N., pupil of J. S. Bach, 176.
Geronimo of Bologna, 20, 111.
Gibbons, Christopher, organist of
  Westminster Abbey, 27, 141.
Gibbons, Orlando, 37, 41, 43, 44, 46,
  49, 53, 54, 72, 118, 120, 185, 223.
  Fantasias of, 126.
Gigue, The, 80, 85, 86, 226, 228.
Gluck, Christophe Willibald, 69, 71,
  72, 134, 215.
  Iphigénie en Tauride, 71.
Glynn, Miss M. H., 42, 43, 51.
Goldberg, Johann Gottlieb, flugel
  player, 156.
Gossec, François Joseph, 72.
Gossec, Madame, 68.
Graun, Johann Gottlieb, 181.
Greene, Maurice, organist of St.
  Paul's, 217, 219.
Gresham, Sir Thomas, 34.
Gretry, André Ernest Modeste, 69,
  72, 91.
Greville, Fulke, 206.
Grimm, Baron, 67, 69, 78.
Guerre, Madame de la, 69.

Gwynn, Nell, 27.

Hamburg, 175.
Hamilton, Lady Emma, 101, 117.
Handel, George Frederick, 37, 72, 75,
  80, 81, 85, 88, 101, 103, 104, 105,
  106, 109, 112, 115, 117, 119, 120,
  124, 128, 129, 134, 143, 146, 177,
  178, 179, 187, 195, 201, 202, 204,
  227, 208, 209, 214–17, 218, 224,
  207, 228, 229, 234, 236, 239.
  Affinity to Beethoven, 162.
  a naturalized Englishman, 214.
  Brawl with J. Mattheson, 137.
  Clavichord of, 201.
  Harpsichord improvisations of, 234.
  in Rome, 116.
  Meets Domenico Scarlatti, 105, 116.
  Meeting with W. F. Bach in Halle,
  183.
  Messiah and inspiration of, 151.
  Ornamentation of the pianoforte,
  148.
  Smith, John Christopher, concert
  organizer of, 214–15.
  Suites of, 228, 230.
  Visit to Naples and Venice, 116.
  Acis and Galatea, 215, 218.
  Agrippina, 116.
  Allemandes, 50.
  Almira, 116.
  Concerto Op. 4 No. 1 in G minor,
  230, 233.
  Concerto in D major, 233, 234.
  Concerto Op. 4 No. 5 in F major,
  233.
  Coronation Anthem, The, 206.
  Fantasia in C for harpsichord, 215.
  Israel in Egypt, 233.
  Israel in Egypt, "Darkness" chorus
  from, 201.
  "Largo," 195.
  Messiah, 227.
  Rinaldo, 216, 225, 226.
  Siroe, 217.
  *Six Fugues or Voluntarys . . .
  Troisième Ovarage*, 233.
  Suites de Pieces pour le Clavecin, 217,
  228.
  Three Lessons, 229.

Harlington, Middlesex, 30.
Harpsichord, The, 13, 14, 15, 16, 17, 25, 27, 60, 61, 67, 84, 98, 99, 122, 132, 136, 140, 145, 148, 149, 161, 162, 169, 172, 177, 202.
  Comparison with organ and pianoforte, 158.
  Composers in England, 222.
Harpsichord Illustrated and Improved, The, 203.
Harpsicon, The, 13, 202.
Hasse, Johann Adolph, 106, 114, 240.
Hawkins, Mr. 38.
Haydn, Joseph, 72, 91, 112, 124, 134, 135, 144, 146, 151, 162, 184–85, 186, 196, 197–98, 204, 221, 235, 236.
  Approached through C. P. E. Bach, 198.
  Influence of C. P. E. Bach on early sonatas of, 197.
  Ornamentation of the pianoforte, 148.
  D major harpsichord concerto, 91, 144.
  Partita in B flat, 198.
  Sonata Op. 14, 185, 186.
  Sonata 27, 123.
  Variations for the pianoforte, 157.
Hayward, John, seller of musical instruments, 202.
Heidelburg, 145.
Hepplewhite, G., maker of spinets, 202.
Henrietta Maria, Queen, 37.
Henry VIII, King, 19.
Heywood, John, dramatist, 19, 21.
Hickford, Great Room of, 208.
Hickman, Dr. Hans, 39.
Hieronymus of Salzburg, 135.
Holbach, Baron d', 67, 68.
Hole, William, 42.
Horwood, William, Master of the Choristers of Lincoln Cathedral, 18.
Hotson, J. L., Death of Christopher Marlowe, 33.

Jigg, The, 50.
Jomelli, Niccolò, 100.

Johnson, Dr., Dictionary, 202.
Jonson, Ben, 35.
Kelly, Michael, Irish singer, 135.
King's Band of Music, The, 19.
Kirkman, maker of musical instruments, 204, 205, 220, 241.
Kirnberger, Johann Philipp, pupil of J. S. Bach, 180, 184.
Krebs, Johann Ludwig, 155, 180, 182.
  Clavierubung, Chorales and Preambles from, 155.
Kuhnau, Johann, cantor of St. Thomas's Church, Leipzig, 138, 141, 178, 185, 186, 187–88.

  Sonatas of, 159.
  "Bible Sonatas, 188.
  Clavierubung, 155, 186, 188.
  Frische Clavier Fruchten, 187.
  Saul malinconico e trastullato per mezzo della, Musica, 190.
Kunz, Viennese comedian, 135.

Lalande, Michel Richard de, 73.
  Musique pour les soupers du Roy, 73.
Landowska, Wanda, 46, 69, 83, 84, 86, 87, 149, 189, 233.
Lautenclaviere, 138.
Leckingfield, Yorkshire, 19.
Leipzig, 175.
Leo, Leonardo, 118.
Leopold, Prince of Anhalt-Cothen, 134.
Levant, influence of, 95, 96.
Leversidge, Adam, 27.
Levi, Sara, 184.
Linley, Thomas, 117.
Liszt, Ferencz, 97.
Loosemore, virginal maker, 26.
Loreto, Italy, 102.
Lotti, Antonio, 107.
Lowe, G., printer, 42.
Lubeck, 140.
Lully, Jean Baptiste, 69, 73, 76, 80.
Lute, The, 24, 53, 59.
Luynes, Duc de, 70.

Manchester, 1st Duke of, 105, 109, 116.
Manichordian, 59.
Mantua, 94.

Marcello, Benedetto, 107.
Marchand, Louis, 73, 75, 139.
Marlborough, Sarah, Duchess of, letter of, 215-16.
Marlowe, Christopher, 33.
Martini, Padre, 102, 103, 109, 117, 147.
Mary I, Queen, 22.
Mattheson, Johann, 137, 224, 225.
  Cleopatra, 137.
Mehul, Étienne 71, 72.
Memoirs of Sir James Melville, 23.
Mendelssohn, Felix, 117, 192, 193.
Mercator, Michael, 20.
Metastasio, 98, 135.
Middleton, Thomas, 25.
Mizler, Lorenz Christoph, pupil of J. S. Bach, 180.
Modena, 94.
Monsigny, Pierre Alexandre, 89.
Monteverdi, Claudio, 222.
Morley, Thomas, 32, 33, 34, 35, 49, 222.
  Pupil of W. Byrd, 32.
  and Christopher Marlowe, 33.
  and Shakespeare, 33.
  Fitzwilliam Virginal Book No. 153, 49.
  Plaine and Easie Introduction to Practicall Musicke, 32, 49, 54.
Mozart, Leopold 66, 102, 103, 144, 146.
  Pour le clavecin Celivre appartient a Mademoiselle Marianne Mozart 1759, 144.
Mozart, Nannerl, 144, 145.
Mozart Street, London, 79.
Mozart, Wolfgang Amadeus, 38, 66, 69, 72, 77, 80, 81, 89, 90, 91, 100, 101, 102, 103, 104, 190, 112, 113, 119, 124, 134, 135, 139, 144, 147, 149, 151, 153, 157, 161, 162, 167, 177, 192, 196, 204, 209, 221.
  At the Hotel Beauvais, Paris, 77.
  At Versailles, 77.
  Chamber music of, 167.
  Comparison with Strauss, 166.
  Death of mother, 79.
  Dislike of Abbé Vogler, 147.
  Of Muzio Clementi, 147.
  Ecclesiastical compositions, 146.
  First flugel concerto, 144.

  Keyboard concertos of, 165.
  Letter to Salzburg, 166.
  Musical shorthand, 150.
  Plays to Lady Hamilton, 117.
  Revisits Paris, 77.
  Sonatas written in the style of C. P. E. Bach and Haydn, 159.
  Use of pianoforte by, 155.
  Variations of, 155, 156.
  Visits the Duchesse de Chabot, 78.
  Visit to Italy, 117.
  Concerto in B flat K.238, 166.
  Concerto in E flat for two solo instruments, 165.
  Eine Kleine Nachtmusik, 230.
  "Fischer Variations," 157.
  Flugel concerto in D major, K.175, 165.
  "La Belle Françoise," 89.
  Le Mariage de Figaro, 90, 100.
  Miserere of Allegri, 98, 117.
  "Paris" symphony, 72.
  Rondo, 81, 82.
  Salzburg Sonatas, 160, 161.
  Salzburg Sonatas, comparison with Fantasia and Sonata in C minor, 161.
  Sonata for two pianos in D, 129.
  Sonata No. K.279, 160.
  Sonatas K.279-83, 159.
  Sonata in F major K.280, 160.
  Sonata No. K.284, 159, 161, 166.
  Sonata in A minor K.310, 91.
  Sonata in C major K.330, 91.
  Sonata in A, K.331, 91, 153.
  Sonata in F, K.332, 91.
  Sonata K.333, 91.
  Sonata in B flat K.358, 162-63.
  "Turkish Rondo," 90.
  Variations on a theme of Gluck, 156.
  Variations on a theme by Salieri, 156.
  "Variations on the Minuet of M. Fischer," 78.
Muffat, Georg, organist of Salzburg Cathedral, 143.
Muffat, Gottlieb, 143, 144, 149, 158.
  Componimenti musicali, 144, 154.
  Sarabandes, 158.]

Mullinar, Thomas, Master of the Choristers of St. Paul's, 39.
Munday, author of "Faire Wether," 55.
Murray, Sir David, 25.
Music in England, Ernest Walker, 228.
  Musick's Handmaid, New Lessons and Instructions for the Virginals or Harpsychord, 211, 223, 232.
  My Ladye Nevell's Booke, 39, 56.
Mysliweczek, Josef, 147.

Naples, 93, 95, 97, 99, 100, 109, 118.
Nares, James, 217, 218.
Naylor, Dr., 55.
Neumeister, poet, 176.
North, Roger, 40, 54.
Noverre, M., ballet-master, 78.

Old English Composers for the Virginal and Harpsichord, 56.
Olmutz, 145.
Opera in Italy, 98.
Organ, The, 19, 53.
  comparison with harpsichord and pianoforte, 158.
Ottoboni, Cardinal, 101, 102, 116.
Overture, The, 227.

Pachelbel, Johann, 178.
Padua, 110.
Palais Royal, Paris, 69, 74, 77.
Palestrina, Giovanni Pierluigi da, 24, 98, 119, 222.
Pangloss, flugel player, 133.
Paradies, Cassandra, 210.
Paradies, Domenico, 118, 120.
Parma, 94.
Paris, 65, 67, 93, 95.
Parry, C. H. H., 124, 155, 218.
Parthenia, 41, 42, 44, 46, 49, 54, 120, 211, 223.
Pasquini, Bernardo, 102, 116, 118, 125, 128, 129, 130.
  La Serva Padrona, 130.
  Sonatas for two cembali, 129, 130.
  "Toccata con lo Scherzo del Cucco," 126.
  Italian Gigues of, 129.
Passacaglia, the, 81.
Pavan, The, 41, 48.

Pepsuch, Dr. and Mrs., 43, 219.
Pepys, Samuel, 13, 26, 202, 211.
Pergolesi, Giovanni Battista, 76.
Philharmonic Society, The, 235.
Philidor, François, 89.
Phillips, Peter, 36, 55.
Pianoforte, The, 14, 17, 22, 61, 84, 91, 105, 111, 113, 119, 132, 146, 158, 161, 163, 167, 170, 189, 197, 202, 221, 224, 236.
  comparison with clavichord, 170–72.
  Haydn's music for, 144.
  Square, 61.
Pierluigi, Giovanni, 99.
Pietro, Signor, 210.
Piggott, Richard, 212.
Playford, musical publisher, 26, 203, 223, 224.
Pompadour, Marquise de, 77.
Ponte, Lorenzo da, 90, 96, 97, 98, 108.
Poplinière, Madame de, pupil of Rameau, 76.
Porpora, Niccola, 135.
Portman, organist of Westminster Abbey, 26.
Poulenc, François, 80.
Prague, 140.
Prelude, The, 54, 153, 226, 227.
Pressburg, 140.
Progressive Lessons for Beginners on the Harpsichord or Piano-Forte for the Use of Schools, 225.
Puccini, Giacomo, 99.
Purcell, Henry, 37, 64, 80, 81, 146, 212–13, 218, 222, 223, 225, 234, 236.
  Financial grant given to, 213.
  Death of, 213.
  Chacone in G minor, 225.
  Choice Collection of Lessons for the Harpsichord, 203.
  St. Cecilia Ode, 223.
  Suites of, 178, 224, 227, 230.
  Timon of Athens, 224, 225.
  Toccata in A, 126.

Quantz, Johann Joachim, author of *Versuch einer Anweisung die Flöte*, 114, 158, 159, 181.

Quatorze Gaillardes, neuf Pavannes, sept Bransles et deux Basses-Dances, 59.

Rameau, Jean Philippe, 63, 68, 69, 72, 73, 74, 76, 78, 79, 81, 88, 89, 125, 224, 228.
  Born in Dijon, 74.
  Operatic success, 76.
  Marriage, 75.
  Plays organ at Dijon Cathedral, 75.
  Pupil of Marchand, 75.
  Returned to France, 75.
  Walks to Italy, 75.
  Allemande in E minor, 88.
  Castor and Pollux, 72, 88.
  "La Livri," 88.
  "La Poule," 76.
  "L'Egyptienne," 88.
  L'Enharmonique, 63.
  "Les Cyclopes," 88.
  "Les Sauvages," 88.
Ravel, Maurice, 168.
Rawsthorne, Alan, 225.
Redman, Mr., 39.
Regals, The, 19, 104.
Rogers, Elizabeth, 44.
Rome, 93, 97, 98, 101, 102, 109, 118.
Rondeau, The, 81, 86.
Rondo, The, 81.
Roseingrave, Thomas R., 106, 204, 218-19, 220, 224, 230, 239.
  Almand, 220.
  Eight Suites for Harpsichord or Spinet, 220.
  Forty-two Suites of Lessons for the Harpsichord by Domenico Scarlatti, 219.
Rossi, Michal Angelo, 118.
  Dieci Toccate, 126.
  Toccatos, ten for cembalo, 126.
  Toccate e Correnti, 118.
Rossini, Gioacchino, 90, 124.
Rosso, cembalo maker, 111.
  Round, The, 50.
Rousseau, Jean Jacques, 67, 69, 71, 76, 90.
  Dictionary of Music, 70, 135, 136, 137.
  Le Devin du village, 67.
  in Paris, 67, 68.

Rutini, Giovanni Maria, 100, 119, 120, 125, 161.
"Rowland, or Lord Willobies Welcome Home," 51.
Ruckers, Hans and André, harpsichord builders, 132, 208, 209.
Ruspoli, Prince, 116.

Saint-Brison, Comtesse de, 68, 69.
St. Gervais, Paris, 64, 65, 74, 77.
Salieri, Antonio, conductor of the Vienna opera, 156.
Salle des Suisses, 71.
Salomon, Johann Peter, 221.
Salzburg, Archbishop of, patron of Mozart, 146.
Sarabande, The, 80, 85, 226, 228.
Saxony, Elector of, 133.
Scarlatti, Alessandro, 102, 103, 104, 105, 107, 113, 114, 116, 118, 127, 128.
  Regole per Principianti, 114.
Scarlatti, Domenico, 80, 85, 91, 101, 103, 104, 106, 109, 112, 113, 114, 118, 119, 120, 121, 123, 124, 125, 128, 130, 146, 208, 219, 220, 224, 228, 232, 234.
  Cembalo music, likeness of to J. S. Bach's Fantasia in C minor, 154.
  Lessons on the Harpsichord, performed by T. Roseingrave, 220.
  in Madrid, 113.
  Maestro di capella of St. Peter's, 113.
  Meets Handel, 105, 116.
  Sonatas of, 121, 122, 230.
Schobert, Johann, 72.
Schubart, Daniel, 133.
Schubert, Franz, 24.
Schumann, Robert, 192.
Schweitzer, Albert, 149, 150.
Scott Thomson, Miss Gladys, 215.
Selection of Pieces composed for the Harpsichord by Bernardo Pasquini, by Mr. J. S. Shedlock, 130.
Shakespeare, William, 33.
Sharp, Cecil, 50.
Sheraton, Thomas, maker of spinets, 202.
Shudi, manufacturer of musical instruments, 204, 205, 206-7, 220, 241.

Sifauchi, singer for whom Purcell wrote "farewell" in D minor, 223.

Silbermann, Andreas, pianoforte maker, 132, 174.

Silbermann clavichord, 174.

Sinigaglia, Italy, 102.

Smith, John Christopher, concert organizer, 214–15, 228.

Sonata, The, 159, 230.

Sonata da camera, 159, 187.

Sonata da chiesa, 159, 187.

Soule's Life, The, 26.

Spinet, The, 13, 14, 15, 25, 59, 62, 77, 110, 111, 161, 170, 177, 202, 210–11.

Spinetta, The, 25.

Spinettegiare, The, 25.

Spinetti, Giovanni, 110.

Spinetto, The, 25.

Stein, Johann Andreas, maker of pianofortes, 89, 134, 146, 159, 166.

Storace, Ann and Stephen, 100.

Strasbourg, 139.

Strauss, Richard, 35.

Suits of the most Celebrated Lessons by William Babell, 225.

Suite, The, 128, 225, 230.

Sweden, Christina, Queen of, 102.

Swelling, organist of Amsterdam, 36.

Tagliapietra, 56.

Tallis, Thomas, 21, 26, 28, 29, 30, 32, 39, 44.
 Felix Namque, 52.
 Granted lease by Queen Elizabeth, 29.
 Organist of the Royal Chapel, 28.
 Teacher of W. Byrd, 21.

Taskin, Pascal, 64, 65, 111, 241.

Telemann, G. P., 179, 182.

Thun, Countess, 134, 135.

Thundertentronckh, Baron, 133.

Toccata, The, 125.

Tomkins, Thomas, 44.

Townsend, Gabriell, 25.

Toye, The, 50.

Tregian, Mr., 42, 52, 55.

Trumpet, The, 104, 154.
 in Dresden orchestra, 136.

Turin, 93.

Ulm, Austria, 140.

Variations, 155.

Vautrollier, Thomas, 28.

Venice, 93, 95, 103, 104, 105, 109, 118, 119.

Verona, 110.

Victoria and Albert Museum, clavichords, harpsichords and virginals in, 13, 200, 215.

Vienna, 104, 134, 135, 140, 145, 241.

Viol, 53.

Violas, in Dresden orchestra, 136.

Viola da gamba, 104, 235.

Violin, The, 68, 104, 167.

Violins, in Dresden orchestra, 136.

Virginals, The, 13, 14, 15, 16, 17, 18ff., 53, 59, 61, 62, 97, 148, 161, 169, 170, 172, 173, 177, 200, 202, 241.

Vittoria, Tommaso, 24.

Vogler, Abbé, Apostolic Protonotary, 139, 147.

Voltaire, 66, 76.

Wagenseil, Georg Christophe, 144, 209.

Wagner, Richard, 162.

Wallace, Lucille, 69, 149, 201.

Walsh, John, musical publisher, 224, 225, 233.

Waltz, Gustavus, 215, 228.

Weber, Carl Maria, 147, 230.

Wesley, Charles, 210.

Wesley, Samuel, 210.

West, J. E., author of Old English Organ Music, 39.

Weston, Father, 31.

White, virginal maker, 26.

Windebank, Sir F., secretary to Charles I, 208.

Wolsey, Cardinal, 20.

Worde, Wynkyn de, 28.

Wurtemburg, Duke of, 133, 175.

Wyatt, poet, 20.

Zipoli, Domenico, 129.